MW01592624

Serial Killers, Mass Murders, & Disorders

Serial Killers, Mass Murders, & Disorders

SGC

Steven G Carley

SGC Production

Boston, Massachusetts

Steven would grow-up in a small town in Boston, Massachusetts playing with other children in his neighborhood. Steven would lead a mostly quiet life spending much of his time devoted to his studies. Steven would view himself more as a curious person than as a genius. He was born on July 13, 1975, his father was a machinist and mother Beverly was daughter to a machinist. Steven liked running and climbing but most of all he liked collecting, match box cars, baseball cards, muscle men figures, and pretty much anything else he could get his hands on. Steven would grow-up with his two sisters who as mentioned earlier would lead a relatively quiet life.

Steven was not a very successful student during high-school and at times would rebel at home by sneaking out of the house at night to join in the endeavors of locals in the neighborhood. Despite Steven's lackluster performance in high-school he would succeed within University of Phoenix receiving a Bachelor of Science degree graduating with honors. During this time Steven would author four works pertaining to his area of study and another on the secrets to self-publishing. He may be most known for his collection of 60+ e-books. He is currently continuing his studies within the IO Psychology Ph.D. program in which he is hoping to complete his Master's degree by 2015 and Doctorate degree by 2018.

stevecarley.us

Contents

Serial Killers, Mass Murders, & Disorders

This book would act as a long drawn out project which over time would reveal pertinent information among certain perpetrators. Serial killers and mass murderers alike tend to be white males. They are usually young but not all, just some are so young the average age drops substantially. Serial killing is often a means of engaging in some sort of sexually sadistic act, but not always. As an example one may point to Harold Shipman (Dr. Death), Ted Kaczynski (The Unabomber), or Herman Mudgett AKA Dr. Henry Holmes who would kill for money more than any other reason. This may make Mudgett the scariest of killers not far behind perhaps the deceitful Mark Barton. The worst may not instill fear, just is the worst in Adam Lanza killing the inhabitants of two first grade classrooms. Whether a mass murder or serial killing the act is horrendous. The serial killer makes the attempt of avoiding capture as his or her in some cases, body count increases. Just as Dr. Harold Shipman would increase his body count to a dreadful 218 deaths. The mass murderer seems to view the act as the last he will ever make claiming his victims and in many cases finishing the job with a self-inflicted gunshot, or in the case of Andrew Kehoe a self-inflicted detonation. The victims of these crimes often go forgotten but the grizzly memories seem to remain with all.

Disorders are not always a means of categorizing the psychotic, deranged, and violent. At other times they can and not all these individuals fit the criteria in consideration as a serial killer or mass murderer. Disorders can characterize situations of a neglect toward a child of a parent or recognize the signs of anorexia which in many cases can lead to a person's unintentional death. Disorders can help people deal with personal issues in one's life, or help one to overcome substance and alcohol use or abuse. No one disorder can fit every individual, especially the wide range of behaviors as described within the book.

Serial Killers, Mass Murders, & Disorders

ISBN-13: 978-1492734192   ISBN-10: 1492734195

Serial Killers, Mass Murders, & Disorders

Steven G Carley

SGC Production

Print Edition

© 2013 Steven G Carley

MASS MURDER

Carley, S. G. (2013). *Serial killers, mass murders, & disorders*. Boston: SGC Production.

Mass Murder

Preferences of the Mass Murderer

The list of American mass murderers continues to grow. A Hawaiian working at Xerox would view himself as the victim of a discriminating society precipitating a 1999 attack. Similarly a Palestinian American by the name of Nidal Hassan would claim discrimination for the reason for his attack on Fort Hood in 2009 against fellow army officers. He would also believe Afghanistan and Iraq Muslims would need to rise up and throw the United States out of the Middle East. In both of these cases the discrimination was nonexistent and a product of a paranoid personality as any discrimination would be against these individuals performance record. Still other cases gain interest and wonder Sandy Hook, Virginia Tech, Columbine, Oklahoma City. Within America the list of mass murderers continues to grow. Two questions which arise are why is the death toll and incidence of mass murder increasing and what can we do to stop this? Whether you were in Oklahoma City at the time of the bombing or joined the military in response to the 9/11 attacks the violence hits home. This is no more obvious than for the military members who would serve in Afghanistan where mass murder and public displays of terror would become part of the normal pattern of life.

Carley, S. G. (2013). *Serial killers, mass murders, & disorders.* Boston: SGC Production.

In defining mass murder it consists of four murders or more within a single location during a single incident in which no pause exists between the killings. One may consider the means at which mass murderers select a target for their aggression. These acts of aggression and violence tend to occur in the school environment with the perpetrator as teenagers, home intrusions with the perpetrator in their twenties, public attacks and executions in which the perpetrator tends to be in their thirties, and familicides and workplace attacks tend to be a peak age of forty often in the 30 – 40 range. The perpetrator tends to possess some sort of connection to the attack location. As an example one who attends a school will select this school as the location for their attack. Similarly one with a family may select his or her home for an attack, or people with a job may choose their workplace as the place of attack. Those attacking public places and the homes of others tend not to fit any description as they are out of school, don't have a job, and possess no family to speak. Hence they are left with the decision of turning their violence elsewhere. The people committing acts of mass murder seem to act as if under military rules of engagement, yet the person committing the act may not put much thought into the reasons for their attack on such a location.

Commonalities Among Mass Murderers

Almost all mass murders are by a single attacker as this would be the case in 98.6% of the attacks. The average age of these single attackers is 34. In the presence of a second attacker the average age becomes much less at 19.4. This may be the result of the young age of school shootings consisting of pairs or teams of shooters. Not including the attacker these mass murderous attacks on average injure 9.6 people and kill 9.0. Over a third of the attackers (38%) would be related to a minimum of one victim and the killing of animals would occur at times within these massacres (3.1%). The gender of the attackers tends to be male consisting of 90% of the

Carley, S. G. (2013). *Serial killers, mass murders, & disorders*.
Boston: SGC Production.

attacks. Six-percent of the attacks would be made by women with 3% of the attackers and attacks remaining unsolved. Consistent with the attacking age made on homes and work, most of the female attackers would be in their 40s. The typical means of carrying out these vicious and disturbing acts is most often through the use of a firearm (73%), other uses still exist such as the use of melee weapons: bare hands, club, or axe (30%). Arson would be the cause of mass deaths in 12% of the cases. The use of more than one weapon would account for the total being over 100%. One-half of the deaths would occur through police confrontation as 39% would kill themselves and another 11% would be shot dead by police officers. In 1% of the cases an angry mob would be the cause of death of the perpetrator. It is a great rarity for an armed bystander to end the attack as only one case exists when an armed Israeli student would kill an attacker. Of the killers taken into justice each would receive a just penalty as 10% of the captured and 5% of the total perpetrators would receive a sentence of death by execution. Over a third of the captured perpetrators (34%) would receive life imprisonment. This statistic represents 19% of the total population of mass murderers. Only 2.8% would receive less than a sentence of life imprisonment averaging a sentence of 29 years. The remaining three-percent would be found mentally unfit to stand trial and be found guilty by reason of insanity. This group would spend the remainder of their lives locked in a heavily secured state institution (Hilshafer, 2013).

The mental instability and extreme beliefs of the perpetrator, regardless of sentencing authorities will typically become aware. No one would perceive the discrimination of Byron Uyesugi the Xerox employee who would attack his workplace. The rampage at Fort Hood in 2009 similarly would be motivated by delusional perceptions of discrimination, instead of the poor individual performance others would profess. Palestinian Nidal Hassan would call for all Americans to be thrown from the Middle East. This

Carley, S. G. (2013). *Serial killers, mass murders, & disorders.*
Boston: SGC Production.

attack would occur during the middle of the war with Al Qaeda. Timothy McVeigh would go to war with the federal branch of the government leading a 1994 revolution transpiring into the attacks on the Oklahoma City Federal building. It would be the womanizing beliefs of Jared Loughner which would propel his attack starting with Gabriel Giffords and continuing onto a dazed crowd of onlookers. Eric Harris and Dylan Klebold would be motivated by a quest for infamy in their attack on Columbine High School in 1999. The tower sniper of Texas Charles Whitman would be dying of a brain tumor writing himself to be a victim before taking his rifle to the tower in 1966. It may be the damage to Whitman's brain may help explain which region of the brain to be responsible for murder or mass murder in this case. The circuitry and hormones driving others to kill may have become a match within the damaged brain of Whitman. Whitman would try to get help, yet when it wouldn't arrive, he acted out the task his tumor would program his brain to perform.

Mass Murderous Attack Warning Signs

A misperception of mass murderers is they attack without warning from some sort of psychotic break from reality. The typical experience of the mass murderer is a steady long-term cognitive decline of a year or more. The life path Timothy McVeigh would take would certainly have something to do with the stress he would undergo while in the 1991 Gulf War. Until his death he would often comment on combat and war. McVeigh would get a job as a security guard after the war, which he would leave to travel the country and visit friends from the military. He would live with his family and start to gamble after romantic rejection. McVeigh would end his relationship with the NRA finding their stance on the pro-gun laws to be weak. This would only be part of the anti-government rhetoric McVeigh would express. McVeigh would even hand-out progun literature at the site of the federal siege in Waco, Texas, involving

David Karesh and the Branch Davidians. It would be here in Waco, McVeigh would meet Terry Nichols, who would teach McVeigh how to make explosive devices.

The person McVeigh would become was a transformation over years and not a single lapse or sudden snap. McVeigh would kill 168 people including 19 children injuring 680, in the process making use of a truck filled with explosives. This would occur at the Murrah Federal Building in Oklahoma City, Oklahoma, on April 19, 1995. McVeigh would state the victims to be collateral in his war with the government, showing little to no remorse for his heinous actions. In acceptance of the premise of McVeigh, agreeance may occur McVeigh's act was, in fact, an act of war. This is not a reasonable viewpoint, and it is difficult to accept McVeigh was at war with the United States. McVeigh's actions should be viewed as nothing less than criminal. The violent delusions McVeigh would demonstrate are compatible with the defining features of mass murderers.

Before the attacks on Columbine killing 15 and injuring 21 by Dylan Klebold and Eric Harris, the two would commit smaller crimes in practicing making pipe bombs and the illegal acquisition of guns. Seung Hui Cho the architect of the Virginia Tech Massacre would see the headlines of the Columbine attacks and would write in an eighth grade assignment, he would want to repeat Columbine. The awkward social behavior and violent writing of Cho on school assignments would cause his college classmates years later to jokingly state Cho to be the kind of guy to go on a rampage killing. Cho's mother would state all along to be something wrong with her son, but when he turned 18 he was now an adult, and her intervention as a parent would no longer be legal. Before the incident a judge would rule Cho would not have to be confined to an institution and could operate as an outpatient. This would be a short 18 months

Carley, S. G. (2013). *Serial killers, mass murders, & disorders*. Boston: SGC Production.

before the 2007 Virginia Tech attack killing 32 (not including Cho) and injuring 17.

Five years before the attack on congress woman Gabriel Giffords Jared Loughner's personality would change. His attack would also include U. S. District Court Judge John Roll among five others. Loughner would be diagnosed with schizophrenia after the attack and forced to take anti-psychotic medications. The motivations of rampage killers can vary ranging from politics, to drugs, to criminal, to the unknown. The act of committing mass murder includes disordered thinking and individuals are diagnosed accordingly. The symptoms of these individuals' disorder tend to get worse over time showing themselves in some form of delusion. Possessing noticeable effects on the person's life is the mental decline which friends and family can observe something is wrong. Mass murderous inspiration appears to feed on itself as with McVeigh, who would be inspired by the Waco, Texas, incident and his experiences within the first Gulf War. Just as McVeigh would find inspiration in David Karesh, Eric Harris would find inspiration within Timothy McVeigh, who in turn would inspire Cho. The Little Rock recruiting station attack would inspire Major Nidal Hassan. A common feature of each of these rampage killers is the want or need to emulate or avenge the actions of previous rampage killers. The trauma most experience from rampage killings, the sociopathic rampage killer will draw energy in committing their own heinous act.

Guns and Violence

Current legislation of gun control proponents is in the process in the reinstatement of the 1994 Federal Assault Weapons ban. The effect this will have is unclear as previous studies involving gun control legislation possess methodological errors, are inconclusive, or inconsistent with the results of other studies. Handguns tend to be

Carley, S. G. (2013). *Serial killers, mass murders, & disorders.*
Boston: SGC Production.

the weapon of choice for homicide attributing for 68% of gun related homicide and 46% of all homicides (FBI, n.d.). This is part of the reason studies on gun control methods and assault weapons show little effect. In addition those who possess assault rifles tend to possess handguns. The elimination of assault weapons demonstrates no significant effect on gun violence as the assault weapon is owned in conjunction with other handguns, infrequently used, and relatively uncommon. The 1994 assault weapons ban did not seem to possess any effect on the incidence of mass murder as during this time 29 murderous attacks would occur including Columbine and the Oklahoma City bombing. The number of mass murder incidents does not change basing upon the availability of assault weapons. The conclusion is killers simply make improvised weapons, obtain illegal weapons, or switch to different weapons. The assault weapons ban would seem to possess a negative effect on the number of mass murder victims. Attacks during the ban would include the 1996 Atlanta Olympic Park bombing and the 1995 Oklahoma City bombing as the number of per incident killed during the ban would rise from 9.4 pre-ban to 11.3 during the ban. Upon the expiration of the ban the per-incident rate would decrease back to 7.6. The injury rate during mass murderous attacks would greatly increase from 8.0 before the ban to 35.0 during the ban to decrease after the ban to 5.6. During the ban 15% more incidents would result in five or more victims as compared to before or after the ban. Before or after the ban 25% more incidents would possess 12 or fewer victims than during the time of the ban. The type of firearm does not possess an effect on the number killed although semi-automatic weapons would appear to result in a higher rate of injury during rampage attacks more so than long guns or hand guns. Semi-automatic weapons resulting in more injuries were no more or less deadly than other types of guns during mass shootings. It would seem a new ban on semi-automatic weapons can expect very little results possessing very little effect on homicide rates or the occasion of mass murder.

Carley, S. G. (2013). *Serial killers, mass murders, & disorders.* Boston: SGC Production.

Legal restrictions on weapons one may make the assumption criminals to ignore. The design of the conceal carry license is to provide the opportunity to law abiding citizens to defend themselves before the arrival of police, which can be five or more minutes. Shooter attacks often do not end until the shooter is disabled physically. The attacker in a crowded area, the armed citizen must be capable of shooting and killing the attacker and if possible make a physical restraint. Others responding to the situation one must also be capable of handling. Gunshots would ring out in Arizona in the vicinity of Joe Zamudio, who would be legally carrying his firearm. Upon approaching the gunfire, Zamudio would witness one man atop the other, the man on top whose handgun would be in a malfunction condition. He would scream at the man he was atop, "I'll kill you, you motherf%*#er. I'll kill you." Zamudio would not draw his weapon and instead would grab the man's wrist instructing him to drop the weapon, which he would. The man on top would be Roger Sulzgeber who along with Patricia Maisch and retired colonel Bill Badger would save many lives by tackling one Jared Loughner when his gun would malfunction (ABC News, 2011). This would not occur until about a minute of Loughner opening fire on a crowd of people having already shot Gabriel Giffords in the head at point blank range. The aggressive comments of Sulzgeber were in the response of having witnessed Loughner shoot 20 people and nearly being shot himself. When Sulzgeber would put the weapon down Zamudio would assist in the restraint of Loughner with Maisch, Sulzgeber, and Badger until the police would arrive four minutes later. Reports would state Zamudio to almost shoot the wrong person, but this is not true as he would never pull his gun from the holster. Zamudio's behavior within the situation would be similar to the expectations of an armed off-duty police officer. The lesson is when doubts exist in taking a shot to resolve these doubts before taking action, or just simply remove oneself from the situation until the police should arrive. In the case Loughner's gun hadn't malfunctioned Zamudio would have been the first person on the scene with a firearm for four minutes until the police arrived. Properly trained armed citizens estimates are could prevent 30 to 40 mass murder deaths annually.

Other gun laws include the Castle or Stand Your Ground laws. The first enaction of these laws would occur in Florida in 2005 followed by 20 other states. Nationwide state law provides the affordance of deadly force in protecting oneself in the home unless an attacker is in a retreat mode. Fights in a public place everyone would be expected to retreat until the enacting of these laws making retreat only one of other options. Studies would show these laws to account for another 600 homicides annually (Hoekstra, Cheng, & Cheng, 2012). Since 2009 of the 13,756 homicides 3,368 would initiate over matters not pertaining to money or property. This is more than felony homicides (14.9%) or non-felony homicides (10.9%). In the United States in 2009, arguments would kill more people than gangs, prostitution, drugs, or alcohol. Only unsolved murders possesses of a higher category. The homicide rates of 2010 would show men to commit most of the acts at a rate of 9.3 to each occurrence of a homicide committed by a female. Of this number 3.8 homicides would remain unsolved. Peak ages to kill and be killed among both genders is between the ages of 20 to 24. This is to say an argument ensues among two young men resulting in a homicide. The explanation for 600 more annual deaths the result of Concealed Carry Stand Your Ground laws is the youthful male concealing a firearm possesses an increased likelihood to escalate an argument in standing his ground. The result is what may have ended in a fistfight erupts into a gunfight.

The reality is the shooting environment is chaotic. These same states permitting conceal and carry permits should establish training requirements on the de-escalation of arguments and gun safety in avoidance of possibly deadly confrontation. Permitting the

Carley, S. G. (2013). *Serial killers, mass murders, & disorders.* Boston: SGC Production.

untrained citizen to carry and conceal and go about their business like they are a police officer will result in more homicide deaths than all mass murder deaths combined. Part of the curriculum within the public school system may consider teaching de-escalation techniques.

Family members and the victims themselves currently are not compensated for death, injury, or emotional distress in the United States. Legislation may take place requiring private liability insurance of a gun owner as a condition of gun ownership or to create a federal tax commissioned to compensate the victims and families of gun violence. Citizens would be afforded the allowance of engaging in risk behaviors and a price to be paid by the people creating the risk. Men would pay more than women for such insurance because of the statistics of gun violence. Means of lowering insurance rates could take place such as through properly securing weapons and partaking in annual safety training. Client testing could occur by the insurance companies pertaining to delusional thinking, psychopathy, among other psychological risk factors. Affording liability insurance would be more difficult for those at higher risks of committing gun violence. The uninsured and untaxed firearms of criminals would be a violation of law permitting yet another means for law enforcement to throw people in jail for illegal gun possession. Gun laws may be viewed as drinking laws in regard to the new legislation for gun ownership. When the number of drunk drivers would increase when the drinking age would be lowered to 18, states would raise the drinking age back to 21. The federal government would intervene establishing a national mandate. Many states do not allow parents to provide alcoholic beverages to their underage child yet establishments such as stores, restaurants, and bars can sell to no one under the age of 21 years. The expectations of parents to control their children can make the parents liable for the criminal acts of a minor pertaining to civil court litigation. Homicide should be part of this consideration as mass murder by gun is the larger part to the homicide issue. Those committing homicide, 90% are under the age of 50 and 60% under the age of 30. In a similar statistic of those committing the act of mass murder 93% are under the age of 50 and 60% under the age of 35. Declines in risks of committing violence do not occur until after the age of 30 to 35. The analysis may suggest raising the legal age for firearms purchases from 18 to 35 or for those under the legal age to have a surrogate of legal age purchase the firearm for them. Use of a surrogate purchased weapon by an under-aged individual, this person committing the act would be legally responsible for his or her actions in court. In terms of a civil case, the surrogate would bear responsibility for the under-aged individual's behaviors. The purchasing of liability insurance and payment of federal taxes would be the responsibility of the surrogate gun purchaser. Civil responsibility for gun violence at the state level can shift toward older more responsible friends or family members, adjudicating personal affairs in a similar means to drinking laws.

In Prevention of More Mass Murders

The fixation of most people tends to be on guns and gun laws with an ignorance to prevention. The primary risk factors of those committing mass murder tends to be a deteriorating individual in terms of mental health who is experiencing some form of delusions and is a male under the age of 35. The prevention of mass murder may point to the treatment of the mentally insane in trying to diagnose before an incident should occur. At the same standard a diagnosis of schizophrenia should not label one a psychotic murderer such as Jared Loughner. Schizophrenia among males typically occurs at the age of 22, yet a first admittance tends to be at the age of 28, six years after the initial onset. The average for the onset of schizophrenia among females is at the age of 25 and a first admittance at the age of 32 (Hiifner, Heinz, Wolfram an der Heiden, Behrens, & Qattaz, 1998). Admissions are typically the result of a psychotic episode most often following four to six years of experiencing negative schizophrenic symptoms, and two years post positive schizophrenic symptoms. Ample time exists to treat an individual before an initial psychotic episode. The term mass murder is in no way synonymous with the term schizophrenic. Many schizophrenics possess delusions which is understandable as a symptom of the disorder. A reasonable assumption is more people experience delusions other than the combination of delusions and hallucinations during a psychotic episode or the combination of a psychotic state. Delusional disorder is very rarely diagnosed comparing to schizophrenia diagnosed within .4% of the female population and .8% of the male population (Hafner, Heinz, Mauer, Loftier, & Riecher-Rossler, 1993). Either delusions are significantly underdiagnosed or the brain mechanisms causing delusions are causing hallucinations and psychotic episodes. The onset of schizophrenic symptoms do not occur all at once and the more likely occurrence is the underdiagnosis of delusions. Symptoms instead should gradually increase over six or seven years, indicative of the separation of symptoms. Typical among the schizophrenic population is a diagnosis after a first episode, as delusionals do not attract attention by not exhibiting a psychotic episode. It seems everyone knows someone suffering from a weird belief system. This is not a personal decision yet the presence of an untreated and undiagnosed disorder. If you should ask this person, they may tell you that you are delusional. At best, the rate of diagnosis among delusionals is negligible.

Schizophrenics and delusionals are not synonymous with violence as delusions do not have to be violent in nature. Mental health concerns voyage beyond the domain of violence. Common among problems relating to mental health is a diminishing of productivity at work, school, or home. Many disorders typify mental health, in fact, as of 2004 according to the CDC 25% of Americans would report possessing a mental illness. As of 2002 the economic cost of mental illness to the United States is $300 billion (Moolenaar, 2011). The implementation of yearly mental health check-ups cannot only assist 25% of the United States population, but may in some manner prevent mass murder. Enforcement would involve a school and work mandate for workers and students especially those under the age of 50, who comprise the more at risk population in committing acts of violence such as homicide and mass murder. The legal precedent for physical health could extend into mental health creating an arising need among the parents of students and employees for expanded insurance coverage. Employers should recognize the association of workplace productivity and site security with paying for family mental health insurance. The type of individual at risk of committing mass murder is most likely not going to seek professional help, hence check-ups alone may not be enough intervention. For millions of years people have lived around the mentally ill evolving the circuits to recognize risk factors. Long before irreversible action occurs friends, coworkers, parents, neighbors, classmates, and others recognize the existence of a problem. Passing this recognition to the parties who can resolve the problem is the primary issue in modern society. Authorities encounter the problem of not being able to act without violating one's rights.

An intervention hotline set up by the department of Health and Human Services or other private aid agency permitting those who notice one with a mental health issue can call to request intervention. A social worker could be dispatched by HSS in the assessment and interviewing of the individual. The assessment could assist the social worker in finding an appropriate health care provider, or if uncooperative can gather evidence to provide before a judge demonstrating the individual's danger to him or herself and others, appointing a legal guardian in treatment of the unwilling person. The building of the hotline may be a challenge. The goal would be no hesitation in using the hotline in the case a person fears for their safety or if the individual simply appears to need help. Intervention should be quick and discrete with operators protecting callers. Hotline abuse should be prevented through the use of simple procedures. The attribution of calls and requests should be to a user or phone of which should be recorded and stored for a period of five years. As a form of independent verification HHS could wait for a second request instead of a response to every request. Before approaching the individual, social workers could interview those who know the person. Psychological evaluations could be a means of deterring prank calling. The initiation of a discrete intervention providing access to the mental health care mechanism will not only potentially thwart mass murder and save the lives of its victims, but also help those experiencing the early and later stages of a disorder. The occurrence of mass murder is a male dominated activity, the participants of which experience some form of delusion whose response is the attack of a target of opportunity. Not addressing the root cause and not demonstrating past success is the increase in armed citizens or the decrease in the availability of assault weapons. In solving the problem, the focus may be more on prevention and less on response. The goal is to prevent irreversible acts before they should take place through social worker operated hotlines and routine mental health check-ups. In the long-run lives will be saved and ultimately everyone will be happier and more productive.

Carley, S. G. (2013). *Serial killers, mass murders, & disorders*. Boston: SGC Production.

Patrick Sherrill

Sherrill Feels Pushed Around

Sherrill was quite the athlete in high school lettering in three different sports and would become a weapons expert upon joining the Marines. Sherrill would join the Oklahoma Air National Guard after receiving an honorable discharge from the Marines. In Sherrill's spare time he would contact fellow ham radio operators while living at home with his ailing mother. Patrick Sherrill would be hired as a letter carrier for the Edmond Oklahoma, post office in 1985 after scoring high on the examination. Through diligence and dedication Sherrill would complete the 90 day probationary period. Sherrill would never understand the lack of satisfaction among his supervisors with his pride to wear the uniform, pride to be a public servant, and pride in his job. Expectations of Sherrill would seem to grow with the more work he would partake. It would seem even Sherrill's 100-percent effort not to be enough for the supervisory team. The frustration would build inside Sherrill to the point of him giving them blood.

Richard Esser Jr. and Bill Bland his two supervisors on August 19, 1986 would take turns giving Sherrill a verbal beating after taking him to an office. The well-rehearsed act was a means of motivating

Carley, S. G. (2013). *Serial killers, mass murders, & disorders.* Boston: SGC Production.

Sherrill to work even harder. Evaluation of supervisors is on amount of mail moved, and not caring how this would occur a reprimand of Sherrill to Bland and Esser would be a means of doing just that. They would figure a scared employee running around picking-up the work load would be a means of motivating other workers as well. Bland would end his argument with a threat of termination, if Sherrill's performance were not to improve. The visibly shaken Sherrill would request a transfer to maintenance, and upon a discouraging response would become enraged. He was aware of his superior performance to other letter carriers giving his best, just as he had done in the Marines and high school football. Sherrill did not think things were supposed to end with him getting fired. Sherrill would make no more sacrifices to the system, and on August 20, 1986 with his anger replaced with determination, he would drive to work as usual at 6:45 AM in his best summer blue uniform carrying in his mailbag ammunition, a .22 caliber pistol, and two government issue Colt .45 semi-automatics.

Sherrill's Attack

Upon entering the building Sherrill would make his way to Supervisor Esser. Concentrating on his .45 caliber Colt Model 1911-A1, he would thumb off the two safeties, and upon taking the weapon out of his mailbag would point the weapon toward the ceiling. With his other hand he would reach across and pull back the slide locking his elbow and taking sight upon the barrel. He would squeeze the trigger expelling a shotgun type blast striking Supervisor Esser with tremendous force tearing a gaping hole in his body. Sherrill's hand would be knocked upward by the recoil as he would lower his hand and again take aim this time at postman Mike Rockne. Rockne would be too stunned to flee and also would be gunned down. Everyone would flee for the exits or hide, Sherrill would chase some toward the exits and shoot one as he would begin to seal the building. Stopping to reload, he would make his way

Carley, S. G. (2013). *Serial killers, mass murders, & disorders.* Boston: SGC Production.

toward the lobby entrance with one bullet to each chamber and seven to each magazine. This reloading process would take less than a minute. Sherrill would flush out hiding employees systematically slaughtering everyone in the rear building work space in less than five minutes. Two hiding supervisors Sherrill would not find, would speak of the speed at which Sherrill would perform the task. In the front of the building still remaining were some office personnel and a few clerks although most had fled through the lobby entrance by now. Sherrill would walk past some and kill others not killing everyone in his path. After circling the interior of the building, Sherrill would return to the corpse of Supervisor Esser having expended 50 bullets, wounding seven and killing 14 in a wild 15 minute shooting spree. Patrick Henry would let off one final round squeezing the trigger and pointing the gun toward his own head. When all was said and done this would be the third largest rampage killing in the United States to date involving a lone gunman. The outraged and shocked postal service would expect the occurrence for some time. The increasing violence would present itself in Atlanta, Georgia, where two supervisors would be killed one year earlier. The following three years would be 355 worker reports on supervisors few of which would become public knowledge.

The flow of mail had to continue and after mopping up the scene, the post office would be ready for business the next day. Charges of worker abuse would be countered by the general manager of the Oklahoma Division of the Postal Service Dick Carleton who would claim if abuse to exist so many would not show to work one day after the tragedy. The former Edmond postmaster Bill Shockey would comment those to show to work to perform as champions. Supervisor Bland would admit to counseling Sherrill before the shooting. Psychiatrists would explain the shooting, the result of self-induced battle fatigue or factitious post-traumatic stress disorder. The problems of Vietnam era veterans would be made public in 1986 through negative articles in the United States. They

Carley, S. G. (2013). *Serial killers, mass murders, & disorders.*
Boston: SGC Production.

would seem not to receive the same respect of veterans of previous wars. The party line to explain the incident of the postal service would be "crazy Pat." Stories would circulate of crazy Pat peeping in neighborhood windows dressed in fatigues. Sherrill smiled too much at his 20th high school reunion and rode a bike built for two solo. Sherrill's insanity would seem to prove the sanity of the postal union. Edmond locals wanted quick answers and since Sherrill wasn't around to defend himself the answers would not necessarily have to be the right ones.

Carley, S. G. (2013). *Serial killers, mass murders, & disorders.* Boston: SGC Production.

George Hennard

George Jo Hennard Luby's Massacre

It was just another day in the life of 35 year old George Hennard who as usual would stop inside the Leon Heights Drive Belton, Texas, convenience store during the early morning of October 16 for a junk food breakfast (Harris & Harris, 2012). For more than a year Hennard had been going there on and off as he would seem always in a hurry. Hennard would possess a brooding and ominous persona as the simmer in his eyes would portray an unsettling hostility. The cashier Mary Mead would claim to be scared of Hennard, claiming he seemed to possess many problems. Ringing-up Hennard's orange juice, donuts and newspaper, candy bar, and sausage and biscuit on this particular Wednesday morning, Mead would claim to sense something different. A sort of calmness and friendliness among Hennard she would not recall. Hennard would arrive in Luby's cafeteria 17 miles away seven hours later. Business was booming as usual as Luby's would be packed with 150 people, when crashing through the plate-glass front window would be Hennard's 1987 Ford Ranger pick-up truck.

As people initially would approach the truck, almost immediately the sound of gun shots would fill the air. Hennard would begin the massacre armed with two 9 mm semi-automatic weapons. Hennard would stalk the restaurant with cold-blooded efficiency choosing his victims, most of whom would be women. Hennard calmly carrying out his executions would yell, "All women of Killeen and Belton are vipers! See what you've done to me and my family! Now we all die!" Most of Hennard's victims would be shot with a single shot to the head at point blank range. "Is it worth it? Tell me, is it worth it? See what you make me do." The terror would increase among his potential victims, many who now would lie under tables holding hands in prayer. There seemed no panic or mad dashes for the exits just an eerie silence as Hennard would take the opportunity to reload his weapons in continuation of the slaughter.

Twenty-two people would already be dead by the time police would arrive and one would die later from gunshot wounds (Harris & Harris, 2012). An additional 27 others would be wounded. Hennard would engage in a shootout with two police officers suffering four wounds before retreating to the restroom, and with the final bullet in his clip would end the madness with a single gunshot to the head. It would take a short 10 minutes for the worst rampage killing in United States history to occur (prior Virginia Tech massacre). Investigators and the people of Killeen would try to piece together the fragments of Hennard's life to answer the question of why he would take such evasive action. All people could remember is the man they called Jo-Jo to be a withdrawn and sullen loner. The disturbed dark portrait of Hennard would trace to a troubled wealthy family of racists and gender biased individuals, whose angry and violent temper could make people scared with his piercing brown eyes. No one could be quite sure what event would trigger the bloody Luby's massacre.

Birth of George Hennard and Beyond

Carley, S. G. (2013). *Serial killers, mass murders, & disorders.*
Boston: SGC Production.

The birth of George Jo Hennard would be in the town of Sayre, Pennsylvania, where his father Dr. Georges Marcel Hennard would be a resident doctor of orthopedics. Hennard and his family from the time George Jr. was the age of five years would travel across the country as their father would work in the various Army hospitals. His other family members would include his mother Gloria Jeanne and younger siblings Alan, Robert, and Desiree. A resident of the White Sands Missile Range Army Base near Las Cruces, New Mexico, Lou Catoggio who would meet young George in grade school would claim him to be an outgoing kid. Everyone thought he was good-looking and cool. People would stop looking up to Jo-Jo when he would get in a fight with his father the following year, who would have a reputation for toughness. Catoggio recalls Jo-Jo going to school like he had been mauled as someone butchered his hair off. Jo-Jo would never be the same after, becoming much more introverted. During high-school Hennard would keep to himself. Hennard didn't hang out with anybody and was never seen with girls. His parents were never around and didn't seem to care much what little Jo-Jo would do. Hennard would join the Navy after graduating high-school and three years later would sign-up for the Merchant Marines. Until 1981 Hennard would work mostly in the Gulf of Mexico before setting out for the first of 37 overseas voyages. Hennard's series of brief stays would lead him into troubles.

In Texas of 1981 Hennard would be arrested for marijuana possession and after a racial argument with a shipmate in May of 1982, his seaman's papers would be suspended. Hennard would possess bias toward different groups including among Blacks, Hispanics and Gays. Hennard would even refer to women as snakes always seeming to have something derogatory to say about them. After losing his seaman's license for a second time in 1989 for possessing marijuana on a cargo ship, he would enroll in a Houston, Texas, substance-abuse program. He would drift from job to job

Carley, S. G. (2013). *Serial killers, mass murders, & disorders.*
Boston: SGC Production.

working for South Dakota and Texas construction crews and living part-time with his mother in Henderson, Nevada and his Belton redbrick colonial family home as well.   In February of 1991, Hennard would illegally purchase a Glock 17 and a Ruger P89 in Henderson. Hennard's behavior would become increasingly bizarre since the summer of 1990. Hennard would send a letter to two of his neighbors who lived together, 19 year old Jana Jernigan and 23 year old Jill Fritz. The two were sisters living only a couple of blocks from Hennard's Bolton home. It would seem Hennard to be admiring them from afar and his five page letter would ask if the three of them could get together someday, stating they would have to allot him the satisfaction of laughing in the face of those who tried to destroy him and his family.

The Hennard Attack Revisited

Less than two weeks prior to the Luby's massacre, he would pick up his pay check from his job at a cement company and quit, wondering the consequences if he were to kill. According to a co-worker Bubba Hawkins, Hennard had some problems with the women of Belton and kept making the comment "Watch and see." Hennard would speak briefly on the phone to his mother on his October 15th birthday.   While at a small grille outside Belton enjoying a cheeseburger and some fries, Hennard would explode while watching television coverage of the Clarence Thomas confirmation hearings. Manager Bill Stringer would claim Hennard just went off during the Anita Hill interview screaming, "You dumb bitch!" October 16 was a bright sunny day with a festive attitude inside the Luby's cafeteria. Sam Wink age 47 would be celebrating National Bosses' Day by treating his boss and several coworkers to lunch at Luby's. When Hennard's truck would crash through the window, Wink's group would be seated at a big round table right where his truck would enter the restaurant (Harris & Harris, 2012). Wink would leap into the aisle and not long after the sound of popping would ring into the air. Hennard would begin shooting before even exiting the vehicle with a gun in each hand, a cigarette in his mouth, and ammo clips bulging from his pockets. The line which had formed for customers to get their food, Hennard would methodically start firing at this group. Hennard would circle the room methodically selecting his victims. He would glare at one woman calling her a bitch and proceeding to shoot her. To a woman hiding behind a bench Hennard would exclaim, "Hiding from me bitch?" She would be shot and killed not long after. It was at this time Hennard would snap in his third clip. Onlookers would describe a sense of calmness among Hennard as he would continue to select his victims, and an eeriness of silence would fill the air between each of Hennard's shots. The age range of Hennard's victims would be from the ages of 30 to 75. At this time the group which huddled on the floor began crashing through windows lead by an oversized 300 plus pound man, trampling each other in the attempt of making an escape. A third of the crowd would escape during this sequence when the police would arrive on the scene. The bystanders who would remain in the restaurant would best be described as paralyzed with fear hiding among a sea of others playing the odds he or she will not be a chosen victim.

The grieving town of Killeen would wave their flags at half-staff as everyone is wearing white ribbons as part of a 30 day unity campaign. Trying to place the tragedy behind them counseling would be in the hopes of diminishing the grief, shock, and stress the incident would accumulate. A mystery continues to persist surrounding George Hennard Jr. as both of his parents refuse to speak publicly saying only, they don't know why their son acted in such a manner. The theories of murder experts pertaining to Hennard's pent-up rage and isolation do little in comforting the residents of Killeen.

Carley, S. G. (2013). *Serial killers, mass murders, & disorders.*
Boston: SGC Production.

James Huberty

James Oliver Huberty The San Ysidro McDonald's Massacre

On July 18, 1984 a rampage killing would occur at the San Ysidro McDonald's restaurant in San Diego, California. The attack would claim the lives of 22 individuals including the shooter James Huberty, also involved in the attack would be the injuries of 19 others. The birth of James Oliver Huberty would occur on October 11, 1942 in Canton, Ohio. A result of polio at the age of three, Huberty would experience a permanent injury resulting in long-term walking difficulties. His father would buy a farm in the Pennsylvania Amish country in the early 1950s of which his mother would refuse to live, and would abandon the family for the Southern Baptist Church. The effect this would have on Huberty, his mother's adandonment, would be a sullen and withdrawn demeanor. Huberty would enroll in the Jesuit Community College in 1962 earning a degree in sociology. Later he would receive an embalming license at the Pittsburgh Institute of Mortuary Science. He would meet his wife Etna while attending mortuary school marrying in 1965 and having two daughters, Cassandra and Zelia. James would work as an undertaker at the Don

Carley, S. G. (2013). *Serial killers, mass murders, & disorders.* Boston: SGC Production.

Williams Funeral Home in Massillon, Ohio, where he and his family would settle down. After their Massillon home would catch fire, the Huberty would relocate to Canton. Huberty would work as a welder in Canton for Union Metal Inc. Huberty and his wife would have a history of violence. Etna once instructed her daughter to assault one of her classmates at a neighbor's daughter's birthday party. Etna would threaten the child's mother with a 9 mm pistol of which she would be arrested. The authorities were not able to confiscate the weapon. A neighbor who would complain of the Huberty's German shepherd damaging their car would prompt James to shoot the animal in the head. Domestic violence was also common in the Huberty household with police reports stating James to brake Etna's jaw. To calm James, Etna at times would read James future through the use of tarot cards. To complement Huberty's limp would be a twitch in his arm, the result of a motorcycle accident ending his career as a welder. The family would leave Canton, Ohio, in 1984 and move to Tijuana, Mexico, for a brief stay before settling in San Ysidro a community of San Diego, California. There he would get a job as a security guard, yet would be dismissed a short two weeks before the shooting. Huberty's apartment would be a short three block distance from the site of the massacre.

The Day Before and After

One day before the shooting, Huberty would make a call to a mental health center. His name would be misspelled by the reception as Glueberty, and his call would not be returned as no emergency was stated during the call. On the morning of July 18, Huberty and his family would go to the San Diego Zoo and a few hours prior to the massacre, his family would eat at the Clairemont neighborhood McDonald's in northern San Diego. Etna would ask James where he was going before leaving for McDonald's of which he would respond to "hunt humans," commenting earlier "society had its chance" (Simola, 2003). Etna could provide no explanation of why she did not report this strange behavior to police when questioned after the incident. Huberty would proceed down San Ysidro Boulevard with a 9 mm semi-automatic uzi, a Winchester pump-action 12 gauge shotgun, and a 9 mm Browning HP when a witness would phone police. As fate would have it, the dispatcher would report the wrong address to the officers. Upon arriving at the restaurant, Huberty would unload on a crowd of restauranters wounding 19 and killing 22. His victims would be predominately of Mexican-American heritage. The massacre would last for an amazing 77 minutes starting at 3:40 PM, in which Huberty would expend 257 rounds of ammunition until sniper Chuck Foster situated on the post office roof adjacent to the restaurant would fatally shoot Huberty. Emergency and law enforcement crews would initially respond to a McDonald's two miles away at the international border between Tujuana and the United States. It would take fifteen minutes before they would realize they were in the wrong location, and start heading for the McDonald's next to the post office. During the attack, Huberty would claim to kill thousands during Vietnam, despite never serving in any branch of the military. Eyewitness statements would claim Huberty to be seen at both the post office and the Big Bear's Supermarket before selecting McDonald's as the better target. The massive body count would require the use of the San Ysidro Civic Center to hold all of the wakes. In accommodating all the dead, the Mount Carmel Church would hold back to back funeral masses.

The property would be torn down and given to the city on September 26, 1984. The building would be reconstructed into an education center for the Southwestern Community College. As an expansion of its off-campus locations, the location would be built in 1988. A memorial is in place commemorating the massacre victims in front of the school consisting of 21 hexagonal granite pillars ranging from six feet to a single foot. The widow of James Huberty, Etna Huberty, in 1986 would unsuccessfully sue McDonald's and James

Carley, S. G. (2013). *Serial killers, mass murders, & disorders.* Boston: SGC Production.

employer Babcock and Wilcox, claiming the incident to be their willingness to operate amongst poisonous metals. The contention of Etna is, it was the high levels of monosodium glutamate in the food McDonald's would serve combining with cadmium and lead levels in Huberty's body accounting for his uncontrollable rage and induced delusions. Autopsy reports would find high levels of these metals in Huberty's system, most likely the result of fume inhalation during his 14 years as a welder. At the time of the killings, Huberty would have no drugs or alcohol in his system.

Carley, S. G. (2013). *Serial killers, mass murders, & disorders*. Boston: SGC Production.

Charles Whitman

Childhood of Charles Whitman

Charles Whitman is most known as the infamous clock tower shooter. He would traverse to the top of the University clock tower after killing his wife and mother and would begin picking off the remaining stragglers after a lunch break. The scene would turn into a standoff, which would not end until a retired Air Force Tailgunner and three police officers would find their way into the tower, shooting Whitman six times with a .38 caliber including a 12-gauge shotgun at five feet and two face shots.

Charles Joseph Whitman would be born on June 24, 1941. Whitman was a student of the University of Texas when he would go on a shooting rampage killing 14 people and wounding 31 on August 1, 1966 (Gould, 1997). The shooting would take place in the University's Main Building on the observation deck where he would be shot and killed by police. The shootings would start after Whitman would take the life of his wife and mother. Charles Whitman on a family vacation would take a popular image of himself holding two rifles. He would be raised on South L Street in

Lake Worth, Florida, as the eldest of three brothers. At a young age Whitman would test very high on an IQ test 138, and while attending the St. Ann's school in Palm Beach, he would join the baseball team as a pitcher. Whitman would also train five years in the piano. At the Sacred Heart Roman Catholic Church each of the brothers would serve as altar boys, and Whitman himself would select the confirmation name of Joseph. Whitman would be among the youngest ever to achieve the rank of Eagle Scout at the age of 12. Serving as an altar boy at the age of 14, Joseph Leduc the scout leader would serve as a Sacred Heart priest for a month after completing seminary. Leduc a family friend would accompany Whitman on several hunting trips and would later become a confidant to Whitman. Whitman would undergo a routine appendectomy at the age of 16 and following a motorcycle accident would be hospitalized.

Charles Whitman Before the Shooting

Whitman's father would not approve of his marriage to Kathy Leissner, and on July 6, 1959 he would join the Marines. He would explain to Leduc an incident in which his father before pushing him into the family pool would hit him repeatedly. His father would attempt to cancel his enlistment to the Marines while onboard a train to the Parris Island Recruit Depot. The federal government would rebuff this request. Through a USMC scholarship Whitman would be accepted into the mechanical engineering program at the University of Texas following his enlistment to the Marines. Whitman's hobbies would include hunting, scuba diving, and karate. Whitman's hunting hobby would land him in a bit of trouble when one day as a prank, he would shoot a deer and upon dragging it into the dormitory would skin it in the shower. Whitman's scholarship would be withdrawn in 1963 a result of his substandard grades and the incident.

Carley, S. G. (2013). *Serial killers, mass murders, & disorders.*
Boston: SGC Production.

Whitman would marry Kathleen Francis Leissner a University of Texas student in August of 1962 presided over by his old time friend Leduc at a ceremony held in Kathleen's hometown in Needville, Texas. In 1963 Whitman would return to the Marine Corps and his return to active duty would begin at the base camp in Lejeune, North Carolina (Goulde, 1997). Whitman would receive a promotion to Lance Corporal. Around this same time Whitman would be involved in a rollover accident in a jeep. He would rescue the pinned passenger and receive four days of hospitalization to be treated for his own injuries. In November of 1963 would receive a court martial for threats over a $30 loan, possession of a personal firearm on base, and gambling. As a penalty for his crimes he would be demoted to the rank of private receiving both 90 days hard labor and 30 days confinement. Whitman would receive an honorable discharge from the Marines in December of 1964, and would enroll in the architectural engineering program at the University of Texas. To pay for the program without the assistance of a scholarship, Whitman would work as a bank teller and bill collector. In 1965 Whitman would get a job with the Texas Highway Department as a traffic surveyor with Central Freight Lines. While Kathleen would work as a biology teacher at Lanier High School, Whitman would also volunteer as a Scoutmaster for Austin Scout Troop 5.

Dysfunctionality would present itself for some duration among the Whitman family. Whitman's mother would make the announcement in 1966 she would be divorcing her husband. Whitman would help move his mother to Austin, Texas, from Florida where she would get a job as a cafeteria employee. Charles youngest brother John would move out and his other brother Patrick would stay with their father and continue in the family plumbing business. Whitman would receive weekly calls from his father pleading with him to ask his mother to give the marriage another try of which he would refuse. Shortly after John would be arrested and given a $25 fine for throwing a rock through a window. Whitman

Carley, S. G. (2013). *Serial killers, mass murders, & disorders.*
Boston: SGC Production.

would discuss his depression in 1966 with the university doctor who would recommend him to see the campus psychiatrist Maurice Dean Heatly. Whitman would explain his frustrations with Heatly in a March 29, 1966 visit explaining his increasing strains from work and school and the divorce of his parents. He would make a remark of possessing an urge of going to the university clock tower and start shooting people. Whitman would never return, yet the hostility among Whitman was obvious to Heatly. In Whitman's final suicide notes, he would make mention to his visit with Heatly stating the visit to be to no avail. Whitman who would already have a prescription to Valium would be prescribed Dexedrine by the summer. An autopsy of Whitman's body after death could not determine if any prescription drugs had been consumed prior to the attack. What would be revealed was the presence of a cancerous tumor in the hypothalamus region. Affecting emotion is the amygdala of which the tumor may have been pressing against. Neurologists would speculate it to be Whitman's condition precipitating the attack. Two months prior to the shootings Leduc would meet with Whitman for the last time where Whitman would claim to lose faith and was no longer practicing Catholicism. Whitman would regret displaying a violent disposition toward Kathleen and just wanted to be a good husband and not follow the same path of his father pertaining to marital aggression. According to close friends of Whitman they would report he would confide in them and learn he had struck Kathleen on at least three occasions.

Whitman Prepares for the Tower

Whitman would request for two rolls of film to be developed with six images highlighting a trip to the Alamo with Kathleen and John and a trip to Barton Springs. Whitman would purchase Spam for a 7-Eleven store, and binoculars and a knife from Davis hardware the day prior to the shootings. Kathleen and Charles would go to the matinee after he picked her up from her summer job as a bell operator, and the two would meet his mother for lunch at her job. They would visit John and Fran Morgan around 4:00 PM, and would leave in time to get Kathy to her 6:00 to 10:00 PM shift. Whitman would begin typing his suicide note at 6:45 PM.

It Read:

"I do not quite understand what it is that compels me to type this letter. Perhaps it is to leave some vague reason for the actions I have recently performed. I do not really understand myself these days. I am supposed to be an average reasonable and intelligent young man. However, lately (I cannot recall when it started) I have been a victim of many unusual and irrational thoughts."

The note would explain Whitman's decision to kill his mother and wife yet would make no mention of the university attack. He would request an autopsy to see if anything may have contributed to his pattern of thinking and continuing headaches. He would leave his will to mental health research in the hopes they could prevent such demonstrations in the future. Whitman would kill his mother just after midnight by rendering her unconscious and stabbing her in the heart. He would add to his suicide note stating:

"To Whom It May Concern: I have just taken my mother's life. I am very upset over having done it. However, I feel that if there is a heaven she is definitely there now...I am truly sorry...Let there be no doubt in your mind that I loved this woman with all my heart."

Upon his return home to 906 Jewell Street he would stab his sleeping wife five times as she lie naked. Whitman would leave yet another note:

"I imagine it appears that I brutally killed both of my loved ones. I was only trying to do a quick thorough job...If my life insurance

Carley, S. G. (2013). *Serial killers, mass murders, & disorders.* Boston: SGC Production.

policy is valid please pay off my debts...donate the rest anonymously to a mental health foundation. Maybe research can prevent further tragedies of this type."

He would write letters to his father and brothers with instructions to give the puppy Schocie to Kathleen's parents and for two canisters of film on a table to be developed.

On August 1, 1966 at 5:45 AM Whitman would call Kathy's Bell supervisor explaining she would not make it in to her shift for the day. Five hours later he would make a similar call to the workplace of his mother. Whitman would go to Sears and purchase a green rifle case and shotgun. He would also cash $250 worth of checks purchasing an M1 carbine from Davis hardware and renting a dolly from Austin Rental Company. Whitman would proceed to saw off the shotgun and pack it with an arsenal of three pistols, a 6mm Remington rifle, the M1 carbine, a Remington 700 bolt action hunting rifle with a Leupold 4x scope, among other equipment, and store this between his Marine footlocker and a wooden crate. In further preparation for his journey to the tower he would wear a green jacket covering his shirt and jeans which would cover his khaki coveralls. Upon taking position in the tower he would dawn a white headband.

University Clock Tower Shootings

Whitman would obtain a security pass from the security guard Jack Rodman, and while pushing the rented dolly carrying his equipment, he would claim to be a research assistant making a delivery. Shortly after 11:30 AM he would enter the Main Building where he would struggle with the elevator. Fortunately for Whitman, an employee Vera Palmer would power on the elevator as he would make his way to the top floor of the tower beneath the clock face. Whitman would make his way to the observation deck area lugging his trunk up three

Carley, S. G. (2013). *Serial killers, mass murders, & disorders.*
Boston: SGC Production.

flights of stairs. There he would be met by Edna Townsley the receptionist, and with the butt of his rifle he would knock her unconscious. Her body would be concealed behind a couch, and she would later die from her injuries. A young couple sightseeing on the deck Don Walden and Cheryl Botts, upon returning to the attendant's area moments after Whitman's attack on the receptionist, he would be standing there bearing a rifle in each hand. Botts would make the claim of her to believe it varnish making the red stain on the floor. The couple would leave the room after speaking briefly with Whitman. At this point Whitman would barricade the stairway. Two families of tourists would encounter the barricade, and when Michael Gabour would look around the barricade, Whitman would fire his first shot. As the families ran down the stairs Whitman would continue shooting. Dying instantly would be Marguerite Lamport, Gabour's aunt, and Mark Gabour. Permanently disabled from the shooting would be Michael and his mother Mary.

At approximately 11:48 AM the first shots would hail from the tower's outer deck. The first to phone the incident to the Austin Police Department would be a history professor after witnessing several students shot in the gathering center of the South Mall. Unaware of the gunfire many would dismiss reports of rifle fire. As news would spread the shootings would cause panic as all Austin police officers would be called to the scene. Others converging on the scene to assist would include Texas department public safety officers, off-duty officers, and sheriff-deputies. Whitman would use the waterspouts on each side of the tower as loop holes once authorities started to return fire. This would permit Whitman to continue his attack and remain safe from the oncoming gunfire, which now would include angry citizens who would assist police by bringing out their personal firearms. Credited with neutralizing Whitman's threat would be officer Ramiro Martinez who would state the civilian officers should be credited, as their gunfire would

Carley, S. G. (2013). *Serial killers, mass murders, & disorders.* Boston: SGC Production.

make it impossible for Whitman to take steady aim. Sharpshooter and police lieutenant Marion Lee would report from a small aircraft that only one shooter on the parapet to be responsible. The plane would come under fire from Whitman while they would attempt a kill shot and were forced into a retreat mode. Whitman would seem indiscriminate in his choice of victim, yet most were shot on Guadalupe Street a major commercial district on the west side of the campus. Funeral home run ambulances and armored vehicles would be used to get to the wounded. Morris Hohmann an ambulance driver would be shot in the leg responding to West 23rd Street victims. Hohmann would be attended to by another ambulance driver and taken to the local emergency room at the Brackenridge Hospital. At the hospital an emergency would be declared and extra medical staff would race to support the on-duty shift. At the local blood banks many would visit to donate their blood in support for those wounded.

DPS agent Cowan and police officer Conner would cover the windows of the northeast and southeast sides of the reception area inside the university. At this same time three officers and a citizen would make their way to the observation proceed to the northeast corner of the observation deck spotting Whitman on the northwest corner watching for signs from the police from the southwest corner. It is disputed which officer killed Whitman, yet McCoy would fire two shots and Martinez six including a shot from deck: Jerry Day, Houston McCoy, and Ramiro Martinez. McCoy and Martinez armed with a shotgun and .38 revolver would his shotgun upon the limp Whitman. As an indication the sniper had been killed, Day would wave Whitman's green towel to the crowd. Whitman's request for a cremation in his suicide note would not be met, and instead a shared service would occur for him and his mother by the Sacred Heart parish in Lake Worth by Tom Anglim. Whitman's casket would be draped with an American flag for his service to the

Carley, S. G. (2013). *Serial killers, mass murders, & disorders.*
Boston: SGC Production.

Marines, and would be buried in West Palm Beach, Florida, at the Hillcrest Memorial Park in section 16.

Within two hours of the shooting the Extra Houston Chronicle would release consideration of the Charles Whitman shootings in conjunction with the Watts riots as the defense to the establishment of task forces and SWAT teams in dealing with situations beyond the normal procedure of the police force. Stricter gun policies would be set forth by President Lyndon Baines Johnson. The Tower's observation deck would close for two years after the incident. It would close again in 1974 after several suicides and remain closed until September 1999. Guided tours are now strictly by appointment including the use of strict security measures and metal detectors. Still visible on the limestone walls are repaired scars from bullets (Gould, 1997). In 1998 Dr. Mink of the Department of Veteran Affairs in Waco, Texas, would diagnose Houston McCoy with post-traumatic stress disorder the result of the tower tragedy of three decades ago. McCoy would live in western Texas as of 2007. Ramiro Martinez would become a justice of the peace in New Braunfels, Texas, a Texas Ranger, and narcotics investigator. Martinez would publish memoirs in 2003 pertaining to the shootings of Charles Whitman. David Gunby would die of long-term complications from a wound he would receive during the Whitman tower attack on November 12, 2001. Born with only one functioning kidney, it would face nearly total destruction after being shot by Whitman. When his sight would fade, Gunby would refuse treatment and die shortly thereafter. The cause of death listed by the Tarrant County Coroner's report would be a homicide.

Carley, S. G. (2013). *Serial killers, mass murders, & disorders.*
Boston: SGC Production.

Timothy McVeigh

Another Day in Oklahoma City

Parents would drop their children off as they normally would at the Oklahoma City Murrah Federal Building. This would be a day like no other as at 9:03 AM on April 19, 1995 a rental truck with a massive bomb inside would explode. For two weeks to follow the building which was blown to oblivion would have the bodies of men, women, and children pulled from the rubble. When the rescue workers would finally finish their task, the worst terror attack to date would have occurred with the deaths of 168 people (prior 9/11) (McCooey, 2012). This date would represent the second anniversary of the federal siege and fire at the Branch Davidian compound of David Karesh in Waco, Texas. Driving without a license plate, the 27 year old McVeigh would be pulled over by an Oklahoma Highway Patrol Officer just 90 minutes after the explosion. McVeigh would be charged two days later with the bombing as just prior to his release, he would be recognized as a bombing suspect. Terry Nichols, McVeigh's ex-army companion would surrender to police in Herington, Kansas, upon learning he was wanted for questioning pertaining to the bombing. Nichols too would be charged for his role in the bombing. Bringing McVeigh's anti-government hatred to a head would be the federal raids on Randy Weaver and David Karesh. In taking action, McVeigh would pack a Ryder truck with explosives, park the vehicle in front of the federal building, and walk away after lighting the fuse. McVeigh's sentence would be death by execution. Nichols would receive a separate trial and upon his conviction for conspiracy to use a weapon of mass destruction and involuntary manslaughter, he would receive a sentence of life imprisonment without the chance of parole. McVeigh would show little remorse for his actions claiming the United States government to be the terrorist, referencing the child victims of the attack as collateral damage.

The birth of Timothy McVeigh would occur on April 23, 1968 in Lockport, New York. McVeigh would grow-up in a nearby New York town, Pendleton. He would be the second of three children with an older and younger sister. McVeigh would be raised in an Irish Catholic setting and in school would be the victim of bullying. It would be within the fantasy world of McVeigh in which he would retaliate against these bullies. McVeigh would grow to view the United States government as a bully and his enemy. McVeigh would graduate high school from Starpoint Central. McVeigh's parents William McVeigh and Mildred Noreen Hill would divorce while he was still a teenager. Throughout his life, McVeigh would be known as a loner whose only known affiliations would be a National Rifle Association membership while in the military, and a voter registration to the Republican party while living in New York. McVeigh's first introduction to guns would be through his grandfather. He would sometimes take guns to school to show off to classmates, and aspired to be a gun shop owner accounting for his fascination with firearms. McVeigh was an excellent student during high-school graduating with honors and taking an interest in the second amendment of the constitution pertaining to gun laws. McVeigh one may view as somewhat of a groupie of violence with his pro-militia attitude and subscriptions to Spotlight and Soldier of

Fortune. McVeigh would get a job with the Burke Armored Car Service. During high school McVeigh would have only one girlfriend explaining himself to always say the wrong thing in trying to impress women. Upon the divorce of McVeigh's parents he would move in with his father, and his sisters would move to Florida with their mother. McVeigh and his father would often go to the Roman Catholic church. McVeigh would claim to believe in a God, but would lose his interest in religion. Some would claim McVeigh of making statements he was an agnostic, yet prior to his execution he would have his last rites anointed to him by a Catholic priest.

McVeigh Enters and Leaves the Military

McVeigh would enlist in the army in May of 1988. McVeigh would go through a brutal recruiting process including long early morning runs, exhausting marches, and sound offs of mutilating the enemy. McVeigh would be awarded a Bronze Star from the United States Army for his service in the Gulf War. He would be assigned to the United States First Infantry Division scoring as the top gunner in the 25 mm cannon of the light-armored Bradley Fighting Vehicles. Prior to Operation Desert Storm he would serve at Fort Riley, Kansas, where he would complete the Primary Leadership Development Course (PLDC). It would be while in the army McVeigh would learn to switch off his emotions. McVeigh would possess the desire to join the army's elite special forces, the Green Berets. McVeigh would enter the Green Beret program upon his return from the Gulf War, but because of poor equipment, he would obtain blisters on his feet during the five mile march and drop out. He would not take the advice to take some time off after the war to rebuild his stamina. McVeigh would be discharged from the Army a short time after in December 31, 1991. In May of 1992, McVeigh would receive an honorable discharge from the Army Reserve.

Carley, S. G. (2013). *Serial killers, mass murders, & disorders.* Boston: SGC Production.

Upon McVeigh's exit from the army in May of 1992, he would work for brief times at various jobs not committing to any lifestyle. He would work as a security guard near his hometown in Pendleton, and would constantly talk to his coworker Carl Lebron Jr. of his disdain for the United States government. McVeigh would leave his job finding the Buffalo area too liberal and drive around America seeking old army companions. He would meet with one of his old friends Fortier, who he would do methamphetamine with, yet McVeigh's lack of interest in Fortier's drug habit would cause him to part ways. McVeigh would write letters to local newspapers asking odd but violent questions along the lines of, "Does blood need to be shed to change the system? Is civil war imminent?" During the Waco siege McVeigh would drive to Waco, Texas, selling bumper stickers and distributing pro-gun rights literature. He would tell a student reporter the government is taking the guns to have total control of its people, and as the government grows more powerful the people should prepare to defend themselves. McVeigh would find a home in the gun show culture selling flare guns and the Turner Diaries. Some of the more extreme ideas McVeigh would remain critical, yet in general this is where he enjoyed discussing threats to American liberty, the federal government, and the United Nations. It would be during the time of the Waco siege the Nichols brothers would teach McVeigh to make use of readily available materials to make explosives. McVeigh would be more convinced than ever it was time to take action after the siege and destruction of the Waco compound. Further threatening McVeigh's livelihood and propelling his actions would be the imposition of new firearm restrictions in 1994. McVeigh would claim to consider other means of retaliation in the form of an assassination, the eligible targets being Lon Horiuchi a member of the FBI rescue team who at the standoff in Ruby Ridge, Idaho, in 1992 would shoot to death a white separatist's wife. Two other targets include Federal District Court Judge Walter S. Smith handling the Branch Davidian trial and Attorney General Janet Reno. McVeigh would state an

Carley, S. G. (2013). *Serial killers, mass murders, & disorders.*
Boston: SGC Production.

assassination to be too difficult and instead would decide to strike their command centers. McVeigh would attempt to make the loudest statement he could in the bombing of a federal building. After the act he would wish to instead commit a series of assassinations against government officials and police.

Bombing, Conviction, and Execution

McVeigh would construct an ANNM explosive device mounted to the back of his Ryder truck rental. He would create the device in the vicinity of his old army post at a lakeside campground. The consistency of the bomb would include a motor racing fuel nitromethane and 5,000 pounds of ammonium nitrate. McVeigh would drive the truck to the front of the Alfred P. Murrah Oklahoma City Federal Building on April 19, 1995 just as the day care center and offices would open for the day. After igniting the timed fuse according to prosecutors McVeigh would run from the truck. A massive explosion would destroy the north side of the building at 9:02 AM injuring 450 and killing 168 people (McCooey, 2012). The day care on the ground floor of the building would result in the deaths of 19 children. He would refer to the destruction as collateral damage showing no remorse. McVeigh would state he did not know the day care was open and may have selected a different site in his defense. Following the bombing 300 buildings would be damaged and 12,000 volunteers and rescue workers would take part in the support operations. In response to the theories other bombers must have been involved, McVeigh would state they couldn't handle the truth of one man being capable of such carnage.

Among the wreckage a vehicle identification number would be found on a rear axle of the vehicle the FBI would identify as a Ryder truck rental from the Junction City agency. Ryder truck agency workers would work with the FBI in creating a sketch of the renter going by the alias of Robert Kling. The sketch would go public and

Carley, S. G. (2013). *Serial killers, mass murders, & disorders.*
Boston: SGC Production.

a Dreamland Hotel manager Lea McGown would identify the person as Tim McVeigh. While driving on the I-95 in Noble County shortly after the bombing in the vicinity of Perry, Oklahoma, trooper Charles J. Hanger from Pawnee, Oklahoma, would stop McVeigh. Upon passing McVeigh's 1977 yellow Mercury Marquis, he would take notice to the vehicle having no license plate. Hanger would question McVeigh when noticing a bulge under his jacket and arresting him for possession of a loaded firearm. McVeigh would have a concealed weapon permit, but it was not legal in the state of Oklahoma. McVeigh would be wearing an Abraham Lincoln t-shirt bearing the state motto of Virginia, sic semper tyrannis. These are the same words shouted by John Wilkes Booth upon shooting Abraham Lincoln. The back of the shirt would consist of a Thomas Jefferson quote along with the picture of a tree with three blood droplets: "The tree of liberty must be refreshed from time to time with the blood of patriots and tyrants." While in jail three days after the incident McVeigh would be identified as the perpetrator of the federal building bombing during an intense nationwide manhunt. McVeigh would be indicted on 11 federal counts on August 10, 1995 including eight counts of first degree murder, destruction by explosives, use of a weapon of mass destruction, and conspiracy to use a weapon of mass destruction. The government would file notice of its intention to seek the death penalty on October 20, 1995. The court would grant a change of venue on February 20, 1996 ordering the case to be transferred to a US District Court in Denver, Colorado, to be presided by US District Judge Richard Matsch. McVeigh would request his lawyers to defend him using his actions as a defense from the imminent danger he was in on account of the United States government. The argument of the lawyers would be McVeigh's actions were a justifiable response to the siege of the Waco, Texas, compound and the crimes committed by the United States government. The siege of the Branch Davidian complex would last 51 days resulting in the deaths of 76 of its members. A video would be shown to the jury of the happenings at the Waco,

Carley, S. G. (2013). *Serial killers, mass murders, & disorders.*
Boston: SGC Production.

Texas compound. McVeigh would be found guilty on each of the 11 counts of the federal indictment on June 2, 1997. The recommendation of the jury on June 13, 1997 would be for McVeigh to receive the death penalty. The United States Department of Justice would seek the death penalty for the deaths of eight federal officers. The remaining 160 deaths would be under the state jurisdiction of Oklahoma. Upon McVeigh's conviction and sentence of death, the state of Oklahoma would not file murder charges against McVeigh for the remaining 160 deaths. McVeigh would write various essays while in prison such as his, An Essay on Hypocrisy, describing the hypocrisy of the United States government in justifying its attack on Iraq, making the statement their use of weapons in the past is enough a reason to not permit Iraq from the collection of weapons of mass destruction. McVeigh would cite instances in which the United States would use nuclear weapons in the past such as in Nagasaki and Hiroshima. McVeigh would write a letter to Fox News on April 26, 2001 explicitly laying out his reasons for the attack on the Murrah Federal Building.

The execution of Timothy McVeigh would be delayed pending the result of an appeal. McVeigh would attempt to have the higher court make the lower court take a review of the case, which they would deny on March 8, 1999. McVeigh would make the request for a nationally televised execution of which would also be denied. Suing for the rights to the broadcast of the execution would be an Internet company. The maintenance of an upbeat attitude by McVeigh would rest on his belief that even after the execution the score would still be 168 to 1 rendering him to be the ultimate victor (McCooey, 2012). He would state it the nature of the beast why these people had to lose their lives. McVeigh would state, "if there was an afterlife and I were to be in hell, I would be in the company of good fighter pilots, who would bomb innocent people to be victorious in battle." McVeigh's death would come by lethal injection on June 11, 2001 at 7:14 AM in Terre Haute, Indiana, at the U.S. Federal

Carley, S. G. (2013). *Serial killers, mass murders, & disorders.* Boston: SGC Production.

Penitentiary. McVeigh would drop any remaining appeals and would die at the age of 33. He would claim his only regret to be not leveling the entire federal building. David Woodard a California conductor/composer would be invited by McVeigh to perform a mass on the eve of his execution. McVeigh would also request for a Catholic chaplain. Under the baton of Woodard, Ave Atque Vale would be performed at the St. Margaret Mary Church near the Terre Haute penitentiary by a local brass choir on June 10 at 7:00 pm to an audience of the next morning's witnesses. McVeigh's final meal would consist of two pints of mint chocolate ice cream. McVeigh's final statement would be the poem Invictus by William Ernest Henley (Elder, 2010). It hasn't been since March 15, 1963 since a criminal would be convicted and executed by the federal government with Iowa's execution of Victor Feguer. Relatives of the victims would claim McVeigh to get the final word, and that he would do it all over if he had the chance. At the Mattox Ryan Funeral Home in Terre Haute, McVeigh's body would be cremated whose remains would be scattered by his lawyer upon an undisclosed location. McVeigh would write of his thoughts of having his ashes dropped on the site where the Murrah Federal Building once stood, yet would find this to be too vengeful an act. Prison regulations would keep McVeigh from donating organs. According to psychiatrist John Smith who would find McVeigh to be a good fellow who simply had too much rage fill him and would engage in the irreversible act.

McVeigh's Motivation and Conspiracy Theories

The motivation behind the terrorist attack by Timothy McVeigh upon the Murrah Federal Building would be an act of revenge for the actions taken by the United States government in Waco, Texas and Ruby Ridge. Speculation also exists a 1994 federal weapons ban against the purchase of semiautomatic weapons also may have been the motivation to the attacks by Tim McVeigh. The white supremacist novel The Turner Diaries, McVeigh would often quote. The terrorist acts described within the book would be similar to the terrorist act McVeigh would carry out. McVeigh would be more interested in the discussion of firearms within the book than the discussions pertaining to race. In McVeigh's car would be photocopies of page 61 and 62 from the Turner Diaries depicting a fictitious mortar attack on the Capitol building in Washington. Documented in the American Terrorist before the execution of McVeigh would be McVeigh's claim of decapitating an Iraqi soldier with cannon fire. It would be to the shock and dismay of McVeigh to carry out orders of execution, and the carnage which would be left behind in Kuwait City after routing the Iraqi army. It would be during the Gulf War, McVeigh would first harbor anti-government feelings. On many occasions McVeigh would contemplate suicide in anticipation of being caught and executed. The bombing to McVeigh would be a form of state-assisted suicide.

An accomplice to Tim McVeigh would be Terry Nichols whose role in the crime would leave him with a federal sentencing of life in prison with no chance of parole. The suggestion at Nichols' trial would indicate other accomplices may exist. Where the alleged bomb was assembled at the Geary State Lake both a retired army NCO and George Rucker would testify to noticing two trucks. After being looked at by a group of surly men aggressively, the retired NCO would leave the lake on April 18, 1995. McVeigh would stay in the Grandview Plaza motel in room 26 the weekend before the bombing, and according to a Dreamland Motel operator two trucks would park outside. Despite no other individuals being indicted for the bombing, McVeigh may have had several other accomplices. Carol Howe an informant of Alcohol, Tobacco, and Firearms (ATF) would warn her handlers of Elohim City, Oklahoma, guests who would be planning a major bombing attack. The McVeigh speeding ticket in Elohim City would be the only connection among McVeigh and a group of Midwest Bank robbers. The FBI would announce in

Carley, S. G. (2013). *Serial killers, mass murders, & disorders.*
Boston: SGC Production.

February of 2004 a review of its investigation after learning explosive caps would turn up belonging to the Midwest bank robbers matching those triggering the Oklahoma City bombing. Surprise would exist among the agency, bomb investigators were not provided information pertaining to the Midwest bank robbery. Prior to the execution of McVeigh he would be given a one week delay while evidence would be collected pertaining to the Midwest bank robbers' gang. McVeigh would maintain himself to act alone and no need for a delay to exist.

McVeigh's first court appointed lead defense counsel Stephen Jones would discuss the possibility of the presence of several other suspects in the bombings continuing to implicate James Nichols the brother of known accomplice Terry Nichols. Jones suggestion is before the attacks during frequent visits to the Philippines, Nichols would come in contact with suspected Islamic terrorists. Nichols father in law would own an apartment building as a Philippine police officer, and would often rent to alleged terrorists posing as Arabic speaking students. The suggestion of the U.S. National Security Council and counter terrorist advisor Richard A. Clarke is the improvements to Nichols bomb-making skills would be a link to Philippine Islamic terrorists in the southern islands. A theory submitted by the defense attorney of McVeigh would be American Neonazis and Islamist terrorists would conspire in the bombing. The day and location of the attack would suggest the bombing to be a revenge attack for the execution of Richard Snell. These theories were not permitted by Judge Matsch to be part of the official defense.

A separate theory would suggest the government to conspire in planning the attack in justification of right-wing organizations. These analysts would point to the Reichstag fire and the Nazi prosecution of legislators. A bombing analysis published by retired Brigadier General Benton K. Partin would claim the destruction of the building could not have possibly been the work of a single man. The pattern of damage to the Murrah building would need to possess demolition charges among several of the supporting column bases of which the locations are not street accessible. A photograph of the collapsed column would support demolition charges and not the explosion of a truck bomb. The truck bomb responsible for ripping out second and third level floors would have insufficient power to destroy columns. Another suspected accomplice to McVeigh would be Jose Padilla. Timothy McVeigh and Jose Padilla would both live in Plantation, Florida, and Padilla would bear a striking resemblance to John Doe # 2 in the police sketches of one of the bombing suspects of the Oklahoma City Murrah Federal Building bombing.

In 2007 Terry Nichols would make the claim McVeigh was directed by a high ranking FBI official, and that the Murrah Federal Building was a secondary target. Nichols would also make the claim, the government was protecting the identities of the official among other conspirators to hide their role, and escape responsibility for the attacks. The FBI director Nichols implicates is Larry Potts. Allegations would arise when Kenneth Trentadue was mistaken for a bombing conspirator, the guard would kill him during an out of hand interrogation. The death of Trentadue months after the Oklahoma City Murrah Federal Building bombing would be ruled a suicide as the government continues to deny any wrongdoing. Attorney Jesse Trentadue brother to Kenneth Trentadue to support his belief in the FBI involvement in the Oklahoma City bombing is suing for FBI teletypes. Federal authorities who knew of the plan would not only fail to stop the bombing, but also permit key conspirators to walk away from prosecution. A September 21 ruling in 2007 by U. S. District Court Judge Dale A. Kimball would permit Trentadue to question and videotape both Nichols and David Paul Hammer. Opposing these videotapes is the FBI, claiming no sufficient controversy continues to exist to confer subject matter jurisdiction after the previous document disclosures of the agency.

Carley, S. G. (2013). *Serial killers, mass murders, & disorders*.
Boston: SGC Production.

The FBI response marked by an absence of documents referencing other documents would result in disagreeance among the court. In Nichols February 2007 affidavit, he would claim to want to bring closure to the survivors and families, alleging to write to Attorney General John Ashcroft in 2004 in helping to identify all parties involved in the bombing. Ashcroft would never reply to Nichols. The only indictments in the bombing would be of Nichols and McVeigh, yet Nichols contends others were involved. According to Nichols, McVeigh would tell him of undercover missions he would be recruited while serving in the military. During 1995 Nichols would learn of a change of target which would upset McVeigh.

Carley, S. G. (2013). *Serial killers, mass murders, & disorders.* Boston: SGC Production.

Seung-Hui Cho

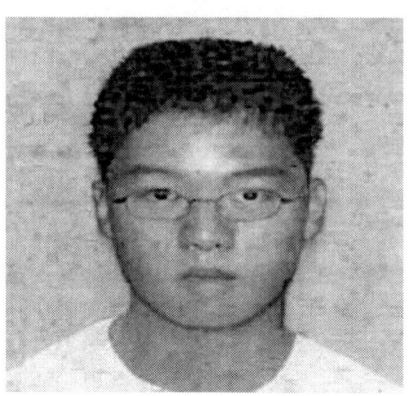

Cho's Preparation

The emergence of basic facts would occur within the first few days as the so-called "shooter" would be an immigrant whose family would move to the Washington suburbs. This would occur when the 23 year old South Korean was only eight years of age. His older sister who would work for the state would be a graduate of Princeton, and whose parents would operate a dry cleaning business in northern Virginia. Seung-Hui Cho was born on January 18, 1984. He would grow up in Seoul, Korea, where he and his family would live in a basement apartment. Seung-Hui Cho in February and March of 2007 would purchase a pair of semi-automatic European made pistols waiting the necessary 30 days between purchases as the law stipulates. With his purchase would be a large stock of ammunition including the purchase of extra magazines. Cho would spend his time over the next few weeks practicing shooting his guns at the local shooting range. The fellow students to Cho and his creative writing teachers would find him a troubling, disturbing, and frightening presence. In late 2005 he would be referred for counseling after the declaration from a judge as possessing an imminent threat to oneself and others, he would

Carley, S. G. (2013). *Serial killers, mass murders, & disorders.* Boston: SGC Production.

spend a night in the local mental hospital to receive an evaluation. Cho's mental health would first receive attention while he was in middle school when he would be diagnosed with selective mutism, a severe anxiety disorder. He would also be diagnosed with major depressive disorder. Until his junior year in high school he would receive special education support and continue to seek therapy. Cho's firearms purchase would hence be a violation of the federal law on account of his psychiatric history. He would require some sort of letter from the psychiatrist to permit his handling of firearms. In any case databases do not provide this information in protection of state measures to maintain the privacy of mental patients.

Supporters of more gun restrictions may point to the Virginia Tech killings to support their claim. Not to defend the mentally ill but it would seem mental health does not receive a diagnosis most often until after such an act. In any case the individual who has committed no crime should not be treated or viewed as the despicable Cho. Cho's act would propel anti-American hostility revealing a darker side of the American at home with his firearm. Outsiders would view the American society as a ruthless and divided group. Psychologists from other countries would make the ignorant statement of one being capable of purchasing automatic weapons in any supermarket. The facts to the matter are automatic weapon bans have been in place since the 1930s, and the only deadly weapons supermarkets are selling are junk food. Gun laws are actually fairly strict in the United States where some cannot purchase a weapon without recommendation of a psychiatrist, and still others who may require a gubernatorial or even presidential pardon. One can be assured certain individuals to be sitting around with no more than foreign antiques with no ammunition to speak of. Some would view the unknown killer at the time as a product of the societal unrest of the United States. It may be the war in America is against an enemy who in protecting themselves must risk such happenings as in the Virginia Tech shooting.

The Media

From the initial moments after the shooting the media coverage was insatiable. Television crews would be sent with multiple reporters and multimillion dollar anchors would be on the scene. This would include the likes of Geraldo Rivera and profilers and retired cops who in speculating of such gaudy crimes would make a living. The crime scene the Virginia Tech campus would become would be described as the loss of innocence of America. Emphasis would be drawn to the fact the incident would represent the worst shooting in American history in terms of fatalities.

For days the rage filled face of Cho would occupy newspaper front pages and the television screen, headlined as the worst shooting in history. This monstrous act would act as the fuel to one of the country's largest news stories of the young century. Virginia tech's technical name is Virginia Polytechnic Institute and State University occupying a student body of 26,000 in the southern Appalachians off of the Interstate Highway 81. The school is in quite an isolated region of Blacksburg three and one half hours from the state capital of Richmond. Cho was a senior English major who was due for Bible as Literature class this same morning 32 faculty members and students would be gunned down. In dealing with troubled and disturbed students part of the problem is not the rarity but the commonality of the issue. Even when Cho was a small child in Korea his withdrawn and sullen mental state would be painfully obvious to his family. Despite this it is only a very minute percentage of troubled youths who will grow to commit acts of violence. What can a free society do in distinguishing the harmless from the potentially murderous? The psychiatrist appointed by the court would state Cho was not an imminent danger and despite being

Carley, S. G. (2013). *Serial killers, mass murders, & disorders.* Boston: SGC Production.

mentally ill was doing well as an outpatient. Cho would make use of his right under Virginia procedures in not seeking treatment. In this sense no laws were broken.

On Monday April 16 at 7:15 AM Cho would enter the West Ambler Johnston dormitory and shoot and kill Emily Hilscher in her room. Cho would next kill the residence adviser Ryan Clark who would come to her aid. In another dormitory Cho would return to his room. He would walk to the downtown post office around 9 AM and mail a bizarre collection of written text, videos, and pictures to NBC News in New York. As no survivors could identify Cho town police would be questioning another suspect at 9:40 AM when Cho would enter Norris Hall, a Tech classroom building. Cho would chain three entrance doors shut from the inside, and wander from room to room shooting students and faculty. Cho would shoot 50 more people killing 30 and wounding 20 and as police would storm the building would shoot himself in the head. Estimations were the attack would last nine minutes with 170 rounds being fired.

Motives of the Killings

The motives behind the attack were not political and no obvious social lessons would be conveyed. It would seem the meaning to the crime would take on many interpretations divulging more information of the interpreter than the thought processes of Cho. Much of the media time would be spent on gun control, and Europeans would speak of the inadequacy of psychiatry and the uniqueness to American violence. The media would almost obnoxiously depict America as grief filled. Tech would begin in 1872 as the Virginia Agricultural and Mechanical College. It would belong to the Corps of Cadets as a small all-male institution. The institution would expand during the 1960s shedding its military tradition in creation of a comprehensive university with both a broad span of students and programs. Immediately striking to an outside observer may be the wide range of the victims of Cho. Cho's first two victims one female, one male, one black, and one white. The Norris Hall killings would include Americans of different backgrounds, but also people from different countries including Egypt, Indonesia, India, Romania, and Peru. The oldest would be 76 years of age an engineering professor and holocaust survivor Liviu Librescu (Clausen, 2007). The younger of the victims would include 18 year old Austin Michelle Cloyd a local freshman from the town of Blacksburg who would provide swimming lessons for children. Cho's victim list would suggest a diverse environment among the Virginia Tech population as is the case among most American Universities.

Those journalists and academics viewing American life through the lens of racial categories may be perplexed by Cho's actions given his own background. A black or Hispanic killer may have received different treatment for the shootings finding the incident to be race related blaming past or present white prejudice in a once segregated Southern university. One of Middle Eastern or Muslim descent the issue would point to terrorism regardless of any connections to extremist or fascist Islamic groups. In the even more improbable scenario of a female killer the issue may have arose of female empowerment and women's oppression. The killer would belong to the most successful of American immigrant groups, the East Asian, representing a high proportion of the inhabitants of higher education and especially so among the student body of V Tech. Difficult to imagine may be a backlash against Koreans, yet one may expect a stronger reaction to the relative ease one could acquire these weapons of destruction. Despite this many polls would show people to believe gun control could make little difference in the matter. The more stringent regulations of Canada and Europe pertaining to the regulation of firearms has not prevented school shootings. Still many Canadians and Europeans possess difficulty comprehending American attitudes pertaining to the private ownership of guns. Urban American liberals too find difficulty comprehending this attitude.

The confiscation of firearms by the British government during the colonial times would influence the enshrinement of the right to bear arms, the fundamental liberty of the Bill of Rights. This right may not possess the same significance as during the 18th century, yet attacking this right may appear politically unpopular as the 2000 Democratic election may demonstrate. Often blamed for this state of affairs is the National Rifle Association, but the NRA would have less influence if voters want more restrictions. As compared to 50 years ago the buying and owning of handguns is more expensive and regulated. Remaining a matter of endless debate among the United States and elsewhere for that matter are the effects of increasing regulations on crime. Despite the draconian gun laws of the United States, the once safe Britain possesses a higher rate of violent crime. Proponents for restrictions on gun control or the outright forbiddance of ownership of guns would assert their point proven by the Virginia Tech killings. Commentators in Europe would take this point of view. The event would fuel anti-American protests. America can feel at home with its firearm and Cho would reveal the dark side of its heart. An independent viewpoint of the American society may be it is more ruthless, pressured, and divided in every manner than the European society.

The response of gun law opponents may be were Cho to be denied access to firearms chances are he would turn to bomb making out of readily available materials. It is against the law at Tech as well as at all or nearly all other academic institutions to carry a firearm on campus. National advocacy groups after the shootings would make proposals on one continuum of banning private firearm possession altogether to the other continuum of encouraging the student body and faculty to carry weapons for their protection. One may safely say that neither of these extremes have any chance of being enacted. A more likely proposition is for the existing gun regulations to possess better enforcement and new legislation may put in place a ban on the large clips Cho would make use in firing so many shots in between reloads. A faculty member of Virginia Tech would state, he would never forget the sound of blaring sirens and the blare of the emergency broadcast system. A friend of the teacher a few hours after the shootings would send a depressed email stating the students and school are going to be traumatized forever. Despite a traumatized institution in the subsequent days of the scrutiny the university would give an impressive account of itself. With a mixture of anguish and stereotypical Virginia grace the president and campus police would answer the impertinent and repetitive questions of reporters. The vast majority of the hundreds of students who would appear on camera would come across as articulate and intelligent.

The Next Day

One day after the shootings the university would hastily plan a memorial service broadcast by all the networks conveying a resurgent community spirit, ecumenical religiosity, and a mixture of disciplined grief. The Bush family would attend the service. Following over the next several days would be makeshift memorials, informal prayer services, pictures of candlelight vigils, and the collective spontaneous grief of a country unaccustomed to ritual. The Virginia Tech response to its worst day in history would bring them out of the national shadow of Charlottesville. From the first few moments after the shootings the media menagerie would be insatiable. Big city reporters would find Blacksburg as alien as Europeans viewing it supposedly as the place of the rural values of America. The suggestion of quality newspapers such as the New York Times or Washington Post is they would not understand small town life or universities for that matter. In uniting them impatiently for the next press conference would be the search for a theme. Upon the arrival of television reporters to Blacksburg, the fault would be placed on the local police who would not lock down the university. The reality to the matter is sealing off such a large campus with over a hundred buildings would be a Herculean task requiring the assistance of a small army. Confining students to the dormitories after the shooting would seem illogical in any matter because of a dormitory shooting. This criticism would gain little traction causing a shift toward the lax gun laws of Virginia. Then it would be Cho and the lack of recognition for his mental problems in allowing him to slip through the proverbial cracks.

It may be difficult to believe these reporters to care of any of the issues passed providing social responsibility to their employer. It seems no more than a storyline to be created of a brief horrific event which the cable broadcasts would find the need to discuss hour after hour turning into day after day. Every morning it would seem the newspaper to find something new to say about Tech and place this information right there on their front page. The ratings for NBC would go through the roof when they would finally receive the package from Cho. He would depict himself as some sort of jihadist Rambo, yet the network would contribute little to an understanding of the causes for his actions. The moral to the Virginia Tech murders may be no more than it being an act of a monster. The act may resemble that of the assassination of then president John F. Kennedy who despite convincing evidence the act would be blamed on the American culture of violence, the Mafia, the anti-Castro Cubans, the CIA, and even the KGB. In the end it may simply be such a powerful event would make the pathology of a single individual too inconsequential a cause. There is not much to make of the massacre other than it was unique and a nightmare. No perfectible defense exists against psychotic rage and despair and the loner of no accomplices to give him away, it may be such an act could happen among any large institution. A sad but true conclusion.

Carley, S. G. (2013). *Serial killers, mass murders, & disorders.*
Boston: SGC Production.

Joseph Westbecker

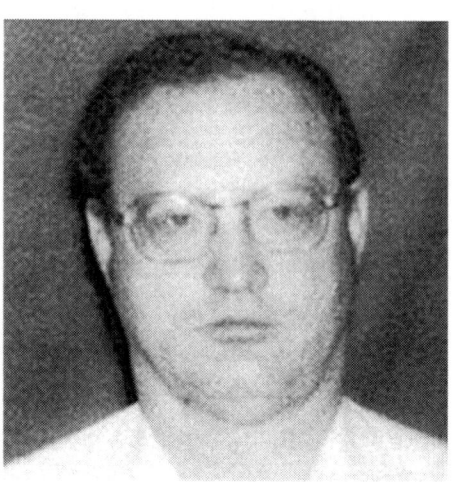

Association of Mood Disorders and Suicide

Although not normal the experience of depression and suicidal thoughts may occur among most people during the course of the lifespan. In the modern society mood disorders seem especially prevalent (McCullough, 2002). The term affect of affective disorders a parallel to mood disorders references emotional subjective experiences. Mood makes reference to the designation of pervasive or consistent emotion influencing our world view and ourselves for that matter. The broad definition for affective disorders is as a primary disturbance of affect and mood contrasting disordered thinking. This is according to the DSM. Affective disorders are characterized by the severe disturbances of schizophrenia and other paranoid disorders. The DSM includes among the affective disorders classification patterns of symptoms which would previously label cyclothymic personality disorder and depressive neurosis. The pattern of symptoms among this category include depressive episodes either mild or moderate to psychotic affective reactions. The major categories include affective disorders

Carley, S. G. (2013). *Serial killers, mass murders, & disorders.* Boston: SGC Production.

(cyclothymic disorder, substance induced mood disorder), major depression, and bipolar disorder (I and II).   The traditional terminology for bipolar disorder is manic depressive psychosis. The categorization of major depressive disorder involves severe and chronic depression.

The characterization of normal depression involves minimal disruptions of normal cognitive functioning accompanied by a brief period of sadness, grief, or dejection. Increased guilt, impaired concentration, and apathy manifests mild disturbances of mood and thought. Such reactions are in response to environmental events discrete in nature such as career disappointments or the loss of someone important in one's life. This form of depression may not require treatment and over time will dissipate. More disruptive to normal functioning are moderate episodes associating with skill deficits and distorted cognitions requiring various psychological therapies. Necessitating a multimodal therapeutic approach are the more severe depressive and psychotic syndromes. These forms of therapy include cognitive behavior modification, psychotherapy, and chemotherapy.

Association Among Major Depressive Disorder and Suicide

A disorder of mood and affect is depression the primary symptoms of which include anhedonia, decrease in stimuli potency, and dysphoria. Anhedonia is an inability to experience pleasure. It is the death of an important other resulting in decreases in stimuli potency, and dysphoria is feeling bad or possessing of an apathetic mood. Associating with these primary symptoms are a mixture of secondary symptoms including crying for no reason, increase in alcohol or drug use, lack of decisiveness, lack of concentration, feelings of guilt and worthlessness (self-blame), disruption of eating behaviors, psychomotor agitation, sleep disturbances, rumination of death or suicide, feelings of hopelessness, and withdrawal of contact with others. At one time or another everyone has been depressed during his or her lifetime. This is the normal response to disappointment or loss. It is when depression becomes severe significantly disrupting a person's world in which depression becomes pathological. A quarter of the office practicing physicians focusing on physiological disorders, in actuality are focusing on depression based symptomologies. In terms of dispensing psychotropic medication for depression psychiatrists only represent a small portion of the percentage consisting of 15%. The other 85% involve non-psychiatrists such as pediatricians, family practitioners, gynecologists, and internists (Phelps, 2002). The FDA would require black box warnings in 2004 on all antidepressant drug containers making aware the increased risks among children of suicidal ideation.

The DSM makes mention in reference to a major depressive episode labeling as severe, moderate, or mild without the presence of psychotic features. At the same time can be labeled severe with psychotic features. The norm is before the age of 30 for manic disorders and depression consisting of manic components to surface. The onset of depressive disorders can occur at any age. The normal age range for the peak occurrences of depressive disorders occurs between the ages of 20 to 45. Depressive episodes among an older crowd tend to possess a more precipitous onset including more severe symptoms. The DSM-IV-TR makes the statement 60% of people demonstrating a major depressive episode will have repeat episodes. Certain predisposing factors exist pertaining to major depressive episodes including physical disorders, history of chronic illness, chronic low self esteem, a recent loss, high levels of negative stress, alcohol abuse, episodes of non-medically based physical symptoms during the teen years, childhood depressive episodes, and family history of depression. The prognosis of a panic disorder or comorbid anxiety is predictably more negative, along with melancholia. The symptoms of melancholia involve severe dysphoria, anorexia, psychomotor retardation, and the inability to experience pleasure. Features of the melancholia syndrome associate with a better response to tricyclic antidepressants and ECT and a family history of depression. Statistics would show one in seven diagnosed with major depression will make a suicide attempt, and one in three will develop some form of substance dependency (Nathan et al., 1995). Research would show susceptibility to depression to increase with each successive recent generation. As an example those born prior to 1905 only one percent would experience major depression before the age of 75. This compares to a 600% increase in those born after 1955 experiencing major depression even before the age of 30. A factor may be better recognition of the symptoms of depression by a professional, but the stressors of modern life would seem to be making coping more difficult. Depressive episodes are twice as likely among women than men according to the DSM IV TR who three percent would experience. This statistic only rates those episodes which would require hospitalization. For those under age 40 this gender gap would appear to narrow. It may be the accentuation of traditional sex role expectations accounting for these differences. Other predisposing factors of depression among women involve a large number of children in conjunction with low socioeconomic status, infertility, patterns of victimization, and childhood abuse. Other factors more predictive of depression in women include narcissistic vulnerability, pessimism, feelings of helplessness, preoccupation with failure, low self esteem, and economic hardships. Depression one may view as lying upon a continuum of normal-pathological. Depression too may lie upon other continuums unipolar-bipolar, primary-secondary, neurotic-psychotic, agitated-slow, and acute-chronic. Another continuum of importance may be endogenous-exogenous. The assumption of the origination of endogenous depressions are from physical and internal psychic causes. External causes would form exogenous depressions. Endogenous depression consists of four significant traditional behavioral indications in

Carley, S. G. (2013). *Serial killers, mass murders, & disorders.* Boston: SGC Production.

significant weight loss without dieting, severe problems with mood, sleep disruption, and slow response patterns.

Joseph Westbecker

Joseph would get married in July of 1960 obtaining a job at a printing company. Joseph could not necessarily be characterized as joyful or gregarious yet the best times in his life were before and during the initial stages of his first marriage. Joseph could often be found working overtime at his job which over time he would obtain tacit knowledge pertinent to the required tasks. Joseph's long work hours and general personality disposition would take a toll on his marriage. Joseph would urge his wife not to work which she did, and in 1978 he would move out in the hopes his wife would give up her job. When Joseph's wife did not give up her job this would act as the catalyst for the psychiatric symptoms Joseph would go on to display. A physician treating Joseph for bursitis in 1980 would first notice the symptoms associating with Joseph's mental disorder. Joseph would spend a week of inpatient treatment at the psychiatric unit of the hospital for agitation and depression upon referral by his physician. The summary of the psychiatric report would state Joseph to work long 16 hour days to then frequent the bar at nights. This would leave Joseph only two to three hours sleep daily as Joseph would seem to drive himself mercilessly.

Joseph would begin another relationship and marry Brenda in August of 1981. This relationship would not be exactly a happy one the result of problems with stepchildren, depression, and Joseph's anger attributing to Brenda's ex-husband. Joseph would follow Brenda's ex-husband for a month and claim, "If he didn't always have a witness with him I would've blown his brains out." Joseph's personal disputes with his oldest son and mother would result in a break of contact. In 1984 Joseph would make his first of several suicide attempts. The catalyst to his wife filing for divorce would

Carley, S. G. (2013). *Serial killers, mass murders, & disorders.* Boston: SGC Production.

be Joseph wielding a gun threatening to commit suicide. A month after Joseph was released from the psychiatric unit in May 1984 Joseph and his wife would separate. Their relationship would continue until Joseph's death, at times living as husband and wife. The pressures of Joseph's job would increase at this time. Upon the request of Joseph's psychiatrist, a result of Joseph's believed inability to sustain concentration and make adequate decisions, he would be excused from operating a piece of machinery at his job. Joseph would never work on the "folder" again, which would brew anger and hostility inside Joseph toward his company and management personnel. Joseph's diet of cookies and ice cream may have contributed to Joseph's increasing depression and agitation. Joseph would undergo another hospitalization in March of 1987 and upon reply to the sentence completion test when asked, "How do you feel about yourself?" Joseph's reply would be, "I don't like feeling weak. I feel I've been screwed. I'm angry." Joseph would have continual concerns regarding working the folder, and would even make a written complaint of discrimination against his mental handicap. The union would not support Joseph's case, and the human relations committee would find jurisdiction of the case to be out of their hands. Joseph would insist he would continue to be requested to work on the folder though this is doubtful. Joseph would complain of his co-workers calling him Westbecker the Whacko, the sicko, among other names. It was at this time Joseph would start buying guns and reading magazines the central topic of which would pertain to guns. Joseph would even on occasion bring a gun to work.

From 1987 on the treating psychiatrist of Joseph would be Dr. Lee Coleman. Dr. Coleman would give Joseph a diagnosis of atypical bipolar disorder because of the paranoia Joseph would display. As a result Dr. Coleman would prescribe Joseph medications of which none would work. Joseph's condition would deteriorate with time and Coleman would suggest Joseph to take a medical leave.

Carley, S. G. (2013). *Serial killers, mass murders, & disorders.*
Boston: SGC Production.

Joseph's last day working at Standard Gravure would be August of 1988. A short time earlier Joseph would tell Brenda he wanted to kill a bunch of people at his work. It would be determined Joseph would have a disability and as entitled to benefits, the Social Security Administration would award him $892 monthly. Joseph's unremarkable behavior would occur over the following year, minus the thoughts of enacting revenge upon his acquaintances, not the psychiatrist. Joseph would purchase guns during this time, and lose his grandmother, who he was fond of in July of 1989. Joseph would continue monthly visits with his psychiatrists, who would note increases in cognitive disruption and agitation. During one such session a crying Joseph would relate a story in which he was forced to have oral sex in the presence of employees to be excused from his work on the "folder." This story would never be corroborated and the psychiatrist would find Joseph's story delusional. The psychiatrist would recommend Joseph to commit himself to a mental hospital of which he would refuse. The psychiatrist would also recommend Joseph to discontinue his use of Prozac. After the shootings at the Standard Gravure high levels of Prozac and lithium were found in Joseph's blood along with other antidepressants and sleeping medications. Joseph would be taking these by his own choice according to the psychiatrist. Joseph would leave $1720 in cash on his dresser the day of the shootings, and the February 6th, 1989 issue of Time magazine on his kitchen table devoted to Armed America. The magazine would be opened to a story on Patrick Purdy. Joseph would visit the plant with a bag full of guns (AK-47, two Mac-10s, and two other pistols) and bullets as he would move from floor to floor shooting and killing those he knew and some he didn't know. He would even kill some he got along with and never find the one's he would view as his enemy.

Causes for Joseph Westbecker's Behaviors

Carley, S. G. (2013). *Serial killers, mass murders, & disorders.* Boston: SGC Production.

There would not be a single factor to point out as the significant cause for Joseph's behavior. Genetics would give Joseph a bad start and the losses and severe disruptions during his early childhood would compound this problem. It is these factors robbing Joseph in the opportunity of developing personality and cognitive variables, the majority use to effectively overcome emotional hardships. It is these same childhood disruptions predisposing Joseph to depression. Leading to hyperactivity of the hypothalamic-pituitary-adrenal axis are early stressors resulting in an oversecretion of stimulating hormones the result of stress. The impact is the facilitation of agitated depression. Voiding options to develop better coping patterns, would be Joseph's often negative relationship with his mother increasing pain and distress. Joseph's chances of turning his life around would become virtually nonexistent as he would increasingly distance himself from those who cared about him including his eldest son. Joseph may have taken the wrong approach in turning his life around by accumulating weaponry and permitting himself to be influenced by the models of destruction and deviance present within the media. Police would find after the devastation of Joseph's actions a copy of Soldier of Fortune magazine written for violence groupies. They would also find the Time magazine issue focusing on Patrick Purdy who too would use an AK -47 in wounding 30 children and adults, killing five children in 1989 in a Stockton, California, schoolyard. It may be the media portrayals of these acts contributing to the violence toward others (Bartol & Bartol, 2008).

Civil Trial Against Joseph Westbecker

After his death the fame of Joseph Westbecker would increase as the survivors and the estates of those killed by Westbecker would join forces in a civil suit. The defense for Westbecker would claim it to be his use of Prozac responsible for his actions. This defense would point fingers toward psychiatrist Dr. Coleman and the manufacturer of Prozac Eli Lilly. This would be the first case in which civil action would allege SSRIs as facilitating violence. The court case would take 2.5 months, and the jury which would deliberate for hours would return with a 9 – 3 decision finding Westbecker solely responsible exonerating the Prozac company. It would later be discovered Eli Lilly to secretly provide large settlements to the survivors of the attack and their lawyers. The official record of the case would be changed by the judge in 1997 to a dismissal of a settled case from the original jury verdict. Until 2001, this case would set the tone for similar litigation upon the reward of eight-million dollars by a Wyoming court to an oilfield worker who killed himself and his entire family including his wife, daughter, and grand daughter. The guilty party would be the makers of Paxil who did not include a warning on their labels of the increased risks of homicide or suicide. The jury would hold the pharmaceutical company 80% responsible and they would be liable for 6.4 million dollars in damages.

Causes and Treatments for Depression

The biological and psychological factors present within the most serious cases of depression would show themselves in the case of Joseph Westbecker (Dilalla, 2004). The combination of internal and external factors combine to form depressive symptoms producing a self perpetuating sequence. The primary treatments for cases of major depression include chemotherapy and supportive therapy involving office visits of no particular theoretical orientation. Interpersonal psychotherapy involving formal psychotherapy aims at promoting effective interpersonal relationships and in the process improving cognitive behavior modification and self esteem (Beck, 1976). The aim of cognitive behavior modification is to determine the governing rules of the depressed individual. Another effective method can be dynamic therapy (Chambless et al., 1996). In the case the client suffers early trauma, the psychological treatment may be more effective. Such early trauma can involve the loss or abuse of a parent. Adult depression without evidence of early trauma, typical indicators tend to be medication with psychological treatment. Among depressed individuals with lesser levels of deterioration, mindfulness training can be useful (Williams, Teasdale, Segal, & Kabat-Zin, 2008). Interpersonal psychotherapy and cognitive behavior modification are treatable with antidepressant medication. Antidepressants such as selective serotonin reuptake inhibitors are often prescribed by physicians, other than psychiatrists. This may raise concern of the overprescription of such drugs, which may diminish the anxieties of life instead of treating a disorder. Clinical depression occurs in children, and a sharp rise has been noted in the prescription of antidepressants in treating these cases. This is despite the administration of antidepressants to children increasing suicidal ideations and violent behaviors (Novak & Pelaez, 2004). The drug Prozac accused of being the propelling force behind Joseph Westbecker's actions would be the first approved antidepressant for use on children. The attainment of change, no matter how abundant, relapse can be common. Signs of relapse among depressives exist, including a clinically depressed episode during late childhood or adolescence, a high level of dissatisfaction with roles in life, poor physical health, a family history of depression, high depression level at time of treatment, and a large number of previous depressive episodes. It is best if during the first three months of a depressive taking medication, to receive constant monitoring of the effects of the medication.

Carley, S. G. (2013). *Serial killers, mass murders, & disorders.* Boston: SGC Production.

Adolph Hitler, Joseph Stalin, & Saddam Hussein

Malignant Narcissism

The general definition of the term narcissism is the presence of excessive self love. All cultures possess of the narcissistic, yet it would appear even more common among our more modern culture encouraged emphatically by individualism and the self (Lasch, 1978). It would not be until the third edition of the DSM in 1980, including narcissistic personality disorder (NPD) among its list of diagnosable disorders. The continuation of narcissistic personality disorder would occur into the fourth edition of the DSM, and expects to continue into future editions of the publication. The requirements for a diagnosis of NPD beginning during early childhood with a lack of empathy, need for admiration, and pervasive patterns of grandiosity, must include the following symptoms according to the DSM-IV-TR: arrogance, envy for others or belief people are envious of the individual, absence of empathy, exploitive interpersonal behavior, sense of entitlement, and a need for excessive admiration. At least five of these criteria must be met to qualify a diagnosis of NPD. The concept of NPD would be extended to a smaller group labeled malignant narcissists (MN) applying to Stalin and Hitler (Kernberg, 1984). In summary of

Carley, S. G. (2013). *Serial killers, mass murders, & disorders.* Boston: SGC Production.

Kernberg's theory Eric Goode would find Saddam Hussein to accurately fit the description of MN. Malignant narcissists possess the components of NPD and in addition display aggression, lack remorse for damage to others, lack moral judgment, paranoia, and display psychopathic characteristics.

Adolph Hitler

Adolph Hitler was born in the Austrian village of Branau Am Inn across the border of German Bavaria on April 20, 1889. Adolph would be the third of five children. His siblings would have four different mothers, only Adolph sharing the same mother (Klara Polzl) with another sibling. Adolph's early childhood would remain a mystery, yet in 1895 Adolph would enter the Austrian primary school who were strict disciplinarians. At this same time the father of Adolph, Alois Hitler, would retire collecting an Austrian civil service pension. Adolph's father an alcoholic was a very strict disciplinarian, himself possessing little tolerance for those who would not obey. As a result Adolph and his family members would be subject to numerous emotional and physical beatings. Adolph would possess a fine singing voice and would sing in the Catholic Church choir. Adolph would consider joining the clergy and in a playful gesture at times would dress up like the priest.

The Hitler family would move in 1898 to Leonding a village close to Linz. Adolph's talent for architectural drawing would assist him in attaining good grades with little effort. A favorite picture book of Adolph would depict the German/French war of 1870 – 1871. Hitler would make the statement in his book Mein Kampf, "My greatest spiritual experience would be the great historic struggle. My enthusiasm for war and soldiering would increase." Alois Hitler would die of lung hemorrhage on January 3, 1903. The family would be left well off financially, and Adolph would enroll in a private boarding school dropping out at the age of 16. Adolph's dream of becoming an artist would become a reality with his enrollment to the Vienna Academy of Fine Arts in October of 1907. At this time a jewish doctor, Dr. Eduard Bloch would diagnose Adolph's mother with breast cancer. Adolph would visit his mother but then return to art school. He would be told he possessed little talent and fail his next exam. Adolph would return home depressed believing himself to possess talent. Adolph would anguish over his mother's suffering who was in the final stages of her painful disease. She would die on December 21, 1907, as Hitler would in part blame her doctor, Bloch, which may in part attribute to Adolph's hatred of Jews.

Adolph would room with his best friend August Kubizek upon moving back to Vienna in February of 1908. Kubizek's recollection of Adolph would be an increasing display of instability among his personality marked by raging outbursts when people would disagree with him. Adolph's second attempt in joining the Fine Arts Academy would fail in October of 1908 further destabilizing Adolph. Adolph would be rejected again, this time for service within the Austrian military on February 5, 1914. Upon rejection Adolph would petition the king of Bavaria Ludwig III, and in August of 1914 Adolph would be enrolled in this military. Within four months Adolph would earn a second class Iron Cross. On November 11, 1918 World War I would come to an end and German Jews would become the focus of Hitler's rage whom he felt would betray Germany. Hitler's interest in politics would guide him toward the Nazi party whom he would join in 1919. This is one year after Hitler's episode with hysterical blindness, who under hypnosis by Dr. Edmund Forster would suggest to Adolph his sight was necessary to redeem the lost honor of the German people. Hitler's sight would return.

The beginning of Hitler's political career would be marked by a speech given in Hofbrauhauskeller on October 16, 1919. Hitler's

Carley, S. G. (2013). *Serial killers, mass murders, & disorders.*
Boston: SGC Production.

political activities would twice land him in prison, and the publishing of the Mein Kampf's first volume would occur on July 18, 1925. The power of the Nazi party would increase basing on the pledge to restore Germany's lost honor blaming economic and social troubles on the jewish people. Hitler would become Chancellor on January 30, 1933, and Fuehrer on August 1, 1934 upon the death of Hindenberg. The rebuilt military power of Germany would result in the invasion of Czechoslovakia, Sudetenland, and Austria. A pact would be signed among Poland and England on August 25, 1939, yet Hitler would decide to invade Poland just a week later. On September third Britain would declare war with Germany followed by France one day later. Hitler again would go against the advice of his military experts invading Russia on June 22, 1941. Hitler would be wrong in expecting a quick victory as the Russian soldiers and winter would decimate the eastern front of the German army. Along with the entry of the United States into the war in 1941, the tide would be turned (Mosier, 2004). Hitler would insist Germany would eventually win despite increasing defeats. This would come under the assumption, in an attempt to stop Russian communism the United States and Britain would join Germany. Hitler viewing only his ideas as valid would continue to display a propensity toward rage and tyrannical outbursts.

Hitler would be responsible for the death of millions of Jews over the course of WW II among others, including those captured from other countries. The majority would die in concentration camps as medical experiments, acts of cruelty, shooting, gas chambers, extreme labor, or starvation. As the architect of the massive and horrific killing no evidence exists Hitler would kill anyone by his own hand. Upon Hitler's realization he would be captured by his enemies, he would retreat to a bunker under the Reich Chancellory in Berlin with his closest advisors and household. It was here on April 29, 1945, he would marry his mistress Eva Braun. Supplied by Dr. Stumpfegger, Hitler and his wife would plan to commit suicide through a lethal dose of prussic acid. Hitler would first test the acid on his favorite dog Blondi. On the evening of April 30 Eva and Hitler would be found dead, Eva dying of poisoning and Hitler from a single gunshot wound to the temple with his 7.67 mm Walther pistol. Hitler would shoot himself just as he took the prussic acid. Upon order of Hitler himself, their bodies would be covered in petrol in the courtyard and burned to ashes. The parts of their jaw bones not incinerated would be used as identifiers.

Joseph Stalin

Joseph Stalin was born in the Caucuses in the Georgian town of Gori to a family of poor socioeconomic status. Joseph's listed birth date when he would come to power is December 21, 1879 although his birth records would show Joseph to be born on December 6, 1878. Joseph's father a severe alcoholic would work as a shoemaker. Joseph's father in a violent manner would beat both his wife and children. His mother an orthodox Christian was a maid and washerwoman and too would beat her son on occasion. No evidence would suggest Joseph to ever feel affection toward his mother, who he would give orders to be constantly watched despite Joseph's supposed public expression of devotion toward his mother (Medvedev & Medvedev, 2003). A model for Stalin as a politician would be his great grandfather Zara Dzhugashvili, leader of a bloody peasant revolt. Stalin would be self conscious pertaining to his looks, consisting of one arm shorter than the other the result of an accident and facial scars from smallpox. He would often wear high wooden shoes to hide his short stature. Stalin's sense of inferiority would increase being from Georgia, a place Russian born Soviets would look down upon.

Bolshevism would lead Lenin's political movement. This is a concept of the working class possessing control instead of politicians. This concept would evolve into communism. To fuel the cause, Stalin would join the Bolsheviks in committing robberies. Stalin is suspected of murdering as part of his involvement in these robberies. The tsar's police would often arrest Stalin and his comrades leading to Stalin's exile. Russian morale would diminish with the end of World War I, and a civil war would ensue with the assassination of the tsar on July 17, 1918. Upon the prevalence of the Bolsheviks, Stalin would receive the title of Commissar of Nationalities. Stalin's ruthless personality would be perfect for such a job as he was to enforce the party line. Russian communist leader Leon Trotsky would send a detachment of army specialists to Stalin in 1918. Stalin because of a lack of trust would imprison the men whose fate would be to drown mysteriously on a sinking ship. Many others were executed on order of Stalin by shooting. Stalin would marry Yekaterina Svandize at a young age, and they would have one child Yakov. She would die shortly thereafter, and her family would raise her son Yakov. Stalin rarely would see his son. Stalin would marry a second time to a 17 year old when he was 39, Nadezhda Alliluyeva, who would kill herself in 1932. Stalin would have two more children Vasily and Svetlana, who again he would seldom see.

Stalin would be placed in charge of the Soviet Secretariat in 1920, permitting him powers of appointment to the Communist Party and government positions. Those Stalin did not trust he would eliminate and those who he did trust would be appointed. Stalin's growing circle would not be enough to gain power as Stalin would set to downgrade Trotsky's influence. Stalin would demote and exile Trotsky in 1927 making Stalin a dictator by the end of the 1920s. This would be a time Russia would experience a great famine, and Stalin who would hoard the available wheat from the lowest classes, would initiate 5 million deaths. Stalin would make a law against mentioning the existence of any famine. The Soviets would attempt to increase industry to support Stalinian views of a powerful Russia. Despite the strong traditional rural economy of Russia, it would

Carley, S. G. (2013). *Serial killers, mass murders, & disorders*. Boston: SGC Production.

continue into a recession. The accountants of Stalin would lie about productivity in fears of being put to death by Stalin. Stalin would force dissenters to work long hard hours often leading to their deaths at the Gulag camps. Stalin would be looked at as a god in 1929 when Russia would recover from the recession. Russians would blame Stalin for the revolution. Stalin would be viewed as infallible, a concept taught to the school children. Blanketing the Soviet Union would be pictures and statues of Joseph Stalin. The new religion within the Soviet Union would be the worship of Joseph Stalin. Anyone Stalin would see as a threat during the 1930s he would kill including members of his own party. In order to look blameless for any problems, Stalin would force his party members to confess to treason using false promises, threatening family members, and even torture. The only one who could speak out against Stalin would be Trotsky, who would again be exiled and beaten to death. Anyone speaking out against Stalin would be killed, and others made aware of their elimination.

Stalin would admire Hitler and share in his anti-Semitism. It was this shared belief creating an alliance among the two. Hitler would betray Stalin because of his hatred and fear of communism (Montefiore, 2004). Stalin's son Yakov would be taken prisoner by the German army along with many Soviets during the invasion of Kiev. Upon the negotiation by German troops to exchange Yakov for fellow Germans, Stalin would claim to have no son. Upon this Yakov would be executed as Stalin would sacrifice his own son for the Soviet party. Stalin would rule the Soviet Union with an iron fist during and after the second world war, exiling and killing anyone he would not trust. Referred to as Uncle Joe the people would view Stalin as a benevolent patriarch. This is despite a death count of 20 million people or more through suppression of revolutions, Gulags, purges, and famines. Stalin would suffer a pair of paralyzing strokes on February 28 and March 1 of 1953 and would slowly suffocate to his death on March 5, 1953.

Carley, S. G. (2013). *Serial killers, mass murders, & disorders.* Boston: SGC Production.

Saddam Hussein

The presidency of Iraq would belong to Saddam Hussein from 1979 to 2003. The termination of this presidency would occur in December of 2003 with the invasion of Iraq and capture of Hussein by U. S. troops. It would be the family background and childhood of Hussein, along with the acts of psychopathic violence classifying Hussein as a malignant narcissist among other diagnostic categories. The impoverished Hussein would suffer through an unhappy childhood. His birth would occur on April 28, 1937, in a neighboring village of Takrit, Iraq. Hussein would not know his father, who would either abandon him or die around his time of birth. At the time Husseins's mother Subha was pregnant with him, his elder brother would die. Both before and after the death of Hussein's father his mother would reject him. She would even attempt to abort Saddam. Subha would have several suicide attempts before and after Saddam's birth, and at times others would care for him. At various points in time it would be his mother and stepfather Hassam who would raise him (Coughlin, 2002).

Hassam was a sheepherder by trade and would possess a violent disposition. He would abuse Saddam and make him steal livestock so Hassam could later sell the product. Saddam would be illiterate until the age of 10 as Hassam would forbid Saddam from going to school. This would stir jealousy among Saddam of his cousin who could both read and write. Saddam's childhood friends would characterize him as quiet and lonely yet constantly angry. Saddam would be sent to live with his uncle Khairallah in Baghdad at the age of 10. Saddam's violent childhood would continue into his teenage years trying to kill his school teacher at the age of 14. At this time Saddam would be linked to a double murder of a school teacher and his cousin. Saddam would be encouraged by Tulfah to possess dreams of being the hero Saladin, who would fight the

Crusaders. Saddam would model the bitterness of Tulfah toward the British and Westerners.

Saddam would turn to politics upon finishing his schooling at the age of 24 leading him to power within the Baath party. Saddam would attempt his first political assassination in 1959 with the unsuccessful attempt on military ruler Abdul Qassim. Saddam would be sentenced to death upon his conviction yet would escape to Cairo, Egypt. Saddam would be arrested on two occasions while in Egypt for threatening a fellow student and another for chasing someone down the street with a knife. Through a military coup the Baath party would rise to power and Saddam would return to Iraq. Saddam would become deputy chairman in 1974 when his cousin General Ahmed Hassan Al-Bakr would become president of the Revolutionary Command Council. Upon Saddam's leadership of Iraq, he would make his uncle Tulfah mayor of Baghdad. The inner circle of Saddam would consist of his most trusted Baath members and of course his family and friends. Anyone posing a threat to Saddam he would sadistically eliminate. When Saddam's cousin Adnan Khairallah would become defense minister, he would ease him out of military intelligence when he would achieve a power base in the army. Adnan would die in a helicopter crash in April of 1989.

In 1964 Saddam would be thrown in jail by anti-Baathist factions. While Saddam would be in prison he would be elected as secretary general of the Baathist party. Through a coup he would escape prison becoming the leading member of the Baath party. Ahmed Hassan al-Bakr his older cousin would become president of Iraq, and by 1973 Saddam Hussein would be the country's vice president. In 1979 Hussein would take control of the presidency staging a Stalinist style purge. Upon Saddam's appointment, within six days he would condemn to death 20 leading members of the Baath party along with numerous army officials. President al-Bakr's death in 1982 many suspect Saddam to play a role. In September of 1980

Carley, S. G. (2013). *Serial killers, mass murders, & disorders.*
Boston: SGC Production.

Saddam would ignore a 1975 peace agreement with Iran, and invade the country killing thousands over a span of eight years. During this same time Saddam would have thousands of his own citizens killed, especially the Kurds through use of poison gas.

The numerous titles and widespread powers Hussein would give himself would point to his narcissism. Hussein would blanket Iraq with images and statues of himself, and along with showing off his palaces would show off his prized possession, a golden machine gun. His lakeside vacation resort in Baghdad would have his initials carved into each brick, and a 30 foot bronze statue of himself placed at the gateway. A debt would grow a result of the Iran-Iraq war of $75 billion generating political pressure onto Hussein, leading to the invasion of Kuwait on August 2, 1990. Iraq would quickly occupy the entire country before experiencing defeat. In 1993, Hussein would break peace terms, and fail to abide by United Nations inspector mandates in 1998. U. S. President George W. Bush would give Saddam the ultimatum of leaving Iraq in March 2003, of which Saddam would ignore. The United States would invade Iraq and Saddam would go into hiding. Upon Saddam's capture by the United States, the Iraqi government would execute Saddam Hussein for his crimes.

Fitting the Label of Malignant Narcissism

It would seem Hitler, Stalin, and Hussein to each fit the description of malignant narcissist. The trio would seem to demonstrate the characteristics associating with narcissistic personality disorder involving arrogance, lack of empathy, avoiding those not accepting their self-perception of uniqueness, need for admiration, sense of entitlement, preoccupation with power and success, and grandiosity, along with the characteristics associating with MN of aggression, paranoia, lack of remorse, lack of moral judgment, and the antisocial factors contributing to psychopathy. Playing a part may be the fact each of these men would experience physical abuse and feelings of inferiority early in life, as genetics too may contribute without a doubt. It continues to be a difficult process of fully explaining the evolution of MN provided the insufficient data. Differences certainly continue to exist among these three men. Marking Hitler would be a lack of moral judgment, paranoia, and sense of a unique mission. The indications are Hitler never killed by his own hand, except perhaps during his service in World War I in the German army. It was not sadism or the enjoyment of personal cruelty architecting the death of millions of people, but instead a delusional belief system. Stalin would be viewed as more stunning and materialistic than Hitler, yet would continue to be deceitful, sadistic, ruthless, and somewhat paranoid. Hussein's needs would stem more from sadistic aggression, psychopathy, deification, and excessive admiration. In the delight Hussein experiences in brandishing his golden machine gun, this may signify his personal aggression and need for admiration. On April 4, 2004, in Iraq Hussein's legacy would continue, when an army of his followers were unleashed on occupation forces by the Shiite cleric Muqtada al-Sadr. The irony to this act is it was al-Sadr's father who would be assassinated on orders of Hussein. To be a malignant narcissist one does not have to possess undisputed power or show the traditional characteristics of mental illness, such as psychoses in association with severe depression. The predomination of sadism and aggression is likely to develop into criminal behavior. Malignant narcissism may be a success within the corporation, in the absence of aggression or paranoia, but the continuity of an ability to manipulate others, high sense of uniqueness, and lack of moral judgment. A significant other without needs for intimacy or caring may be the perfect mate for a malignant narcissist who may be capable of maintaining a successful personal relationship.

Carley, S. G. (2013). *Serial killers, mass murders, & disorders*. Boston: SGC Production.

Adam Peter Lanza

Lanza Enters the Building

In Newtown, Connecticut, at the Sandy Hook Elementary School, Adam Lanza would fatally shoot and kill 20 children and six adults on December 14, 2012. Just prior to the attack, Lanza would shoot and kill his mother Nancy in their Newtown residence. Lanza would shoot himself in the head as the first responders would arrive on the scene. After the 2007 Virginia Tech Massacre, the incident would represent the second deadliest mass shooting committed by a single individual in American history. After the 1927 Bath school bombings in Michigan, the incident represents the second deadliest of mass shootings at an American elementary school. The incident also represents the deadliest shooting in American history among United States public schools. As a result of the shootings, renewed debate would arise pertaining to gun control within the United States. New legislation would arise of possible bans on semi-automatic weapons and magazines holding more than 10 rounds of ammunition.

The Sandy Hook elementary school would enroll children from kindergarten to the fourth grade consisting of 456 children. As of recent the school security had become more strict requiring

Carley, S. G. (2013). *Serial killers, mass murders, & disorders*.
Boston: SGC Production.

individual admittance of school visitors whose visual identification would be monitored through surveillance cameras. After morning arrivals the school doors would be locked daily at 09:30 AM. Fairfield County is a suburb of New York City in which Newtown is situated. A town of 28,000, homicide would be a rarity with a single killing in a decade's time. This day would be like no other in Newtown as on Friday December 14, 2012 sometime before the doors would close at the Sandy Hook Elementary School, Adam Lanza would fatally shoot and kill his mother Nancy in their Newtown home with a .22 Marlin rifle. Her body would be found later by investigators lying in bed covered in pajamas, four gunshot wounds inflicted to her head. Adam would proceed to take his mother's car to Sandy Hook Elementary. Adam would not arrive at the school until 09:35 AM so he would have to make his way through the locked glass door using his mother's Bushmaster XM-15 rifle. Lanza would be wearing a mask and black clothing as he would enter the building. At the time of the morning announcements some would claim to hear the whistling of gunshots in the background of the PA system.

Lanza Attacks Sandy Hook

A faculty meeting involving the school psychologist, principal, and other faculty members would be interrupted by the sounds of the gunshots. Immediately responding to the scene would be principal Dawn Hochsprung, psychologist Mary Sherlach, and faculty member Natalie Hammond, who upon approaching the source of the disturbing sound would encounter and confront Lanza. The three women would alert colleagues of the ensuing danger by yelling, "Shooter, Don't move!" At this precise moment Lanza would shoot and kill both Sherlach and Hochsprung. Hammond would run for her life as Lanza would pursue in a three-quarter paced jog. Hammond would make her way to the meeting room and press the door closed behind her in hopes Lanza would not be aware of her

Carley, S. G. (2013). *Serial killers, mass murders, & disorders.*
Boston: SGC Production.

location. Lanza would shoot through the door into her leg and arm. Hammond would survive the attack and be treated for her injuries after the carnage at the Danbury Hospital. It would seem the intercom to be left on as scared teachers and students hiding in closets could hear people screaming "don't shoot" followed by the sound of gunshots.

Lauren Rousseau was a substitute teacher who would frantically try to hide her first grade classroom from Lanza when he would enter the classroom. Many were herded in the back of the classroom and Rousseau would open fire on the group. Only one survivor would outlast Lanza who would claim to play dead and remain still. Lanza would next enter the classroom of Victoria Leigh Soto who would have her children concealed in closets and under tables. Lanza would enter just as Soto would go to lock the classroom door. Soto would tell Lanza the children to be in the auditorium. Lanza would search the classroom and upon finding the children hiding under the desks, he would start shooting at them. When Soto would place herself between the shooter and the children he would shoot her too. Jesse Lewis would yell for his classmates to run, and Larza would reply by shooting him. Some of the classmates would run and escape on account of Lewis' efforts. Six children from Soto's class would escape in part due to a jammed weapon, and along with a bus driver would take refuge in a nearby home. When the police would enter the classroom the five children hiding in the closet remained unharmed. A total of eleven students from Soto's class would survive the horrific attack. Other faculty members dying trying to protect their students would be Anne Marie Murphy and Rachel D'Avino. The school nurse Sally Cox would hide in her office under a desk. Lanza supposedly entered the office and after gazing around for a brief moment would turn and exit the room. She could see his boots and pant legs as he stood in the office. Sally and Barbara Halstead would alert emergency medical services hiding in a first aid supply closet for upwards of five hours. Alerting classrooms

Carley, S. G. (2013). *Serial killers, mass murders, & disorders.* Boston: SGC Production.

would be the custodian Rick Thorne as he would run through hallways. Kaitlin Roig's first grade classroom would be hiding 14 first grade students who would be told to keep quiet. A piece of black construction paper on the door glass may have lead Lanza to believe the class to be empty. In any case, he would never enter this particular classroom. Roig would barricade the door. Yvonne Cech and Maryann Jacob members of the school library staff would hide 18 children in a part of the library used for lockdown drills. One of the doors would not lock so the children would crawl into a storage space and the door would be barricaded with a filing cabinet. The fourth grade music classroom would be led by Maryrose Kristopik whose students would hide in a supply closet. Lanza would yell, "Let me in," as the students would continue to hide. Two third graders walking down the hallway when the shooting would begin would be dragged into Abbey Clements classroom where they would be hid from Lanza. Laura Feinstein would hide in her class with two students for 40 minutes until the authorities would arrive.

It would not be until the expenditure of 154 rounds of ammo from his rifle, Lanza would stop shooting between the times of 09:46 AM and 09:49 AM. Lanza would become aware he was spotted by police at which time he would flee to Soto's classroom and take his own life with a single gunshot wound to the head expelled from his 10 mm Glock handgun. The determination of authorities is multiple reloads would occur during Lanza's attack. All of his victims would be shot multiple times with most of the shooting occurring within two classrooms in which 20 of the shooting deaths would occur. The six adults killed in the massacre were all women and the 20 children ranging in ages of six to seven would consist of 12 girls and eight boys. Cars in the parking lot also would have bullets in them leading one to believe Lanza would shoot at escapees as they would flee the carnage.

Carley, S. G. (2013). *Serial killers, mass murders, & disorders.*
Boston: SGC Production.

Investigation of Lanza

At 09:35 AM Newtown police dispatch would first request officers on the scene. Six minutes later Connecticut State Police would receive their first call initiating the mobilization of a state police helicopter, a bomb squad, and police tactical and police dog units. Police would evacuate survivors room by room locking down the school and escorting groups of adults and students from the premises. The authorities would never fire a single shot and they would sweep the building in the possibility other shooters were hiding. The Danbury hospital would declare a state of emergency with the risk and expectation of numerous victims. To assist the authorities the New York City medical examiner would dispatch a portable morgue. The night after the shooting the victims' bodies would be identified.

Lanza would never leave any type of suicide note. Lanza's mother was at one time an employee of the school which may be in some way the reason he would select the school as the location for his attack. He also attended the school when he was young. Police would investigate an altercation the day before the shooting to see if Lanza would be involved in any manner. Lanza would shoot and kill two of the people involved in this altercation both the principal and the psychologist. The initial reports would state the perpetrator to be Ryan Lanza as Adam would carry his identification as he would carry out the attack. Ryan would state not to be close to his brother, and anyone who should post Ryan as the attacker to be subject to prosecution. Lanza would make use of a small arsenal to perform the attack as would be noticed when the attack was finally complete. Lanza would be found with a 9mm SIG Sauer P226 handgun, a .223-caliber Bushmaster XM15-E2S rifle, a 10mm Glock handgun, in his car would be a an Izhmash Saiga-12 combat shotgun, and an abundance of unused ammunition. It would be the rifle Lanza would make use to kill his victims during the shooting

Carley, S. G. (2013). *Serial killers, mass murders, & disorders.*
Boston: SGC Production.

spree. Court records would state the shooting to last less than five minutes with the expelling of 155 rounds of ammo all of which were from the rifle minus the fatal self-inflicted head shot from a 10 mm pistol.

An autopsy of Lanza would search for evidence of medications or drugs and obtain DNA testing information. Lanza would possess no kind of abnormalities of his brain structure. This does not mean Lanza's bout with autism did not affect his decision-making (Flannery, Modzeleski, & Kretschmar, 2013). Prior to the shooting Lanza would damage his hard drive making it difficult for investigators to recover pertinent information. It is suspected Lanza would investigate other mass killings. According to investigation reports, Lanza would create a spreadsheet consisting of 500 rampage killings and the weapons used in the attacks. A safe in the Lanza home would consist of over 1,400 rounds of ammunition among a .22 Marlin rifle, a .30 Enfield rifle, and a .45 Henry rifle. Adam would often play the video game Call of Duty.

The Life of Adam Lanza

The birth of Adam Peter Lanza would occur on April 22, 1992 and along with his mother the two would reside in Sandy Hook a short five miles from the elementary school Adam would once attend. Adam would possess no criminal record. He would be an honor student at the St. Rose of Lima Catholic high school yet would be mostly home schooled by his mother. He would earn his GED in this manner. In 2008 and 2009 Lanza would attend Connecticut State University. Those who knew Lanza during high-school would describe him as intelligent but fidgety and nervous. They stated him to be uncomfortable in social settings and would avoid attracting attention. He did not have many close friends and was suspected of experimenting with homosexuality. According to Lanza's brother this may have stemmed from his autism and disordered personality.

Carley, S. G. (2013). *Serial killers, mass murders, & disorders.* Boston: SGC Production.

Adam was once diagnosed with Asperger syndrome, a spectrum disorder associating with autism, and sensory integration disorder, a neurological disorder.

Adam and his mother would be supported by alimony payments from her husband after their divorce. Nancy, Adam's mother was a bit of a gun enthusiast possessing a dozen firearms teaching her kids to shoot by taking them to the shooting range. Some would defend the rights of the autistic possessing firearms claiming it not to be a mental illness. The truth is it may be even worse as the individual possesses of some sort of control processing disturbance which it would appear affected Adam's decision-making in this case (Walkup & Rubin, 2013).

Government's Reaction to the Shooting

The day of the shootings President Obama would address the nation to a televised audience of stunned listeners stating the nation to need to come together to prevent further tragedies of this kind. Obama would express his sympathy to the affected families. Obama would order flags raised to half-staff. Obama would meet with victims' families on December 16 and speak at an interfaith vigil. Obama would award the six adult victims of the massacre the Presidential Citizens Medal on February 15, 2013. Connecticut Governor Dan Malloy too would speak at the vigil requesting a statewide moment of silence and the ringing of 26 church bells one week after the shootings at 09:30 AM Friday December 21. Throughout the weekend after the shooting many organizations and countries would offer their condolences.

Within 15 hours of the incident 100,000 Americans would show renewed support toward the national debate on gun control. The group would express this opinion over the We the People petitioning website. In a December 19 speech Obama would affirm to make gun control central legislation during his second term. Obama would propose 12 congressional actions one month after the shooting pertaining to gun control and sign 23 executive orders. To address the causes of gun violence in the United States a Gun Violence Task Force would be created by Obama to be led by Vice President Biden. An assault weapon ban would be proposed by Senators Joe Lieberman and Dianne Feinstein. Feinstein would go so far as to introduce a ban bill during the first day of new Congress as similarly Congresswoman Gabrielle Giffords, who was shot and injured in the Tucson shooting, would help raise money in furthering gun control efforts after the Sandy Hook shootings. The weeks following the shootings the result of fears of future restrictions would result in a massive increase in firearm sales toward magazines, guns, and ammunition. The National Rifle Association on December 21, 2012 would suggest the United States Congress to appropriate funds permitting armed police officers to man the schools. Such an act would make the banning of certain firearms unnecessary as the added safety measure would be more than enough of a deterrent to keep a perpetrator from selecting a grade school as an attack site. Another option is to arm teachers with conceal and carry permits. Each teacher could strap a little .36 caliber to their waste, and in the event an attacker should approach the school, the teachers would be more than prepared. Both sides of the issue can be extreme in either case. A new school protection program would be created led by drug enforcement administrator and United States Congressman Asa Hutchinson, which would be announced by the National Rifle Association (NRA). President Obama would cite the incident in his proposals for increased gun control one month after the shooting. Included within Obama's proposals would be a 10 cartridge limit pertaining to magazine capacity, an assault weapons ban, and universal background checks on firearm purchases. Official guests during the announcement would be survivors and relatives of the guests during the shootings. President Obama would receive a letter regarding his demonization

Carley, S. G. (2013). *Serial killers, mass murders, & disorders.*
Boston: SGC Production.

of firearms from the Utah Sheriff's Association on January 17, 2013. They would suggest his proposal as a restriction to the second amendment right to the constitution and as such would not be defending or upholding such federal laws. Following the Connecticut state shooting a multi-state trend would occur in the anticipation of restrictions on gun permit applications and firearms. The bill restricting gun control would fail to pass on April 17, 2013 falling six votes short. The belief among both democrats and republicans is the expansion of background checks cannot possibly correlate in a reduction of violent crime or school safety. Obama would speak out the next day stating Congress to have failed and finding their decision as shameful.

Following the shooting the school would close indefinitely in part because it would remain a crime scene. On January 3, 2013 the students of Sandy Hook would return to school at the nearby Chalk Hill Middle School upon request. Chalk Hill would be an unused facility which after the shooting would be refurbished with equipment and desks much of which would simply be brought in from the Sandy Hook Elementary. In the interim the Chalk Hill School would change its name to Sandy Hook. The surviving members of the shooting would have a scholarship to the University of Connecticut donated on their behalf. The Newtown school board would unanimously vote for police presence in all of its elementary schools on January 31, 2013. Other schools previously would already have this protection in effect. Upon the inundation of media requests to the town clerk's office legislation would be introduced by republican Dan Carter of the Connecticut House of Representatives restricting the availability to public information under the principle tenets of the Freedom of Information Act.

Carley, S. G. (2013). *Serial killers, mass murders, & disorders.* Boston: SGC Production.

Mark Barton

The Barton Murders

Spree killer Mark Barton would be born in Stockbridge, Georgia, in 1955 who would kill nine people injuring 13 others on July 29, 1999. The shootings would occur at the All-Tech Investment Group and Momentum Securities, two day trading firms in Atlanta. Over the previous two months the daytrader Barton, would accumulate losses of $105,000 acting as the motivation behind his actions. Barton would end the killing spree by committing suicide at an Acworth, Georgia, gas station a brief four hours after the Atlanta shootings. The police would order Barton to stop upon spotting him, yet before police could ever reach Barton he would shoot himself. Police would search the Barton home after the shooting to find a disturbing scene. Before the shooting spree Barton would kill his second wife, Leigh Ann Vandiver Barton, and two children, Mychelle Elizabeth Barton age 10 and Matthew David Barton age 12. Barton would murder his children by smashing their head with a hammer in their sleep and drowning them in the bathtub in an unconscious state. He would bludgeon Leigh Ann to death. According to a note Barton would

Carley, S. G. (2013). *Serial killers, mass murders, & disorders.*
Boston: SGC Production.

leave on the scene the killings would occur one day apart killing his wife on the 27th, his children on the 28th, and going on a shooting spree on the 29th. In 1993 Barton's first wife, Debra Spivey, and her mother, Eloise Spivey, would be murdered of which Barton would be a suspect of the 1993 beating deaths occurring in Cherokee County, Alabama. Barton would never be charged in the crime and would even deny his involvement in the note he would leave with his children and second wife when they would be found dead. Despite this, it is suspected Barton to be behind the Spivey deaths.

It would be just another day at the All-Tech Investment Group as the manager and secretary would greet Mark by name as he would gather with them to discuss the news of the 200 point slide in the Dow. Without a doubt it would seem like the same old Mark. Mark would be a little different though on this day as unaware to others he was packing two handguns. Barton killed his wife on Tuesday and two children on a Wednesday. Barton would have just returned from the Momentum Securities brokerage across the street where he would engage in small talk about the stock market and its recent decline. This is just prior to opening fire and killing four people with a .45 caliber Colt and a 9 – mm Glock. So the oncoming scene within the All-Tech Investment Group would be like no other as from the meeting room five shots would ring-out. Lying on the floor seriously wounded would be the manager and his secretary. Barton would march onto the main trading floor with a Colt in his left hand and Glock in his right preparing to let 'em fly like just another day at the range. Barton would utter, "I hope this won't ruin your day," as he would make his way through the All-Tech main trading floor claiming five victims when the carnage would eventually come to an end. As police would corner the 44 year old Barton at an Atlanta suburb gas station, he would turn both Colt and Glock on himself putting an end to the day's madness. By the time Barton would turn on himself four hours after the shootings, the event was a national

Carley, S. G. (2013). *Serial killers, mass murders, & disorders.*
Boston: SGC Production.

drama as American television would view image after image of the panic in the city's financial center and Atlanta streets.

The mourning of Barton's victims would coincide with the unfolding of a dead murderer's grim story of previous suspected murders, financial folly, suspected fraud, suicide notes, brutality, and adultery. Shooting sprees of this nature would only increase the public's anxiety as onlookers can do nothing but gaze with horrific astonishment. The questions would continue to arise of who the shooter was and why he would go berserk. Many of the answers Barton would leave in a note left on the murdered corpses of his wife and two children, Leigh Ann, 27, daughter Mychelle, 8, and son Matthew, 12. Barton would write planning to live only long enough to kill as many of those who would seek his destruction. Barton would be trying to collect insurance money from the deaths of his first wife and her mother in the sum of $600,000. The murders were more than suspicious, police viewing Barton as a suspect. The insurance company would be forced to investigate Barton pertaining to his role in the murders subjecting him to six hours of scrutiny. Barton would talk about his life pleading his case along the way discussing his deteriorating relationship with his wife Debra Spivey and his affairs with Leigh Ann Lang who would be Barton's second wife.

Leading-up to the Barton Killings

Barton's parents were in the Air Force and he was their only child. Barton would work manual labor jobs and would settle among a second college University of South Carolina graduating in 1979 with a chemistry degree. It would be in 1979 Barton would marry Debra who he met as a night auditor at a local hotel. Debra would also attend the University of South Carolina. The couple would move from Atlanta to Texarkana, Texas, where in 1988 Barton would accept a position as company president of TLC

Manufacturing earning in the arena of $86,000 annually. This was a company constructed by Barton and some friends. Barton would be fired from the company in 1990 and on his last day someone mysteriously would break into the offices of TLC erasing computer files and stealing secret formulas. Barton would be arrested by police for burglary, yet a detective in the case would claim it was not formulas being stolen instead inventory discrepancies and kickbacks were being hidden. The charges would be dropped upon an agreement with Barton made by the TLC company. Barton and his wife would move to Georgia and would accept a sales position with a chemical company. It would be while in this position he would meet Leigh Ann Lang a young attractive receptionist. She was unhappily married at the time and would not hide the fact she would like other guys. Barton and Lang would be engaged in an extramarital affair by May 1993. Barton would start buying Leigh Ann gifts and going tanning, and his suspicious wife Debra would start to display jealousy. Barton was once accused by Debra of having another woman's hair on his clothing.

It would be during this time Barton would take out a rather substantial insurance policy on Debra totaling $600,000. Barton would go for a cool million but could not afford the premiums. Barton would rationalize to the insurer the policy to be his wife's idea. Barton's position as a company president would make her enjoy her title as wife, and she would develop an extreme sense of self-worth feeling just as important as her husband. Barton and Leigh Ann would take a trip to Charlotte, North Carolina, in June of 1993 where the pair would have dinner with some friends. Barton would confess over dinner to never love anyone quite the way he would Leigh Ann and would be available to marry her by October. Leigh Ann would find an apartment and move in with her sister ready to end her own marriage by the beginning of September. Debra would visit her mother a few days later traveling to Alabama to spend Labor Day weekend. According to authorities Barton

Carley, S. G. (2013). *Serial killers, mass murders, & disorders*. Boston: SGC Production.

would spend a quiet weekend at home with his children Matthew and Mychelle. By the end of the weekend Debra and her mother Eloise would be found dead in Eloise's trailer hacked to death by an ax-like instrument police have yet to recover. Police would arrive at Barton's home in search for evidence a short hour's time after his wife Debra's funeral. Investigators would search Barton's possessions, spraying the house with Luminol in search for blood traces. Some blood would be found in Barton's car on both the seat belt and ignition switch of which he would explain as an old injury from the previous summer in which he had cut his finger to the bone. Barton would continue to deny leaving any DNA samples or to take part in a lie detector. Despite having inconclusive forensic evidence, no witnesses, and no fingerprints, the authorities would continue to suspect Barton's guilt for the crime. Barton would claim to spill a soft drink on the blood traces in the car destroying the only evidence before a retest could ever occur.

Less than a week from the time of Debra's death, Leigh Ann would begin spending nights with Barton and his kids. Leigh Ann's divorce would be final less than a month from Debra's death, and within six months the two would be living together. Barton would now live in Morrow, Georgia where his neighbors would know nothing of his previous wife. It would seem the marriage right from the beginning to not possess any fairy tale endings of living happily ever after. The neighbors would gossip about the problems of the couple, and Leigh Ann would often pick-up and leave. The 2.5 year old Mychelle in February of 1994 would tell a daycare worker her father sexually molested her. A psychological evaluation would find Barton capable of homicide. Mychelle's age would make it too difficult for attorneys to build a sexual assault case and Barton would continue his custody of Mychelle and Matthew. The insurance company would settle for $450,000 in 1997 under the assumption the jury would side with Barton sympathizing for the plight of his children Matthew and Mychelle. A stipulation of the

Carley, S. G. (2013). *Serial killers, mass murders, & disorders.*
Boston: SGC Production.

company was for 1/3 of the total proceed to be placed in a trust for Mychelle and Matthew.   With his new fortune, Barton would become a full-time day trader, yet this summer things would take a turn for the worse.   According to Momentum Securities Barton would lose $105,000 by June on volatile Internet stocks.   Reports would state Barton's account to close on a Tuesday when he could not cover a debt the result of falling stock prices.   Barton would bounce a $50,000 check in an attempt at reopening the account and his privileges would be revoked as he would be denied participation on both Wednesday and Thursday.   During Barton's Thursday shooting spree, Momentum would be his first stop.   The All Tech company whom Barton had not used for months would report his stock market losses to surpass $300,000.   In Barton's suicide note, he speaks of the greedy seeking his destruction, possibly in reference to the world of day trading.   Pertaining to Barton's family there is denial, regret, and blame.   Barton would blame Leigh Ann for his demise and despite it not being her fault, he would find the need to kill her.   Barton would bludgeon Leigh Ann and hide her limp body in a closet out of sight of the children.   Barton would insist his children to die of little pain, smashing their sleeping heads with a hammer to drown them in the tub.   On their dead bodies he would place a teddy bear on Mychelle and a video game on Matthew. Barton would claim any similarities among his children's death and his first wife's death to be a coincidence, and would continue to profess his innocence for the deaths of Debra and her mother.   Barton would claim in his letter to hate his life and to be experiencing feelings of helplessness and its cousin hopelessness. Barton would state you should kill me now if you can, upon this he would arm himself with a small collection of guns and 200 rounds of ammo and take nine more lives with him before taking his own.

Carley, S. G. (2013). *Serial killers, mass murders, & disorders.*
Boston: SGC Production.

Andrew Kehoe

Andrew Philip Kehoe The Bath School Murderer

Andrew Kehoe is most known for his detonation of an explosive device which would tear through the Bath Consolidated School in Bath, Michigan, killing 45 people, 37 of which would be children. After detonating the explosive device, he would place under the school, the maniac bomber Andrew Kehoe would blow up his pick-up truck killing himself and the school superintendent, among others. At the time, Kehoe would serve on the local school board as treasurer, and fueling the act would be the levy of new taxes to pay for the five year old institution.

On May 18, 1927 the Bath School Disaster would take place with a series of bombings in the town of Bath Township of Michigan, 100 miles west of Detroit. The blast would kill 45, 37 of which were children injuring another 58 in the process. In terms of deadliest school attacks in United States history, the Bath School Disaster would represent the deadliest display of rampage killing, claiming three times more victims than the Columbine High School Massacre. Upset over a property tax levy in construction of the school building, school board member Andrew Kehoe would initiate the attack. Kehoe would blame his financial hardships leading to the closing of his farm on the additional tax. These would act as the course of events leading to Kehoe's plan and execution of a deadly bombing attack. Kehoe would start the morning of May 18 by killing his wife and setting his farm ablaze. Fire fighters would respond to the blaze just as a massive explosion would rock through the northwest wing of the school building killing many of the occupants of the building. Over the course of many months Kehoe would secretly plant explosives inside the school and would ignite the dynamite and hundreds of pounds of pyrotol with a detonator. Rescuers would begin to gather at the scene and no sooner would Kehoe arrive in his shrapnel-filled truck of which he would detonate killing himself, the superintendent, and injuring and killing many others. Searchers would discover during the rescue effort unexploded dynamite and pyrotol throughout the southwing basement of the school totaling an additional 500 pounds. It would seem these explosives for whatever reasons to never detonate. Speculation is the initial explosion would cause a short circuit.

Containing the unincorporated village of Bath is the Bath Township situated 10 miles northeast of Lansing, Michigan. The area was primarily agricultural during the 1920s, and in 1922 the funding and construction of a consolidated school would be passed by voters to form a district. When the school would open, 236 students would enroll ranging in grades from the first to the 12th. The disappearance of many small one roomed schools would occur during this time of the early 2oth century. Educators would find it a better system where students of different grades would not share the same classroom, consisting of age-divided classes and a higher quality facility. In creation of the district within the Bath Township, to pay for the project property taxes would be raised. The result being the imposition of new taxes upon landowners including Andrew Kehoe.

Carley, S. G. (2013). *Serial killers, mass murders, & disorders.*
Boston: SGC Production.

Andrew Kehoe

The birth of Andrew Kehoe would occur on February 1, 1872 in Tecumseh, Michigan. Kehoe would come from a large family of 13. When Kehoe was still young, he would lose his mother and his father would remarry at the time. Kehoe would often fight with his stepmother, in fact, when he was 14, she would be soaked in oil fuel the result of a family stove explosion. Kehoe would watch as the flames would burn his stepmother's body, to minutes later dowse the flames with water. As a result his stepmother would later die of her injuries. Kehoe would not be charged for the malfunction of the stove. Kehoe would meet his wife Ellen Nellie Price while attending Michigan State University. The couple would marry in 1912 and live together in 1919, purchasing a 185 acre farm from Nellie's aunt for $12,000. Kehoe was an intelligent man according to his neighbors claiming him to be impatient with those who would disagree with him. Kehoe was known as a neat meticulous dresser at times changing his shirt during the day. Kehoe once beat a horse to death and was known to be cruel to farm animals. Kehoe's farming ability would be described as less than impressive, a result of his constant experimentation with tactics and machinery costing in production in the long-term. The thrifty Kehoe would be elected to the Bath Consolidated School Board in 1924 as treasurer who would fight for lower taxes. Kehoe would blame the superintendent, Emory Huyck, of financial mismanagement and prior tax levies accounting for his family's poor economic condition. In 1925 as Treasurer, Kehoe would receive an appointment as Bath Township Clerk, lasting only a single year as Kehoe would lose a re-election attempt. Further putting the family into debt would be Nellie Kehoe's bout with tuberculosis leading to frequent hospital stays. Kehoe would cease all mortgage and homeowner insurance payments at the time of the bombing as foreclosure proceedings would begin against the farm.

Carley, S. G. (2013). *Serial killers, mass murders, & disorders.* Boston: SGC Production.

No clear indication exists as to when Kehoe would plan and conceive the notions to bomb the school building. An investigation into purchases and activities would lead authorities to speculate Kehoe would plan the attack for more than a year. Kehoe would be requested to perform maintenance in the school building in the winter of 1926. Kehoe would be familiar with electrical equipment and regarded as a talented handyman. Kehoe would have free access to the building as a board member and his presence would never be questioned. Kehoe would purchase over a ton of pyrotol in the summer of 1926 an often used substance among farming for excavation. Kehoe would purchase two boxes of dynamite in Lansing at a sporting goods store in November of 1926. Kehoe to avoid arousal of suspicion would purchase small amounts of the dynamite and pyrotol from different stores. Neighbors would at times hear explosions on the Kehoe farm, which he would explain as a means of tree stump removal.

Warning signs would exist prior to the event as while passing out paychecks the prior week of the explosion, Kehoe would tell a bus driver his check would be the last he ever gets. Kehoe would also make peculiar comments to a teacher, Bernice Sterling, two days before the event. Kehoe would load the back seat of his car with metal debris prior to May 18 including digging shovels, pieces of rusted farm machinery, some old tools and nails, and pretty much anything else old Andrew could find acting as shrapnel for an explosion. Upon filling the back seat Kehoe would place a loaded rifle on the passenger seat and a cache of dynamite behind the front seat. Nellie Kehoe would be discharged on May 16 according to Lansing St. Lawrence Hospital records. Sometime after her release and before the bombings, a period of two days, Kehoe would kill Nellie making use of an unknown heavy object providing blunt force trauma to Nellie's skull. Her body would be found in the rear of the farm's chicken coup in a wheel barrel. Kehoe would pile around the cart a metal cash box, silverware, and jewels. Kehoe would insert

Carley, S. G. (2013). *Serial killers, mass murders, & disorders.* Boston: SGC Production.

pyrotol firebombs in every farm building, wiring the entire farm. To ensure the deaths of farm animals from the fire Kehoe planned on starting, he would tie farm animals to their enclosures. Kehoe would detonate the firebombs at approximately 8:45 AM as fire crews and volunteers would rush to the scene. One hour later at 9:45 AM the school building would explode as rescuers would double back to the school. Community parents too would rush to the scene.

The reports of the explosion would be described as a terrible earthquake, would seem to cause the floor to rise several feet. Children and debris would fill the air as some would be catapulted out of the building. The school's north wing would collapse as the roof edge would fall to the ground and walls collapse. Piles of children would lie under the roof, limbs and head sticking out unrecognizable from the plaster, dust, and blood covering them. The roof was too heavy to lift off the children as volunteers would have to leave the scene and return to move the structure. Needless to say the scene was a chaotic one with mother after mother finding their lifeless child on the lawn, and 100 men frantically tearing away at debris in hopes of finding life under the rubble. Kehoe would drive up to the school a half hour after the explosion and would summon superintendent Huyck over to his vehicle. As Huyck drew close, Kehoe would draw his rifle and fire into the back seat igniting the dynamite resulting in the explosion killing himself, superintendent Huyck, Nelson McFarren his father in law, and Glenn Smith. An eight year old who had crawled from the exploding building would also be killed by the shrapnel of the second explosion. The shrapnel entering the crowd would also injure a few others. The dying and injured would be transported to the St. Lawrence and Sparrow Hospitals in Lansing. Nellie Kehoe's uncle would largely finance the construction of the new facility. Assisting in the relief work during the afternoon would be Michigan governor Fred Green who would cart bricks from the scene. The

Carley, S. G. (2013). *Serial killers, mass murders, & disorders.*
Boston: SGC Production.

Lawrence Baking Company would serve rescue workers loading up their truck with sandwiches and pies.

SERIAL KILLERS

Carley, S. G. (2013). *Serial killers, mass murders, & disorders*.
Boston: SGC Production.

12 Ways to Catch a Serial Killer

Forensics to Serial Killing

Many television shows and movies put an emphasis on crime investigative analysis and forensic science in the capture of homicide perpetrators and serial killers. Many of these shows despite being unrealistic they are a reflection of the technological advance among forensic and criminal psychology over the past two decades. In taking an in depth look at 200 serial killers, it would appear 12 categories to exist, which will lead to police attention and eventual detainment. Most captures are the result of surviving victims informing the police. Forensic science as it would turn is not so important in the identification of perpetrators, yet within the conviction process becomes a useful tool.

Serial killing is both informative and at times through novels and movies a means of entertaining the public. Stories pertaining to forensic science and criminal profile would appear to lead all others within this domain. Pertaining to forensic science and criminal profiling are two perceptive types, one pubic and the other law enforcement. The criminal profiling perception of the public basing on the dramas of the television fantasy world are most likely inaccurate. This is despite the fact many serial killer depictions to be somewhat accurate. Criminal profilers cannot simply have

Carley, S. G. (2013). *Serial killers, mass murders, & disorders*. Boston: SGC Production.

flashes of insight providing the clues to solve who kills who or supercomputers hacking into illegal databanks. In regard to the efficiency of forensic science the public may hold similar misperceptions. Television land depicts field officers collecting and analyzing evidence themselves. The facts are the procedures among these shows are error filled, and the public remains unaware of the happenings in the world of crime fighting. One should realize an informative television show is created as a means of entertainment. Expectations can become unusually high of DNA evidence among every case and perfect personality profile of each defendant.

The rate of advance among criminal personality profiling and forensic science one may describe as exponential. The first application of medical expertise to a crime would occur in the year 44 BC by the physician Antitius. He would deduct which of the 23 stabbing wounds upon Caesar would be the fatal one. This evidence would be presented to a forum, the derivation of the term forensic. Many advancements among medicine have occurred since this time. In distinguishing natural death, suicide, and homicide, in 1247 a Chinese lawyer would write an instructional manual (Ramsland, 2005). Courses in forensic science would be offered during the 1600s to German physicians. An explanation would be provided in 1628 pertaining to blood circulation by William Harvey. The efficiency has increased over the years pertaining to both time and cause of death and victim identification. More differentiation occurs today than in the past regarding post, pre, and anti-mortem wounds. One medical examiner Frederick Zugibe would make the determination a victim to be frozen after death by Richard Kuklinski, a serial killer (Zugibe, 2005).

Toxicology advancements also exist. The discovery of detecting arsenic among different substances would occur in 1790 by John Metzger. Further advancement's to Metzger's discovery would occur in 1806 by Dr. Valentine Rose. James Marsh would enable a means of detecting arsenic samples even when seeping inside the body post-burial. Diagnostic testing would first be used in the detection of arsenic. Still the same, much improvement would be needed in the detection of poisons. The 1856 case of Dr. William Palmer a condemned murderer would leave doubt in regard to the medical profession's proficiency in poison detection, in this case the toxin would be strychnine (Burney, 1999). Medical journals would profess the need for more precision in this domain. Tremendous advances exist today among forensic toxicology as seen through the three most popular methods of screening tests in immunoassay, gas chromatography (GC), and thin layer chromatography (TLC). With such advancements in toxicology this would pose the question of how many serial killers who would use poisons as their modus operandi would be captured through the toxicological investigation? Serial killers in the medical personnel such as Charles Cullen, Donald Harvey, and Genene Jones each would make use of poisons. Trace evidence detection among other foreign substances would also increase, which would assist in the captures of Bobby Joe Long of Florida and the Atlanta Child Murderer Wayne Williams. The first scientific tool used in a court case would be the microscope (Ramsland, 2005). This is a 1590s invention of Zacharias Janssen starting with the single lens microscope. Over the ages more advanced microscopes would arise bringing trace images into more defined focus. The improvement upon the standard laboratory microscope would occur through the addition of polarizing light filters in the creation of the polarized light microscope. This new invention would facilitate detection of minerals in glass, synthetic fibers, soil, and other birefringent materials. Helping investigators view material in three dimensional form would be the stereoscopic microscope. Another technique often used in ballistics permits the juxtaposition of two images into a single field through the comparison microscope. The development of the electron microscope would occur during the 1930s by Ruska forming the basis for the scanning electron microscope (SEM). In terms of examination of small traces of material such as gunshot residue or paint, the SEM is an excellent instrument. As electron optics enhances the efficiency of the electron microscope, trace evidence would be brought more into focus. Within the microspectrophotometer absorption spectrums can be observed, and unseen images can be elicited by adding minute amounts of a reagent to a microscopic sample. Through the use of infrared spectroscopy material associations can be compared in inorganic and organic mixtures.

The killing preference of serial killers tends to be by hand, yet some killers would like to make use of the firearm: John Muhammed, Lee Malvo, D. C. Snipers, Douglas Clark, Thomas Dillon, and David Berkowitz. The first successful link of a suspect to a bullet would be made by Henry Goddard of London in 1835, who would compare a suspect's bullet mold to the bullet. The mass manufacture of guns would create a prominence of rifle cutters in boring a hole in the barrel. The rifling of the majority of mass produced firearms today is through electrochemical etching, hammer-forging, swaging, or broaching. The marks made on a fired bullet or cartridge casing by a firearm can be measured using a comparison microscope in determining whether a bullet was fired from a particular firearm. Making use of the FBIs national database a comparison of recovered bullets and cartridge shells can occur.

In the identification of unknown suspects perhaps the number one forensic procedure is the classification of fingerprints. The Chinese would place fingerprints on contracts two-thousand years ago, yet it was not until the mid 1700s the unique ridge configurations would become well known. The classification system presently used today within the United States would occur in the year 1900 by Sir Edward Henry. Immense improvements have occurred in the science of disseminating the classification and recovery of fingerprints. Through chemical treatment of the print or different types of powders, the discovery of prints left on surfaces by skin oils and salts can occur. In the stabilization process of delicate prints, the print should be fumed with either super glue or cyanoacrylic fumes. To enhance the clarity of ridges, one can make use of digitization among sophisticated software. To make the ridges more definitive the use of dyes now occurs. Each state possesses their own fingerprint data system (Integrated Automated Fingerprint Identification System (IAFIS)) which is managed by the Federal Bureau of Investigation (FBI). The individual classification of fingerprints 30 years ago was much slower. The identification of finger and palm prints is at a much faster rate through use of the IAFIS.

Gary Ridgway, the Green River Killer, would begin killing prostitutes in 1982 dumping their bodies in and around the Green River in the Seattle, Washington area. Ridgway's DNA he would provide police in 1987 would lead to his capture in 2000. It would be newly refined techniques over this period enabling the DNA match leading to the arrest and capture of Ridgway. This would be a long road in the measurement of deoxyribonucleic acid (DNA) in blood. In 1853 a method would be developed in the determination of whether dried stains were blood by the Polish physician Ludwig Teichmann. Teichmann's discovery would withstand the test of time and is presently the preferred means of making this determinant through the microcrystalline test. The development of other presumptive tests would occur resulting in false positives at times. The luminol test would be developed in 1937 by Walter Specht. The chemical reaction releases light as a chemiluminescent compound. Human blood groups would be discovered by Karl Landsteiner in 1940 permitting law enforcement to trace crime scene biological evidence through a narrowing process among suspects. Leading to DNA typing would be the 1985 discovery of multilocus restriction fragment length polymorphism (RFLP). This would be the culmination of many discoveries relating to serology. The genetic material in cells is deoxyribonucleic acid. Enabling the amplification of regional genomes would be the research of Kerry Mullins in use of the polymerase chain reaction (PCR) used for tiny degraded forensic samples. DNA laboratories can now run DNA markers more efficiently and faster using short tandem repeats (STRs). In a similar fashion to the AFIS in matching fingerprint samples, the FBI has the Combined DNA Indexing System (CODIS) in matching blood samples.

During this time of scientific dedication in new techniques of forensic science others would consider the mind of the perpetrator. The physical and psychological evidence left at a crime scene possesses an interrelationship with criminal profiling. The terminology for profiling has changed and is now referred as criminal investigative analysis by the FBI. The term references the details and behavioral aspects of an unsolved violent crime in which the crime scene possesses evidence of psychopathology. Sherlock Holmes the fictional detective would be introduced to the world in 1887 by Sir Arthur Conan Doyle. Holmes would display the uncanny ability to conclude evidential meaning in the mind of the perpetrator. He would also pay attention to the smallest of details of a crime scene. The services of Dr. Walter Langer would be requested during WW II by the United States Office of Strategic Services to profile Adolph Hitler in providing insight to the government in how Hitler would act in certain situations. Langer would predict Hitler's suicide, and Dr. James Brussel in 1957 would accurately profile a New York City arsonist The Mad Bomber George Metesky (Douglas et al., 1986).

FBI special agents Robert Ressler and John Douglas would interview 36 mass murderers and serial killers while in prison. A systematic approach to criminal profiling would occur through these interviews the Criminal Profile Generating Process. As an adjunct investigative tool criminal profiles have been used in hunting the vampire-like Sacramento, California killer Richard Chase, a prostitute killer in Rochester, New York Arthur Shawcross, and a child serial killer in Atlanta, Georgia Wayne Williams. Criticism has taken place on the work of these investigators regarding a lapse in procedural clarity, statistical errors, basing upon impressions and not research findings, and lack of procedural theoretical bases. At the same time methodologically sound research would support this work involving an investigation of the act of profiling, and in validation of the disorganized and organized criminal behavior syndromes (Kocsis et al., 1998).

Different approaches exist to this problem known as the FBI method of profiling. The typical presentation of this process is in five stages: profile construction, looking for perpetrator idiosyncrasies, reconstruction of criminal behavioral sequence, offender classification, and evidence collection. In recent years statistical techniques have been used instead of clinical assumptions in deriving profiles from crime scene data analysis. Particular aspects are the focus of certain approaches. An example is geographic profiling obtaining clues to the offender through the use of location analysis of a series of crimes. In recent years this process has been assisted by computer tool development such as geographic information systems (GIS). Milton Newton would devise a similar system referred to as geoforensic analysis. Particular aspects of the offender have been the focus of recent research such as the perpetrators language or footwear impressions. Tests and empirical studies have also occurred in relation to profiling. An example would be an analysis of 566 rapes committed by 108 serial rapists in identification of the proximity to their homes (Warren et. al, 1998). The suggestion of recent years is profilers be licensed in standardizing profiling processes. The utilization of computers should be toward the classification of particular cases into profiles and deriving profiles. The importance is the lack of reliability and validity among profiling according to the opinions of forensic

Carley, S. G. (2013). *Serial killers, mass murders, & disorders.*
Boston: SGC Production.

psychologists and psychiatrists. A typical conclusion is the majority of serial killers must be caught from the psychological and scientific evidence found on a crime scene. How do police first become aware an individual has committed three or more murders at different times? How does the individual get away with a single murder with so many advancements in technology? These answers are answered through data of 200 serial killers, and to what extent profiling is successful.

12 Categories of Serial Killer Capture

Various sources such as encyclopedias, newspaper articles, journals, and books describe how 200 serial killers would be brought to the attention of the authorities and captured. Cross referencing with other sources would occur pertaining to the subjects. The definition of a serial killer who is one who kills three or more people at different locations with a period of time separating the occurrence of each murder. Perpetrators such as John Wayne Gacy or Jeffrey Dahmer a modification of the definition would have to occur as the killings would occur in the same place, the perpetrators home, but the victims would be abducted from different locations. The same can be said of Angel of Death killers who kill their victims in the same location, the hospital: Charles Cullen, Teri Rachels, and Donald Harvey. Upon analysis of the capture of each serial killer the emergence of 12 categories would arise (White et al., 2011).

The first category involves the serial killer being caught because the serial killer voluntarily releases the victim who in turn reports the incident to the police. This release of the victim can be during or after an abduction. The victim describes the perpetrator, the perpetrator's vehicle, or provides other pertinent information. A victim release would only account for one percent of the captured serial killer population. A second category is the murderer being killed during the crime. This would occur in three instances representing 1.5% of the population of captured serial killers. Some examples include Dean Corll who was killed by his partner Elmer Wayne Henley when he would attempt to murder Henley's girlfriend. Wayne Nance would attempt a murder of a couple and would be killed by the husband. The wife of Joseph Mumfre's final victim would finish him off. A third category is a voluntary confession to the police which would occur in 2% of the cases. Shortly after California's co-ed killer, Edmund Kemper, would kill his own mother and friend he would notify authorities. Before this he would kill six college coeds. When he was a teenager he would kill both his grandparents. Wayne Ford would confess to four murders with a female breast in his pocket.

A fourth category of serial killer capture is identification of a witness of being with a victim prior to the murder. This would occur in four instances or 2% of the cases. Antone Costa would be identified as being with his final two victims shortly before their bodies would be discovered. Costa would be found driving a victim's car shortly after his female acquaintances would be found dead. His claim was he bought the car before she died. Costa would be suspected of committing 10 murders and convicted for four. The night before Wayne Boden's victim would be discovered, he would be seen driving around with her. A witness would identify his car when returning to the scene, he had dumped his final victim. He would confess to three other murders. A fifth category is through communication sent to the police by the suspect. This would account for 2.5% of the serial killers capture. The BTK Killer, Dennis Rader, would send a disc to the police they would be able to trace to the Lutheran Church and Dennis Rader. The stationary William Hance would write on would lead to his capture. The correspondence sent to the local newspaper by Maury Travis would identify him as the serial killer in St. Louis, Missouri who would claim 12 victims. A sixth category is caught in the act. Caught in the act includes serial killers who attempt a murder, but are stopped

Carley, S. G. (2013). *Serial killers, mass murders, & disorders.*
Boston: SGC Production.

before the completion of the act. This category would account for 5.5% of the cases. The would be fourth victim of Harvey Glatman would be captured by police while kidknapping the person. An innkeeper's son would have Jeanne Weber's hands around his throat when she would be caught. This would be the method consistent with the other murders. The sixth murder of Richard Cottingham would be foiled by a police capture.

A seventh category of serial killer being caught is a victim survives after being left for dead. The surviving victim in turn goes to the police and provides the pertinent information leading to an arrest. This category involves 15 cases or 7.5% of the serial killing population among the study. Harvey Carignan's 20 year murder rampage would come to an end with a deserving death sentence. His sentence would be overturned by a legal mistake by the sheriff. Harvey would be released after a few years in prison only to begin killing again. The sloppy Carignan would leave live victims he would believe to be dead who would identify him eventually leading to his capture. An eighth category is an escaping victim. Serial killers committing three or more crimes tend to be highly organized ensuring victim capture, efficient killing, and little to no evidence remains on a crime scene. Even the most organized of serial killers can become careless leading to an escaped victim. This cluster would account for 8% of the captured serial killers. One may think of Jeffrey Dahmer's last attempted victim Tracy Edwards who would escape through a life or death struggle. Edwards would flag down a police cruiser bringing the officers back to Dahmer's apartment. Good thing he escaped or Dahmer may have bore a hole in his skull and filled it with muriatic acid. Two female victims of Gerard Schaefer would be bound to a tree. They would escape before his return and the two females would notify the police. Tommy Sell's would slash a victim's throat before they would be able to escape and inform the police. The ninth category is linked to the crime scene. This category would account for 16.5% of the

Carley, S. G. (2013). *Serial killers, mass murders, & disorders.*
Boston: SGC Production.

captured serial killers. Arthur Shawcross would be caught when investigators would discover the suspect was returning to the dump sites to perform necrophilic acts. When they would find a victim surveillance would be set up, and when Shawcross would return to the scene he would be captured. Dennis Nilsen would flush body parts down his drain causing clogged drains. The clogged drain would link to his apartment and eventually his arrest. America's most prolific serial killer by argument Gary Ridgway AKA The Green River Killer would be questioned for the Green River killings as identifiable as one who would frequent the prostitutes in the area. A prostitution sting would get Ridgway arrested, yet he would somehow pass a polygraph test pertaining to his involvement in the murders. Ridgway being observed with what would identify as a secondary crime scene, his saliva would be procured in 1987 for further investigation. After sixteen years DNA evidence found on several Green River victims would match the saliva Ridgway would leave in 1987. The DNA technology advancements would point to Ridgway as a killer, yet permitting the police to take the DNA was his link to the abduction sites.

A tenth category is linked to victims other than eyewitnesses. This category would account for 16.5% of the captured serial killers. This capture does not involve forensic evidence, instead personal connections among the killer and friends, loved ones, neighbors, or coworkers. One of the victims of the Killer Clown John Gacy would tell his mother he would be doing some work for a local carpenter. He would also tell others he would be working for a Gacy. This would be the information leading to the search of Gacy's home, and the finding of the bodies in the crawl space. The link among Doss and her dead husbands would eventually lead to her arrest as too many of her husbands would end up dead. Over a 13 year period Mary Beth Tinning would kill nine of her own children, and this obvious link as her own children would lead to her arrest. Category number 11 is arrested for a different offense. This would account for 16.5% of the captures. One example is Ted Bundy who would be driving and a suspicious officer would put his sirens on. Bundy would eventually stop but a struggle would pursue, and he would be arrested. While in custody he would be identified as the wanted serial killer. Fred West and Albert DeSalvo arrested for rape would eventually be linked to their serial murders. DeSalvo would confess to being the infamous Boston Strangler and West would meet arrest when his 13 year old daughter would inform her siblings she was raped by Fred. This would create an uproar among classmates and parents eventually leading West to his connection to the serial killings and subsequent arrest. The final category of serial killers being captured is turned in by someone who knows the offender. This is the largest category including 41 cases or 20.5% of the serial killing sample population. This group of people turning in the serial killer can include cell mates, accomplices, family members, friends, lovers, neighbors, or coworkers. An example would be Ted Kaczynski whose very own brother and sister in law would turn him in. Of course they were influenced by a one million dollar bounty on Ted's arrest. Claiming innocence of wrongdoing Carol Fugate the girlfriend of Charlie Starkweather would be one-half of the murderous duo taking part in a murderous rampage. She would make officers aware of Charlie's identity and crimes (White et al., 2011).

When the realization occurs a serial killer is working in your jurisdiction this becomes a formidable and daunting task for police. Paramount in assisting police develop leads leading to the capture of a serial killer are the police interviews of surviving victims, witnesses, among others. Advocating for the creation of an organized police department in London, England would be Sir Robert Peele who in 1829 would produce the Peelian Principles. One such concept embodying the principles is the police and public are one. In catching serial killers this concept is a major aspect. It is investigative skills and public information leading to the capture

Carley, S. G. (2013). *Serial killers, mass murders, & disorders.* Boston: SGC Production.

of serial killers. Nearly three quarters of the serial killer captures (71.5%) are on account of the descriptions, direct observations, and other information provided by serial killer family members, direct witnesses, and surviving victims. Of all the killers in the study not a single one would be captured by forensic evidence alone. These cases making assistance of forensic evidence would also require the help of the police and public through public interviews. Leading to the arrest of John Orr in California would be a single fingerprint left on the scene of one of the fires he would set ablaze. Orr does not meet the definition of a serial killer and would not be part of the study. The advancements in fingerprint detection would not solely lead to the arrest of even a single serial killer. Forensic science seems to have taken the role of solidifying evidence in leading to the conviction of a captured serial killer. Forensic science can further assist in the prosecution process by urging a suspect to confess to crimes committed. With the widening of DNA databases perhaps forensic evidence alone will identify serial murder perpetrators. Until such time the public means of providing information to the police and skills of investigators appear important in the apprehension of serial murderers. Forensic evidence may not incriminate serial killers because in many instances it is the forensic evidence catching perpetrators during their first or second offense. Hence these perpetrators would not fit the categorization of a serial killer. As an example John Orr most likely would have continued setting fires leading to deaths were it not for the finding of his print. This hypothesis may be better enabled of those who may have become serial murderers were they not caught before the third act. The interrelation among physical and psychological evidence defines criminal profiling. Within this study at least seven serial killer investigations would make mention of criminal profiling as a tool in the development of leads and the suspect narrowing process (Holmes & Holmes, 2002). Narrowing the focus of an investigation is not necessarily identifying a suspect as in the case of Wayne Williams. A profile may assist citizens to call police in identification of someone they know may fit the profile, or help link a criminal to a crime scene as in the case of Arthur Shawcross. It is not often serial killers turn themselves in like Wayne Ford or Ed Kemper, or are rarely killed by their victims as is the case of Wayne Nance. The public continues to be relied upon by the police to provide reliable enough information resulting in a viable investigation and leading to an eventual arrest and conviction. An essential aspect to capturing serial killers appears to be good police community relations.

Carley, S. G. (2013). *Serial killers, mass murders, & disorders*. Boston: SGC Production.

Aileen Wuornos

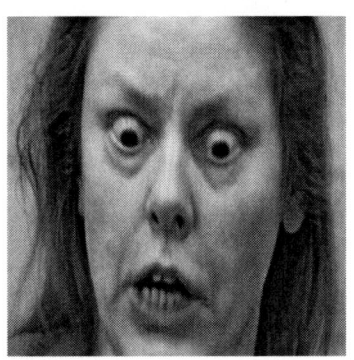

Aileen Wuornos

Aileen Wuornos was a ragged drifter who from 1989 to 1990 along a stretch of central Florida freeway would kill seven men. The victims of Wuornos would include Richard Mallory, Dick Humphreys, Troy Burress, David Spears, Walter Gino Antonio, Peter Siems, and Charles Carskaddon. Her dissolute and desolating life would take her to the roadside as a hitcher who would ring off a song and dance about being separated from her kids and needing to get back to the next state. At some point during these chariot rides an offer of prostitution would take place. The unsuspecting man expecting of sexual gratuity in a secluded arena would in turn face a gun wielding Aileen who would shoot and kill these men. The victims of Wuornos some would be shot in the car expecting of felatio from Wuornos. Still others would be slaughtered completely naked outside expecting some form of sexual gratuity. Wuornos would hide the body in the heavily wooded area and proceed to take the man's money and steal his car. Wuornos would pawn the belongings of Mallory and Antonio of which thumb prints left on pawn shop cards would connect her to

Carley, S. G. (2013). *Serial killers, mass murders, & disorders.* Boston: SGC Production.

the murders. She would only keep the car for a short time abandoning the vehicle in the risks of being caught. These risks of being caught would not keep Wuornos from returning to that lonely stretch of freeway time and again.

Wuornos would be born on a Detroit suburb on February 29, 1956, as Aileen Carol Pittman. Aileen's mother Diane Wuornos would marry her father Leo Dale Pittman when she was 15 on June 3, 1954. Two months before Aileen's birth her parents would divorce. She would have an older brother Keith born in February of 1955. Her father was a convicted child molester having raped and attempted to murder a seven year old girl. Her mother would abandon her and her brother at a young age when she was only four. The two would live with their grandparents who would abuse the children physically and sexually. Wuornos first sexual activities would occur when she was in school at the age of eleven exchanging sex for drugs or cigarettes. She would even have sex with her own brother. Wuornos would become one of street wise savvy and by her early teens she would have already given a child away to adoption. Her child was through a rape at the age of 14 by one of her grandfather's friends. She would divorce, take her maiden name, and squander much of the insurance money she would receive from her brother's early death. Aileen would turn back to prostitution exchanging sex for a means of surviving. At times she would commit petty crimes according to police records. Some of these crimes include driving under the influence, disorderly conduct, failure to appear in court, firing a weapon, assault, armed robbery, forgery, grand theft auto, resisting arrest, and obstruction of justice. Her blonde good looks would erode through the abuse of drugs and alcohol. A curious attractiveness may remain within her, enough to lure her victims. Wuornos was never happy as a hooker, and in avoidance of pimps and madames would choose to work alone. In terms of prostitution, one may say Wuornos to work at the bottom rung standing along the roadsides. Unlike the street prostitute in uniform, Wuornos would

Carley, S. G. (2013). *Serial killers, mass murders, & disorders*.
Boston: SGC Production.

sport sneakers and roadhouse gear. She would take the hitchhiker's pose by sticking her thumb out, shooting a hip provocatively toward oncoming traffic. Homebound husbands looking toward the gutter for affection would find their destination. The sinister urges of rough trade would not treat her well.

Wuornos' nine month killing spree would be captured on film by writer/director Patty Jenkins within the movie Monster. The mainspring to the Wuornos murders according to Jenkins would be romance. Aileen would meet a young woman at a gay bar Tyria Moore. Tyria would seem an unlikely object of Wuornos' desire. The prelapsarian childhood of the innocent and vulnerable Moore may be what would attract Wuornos to Moore. Wuornos' disregard for authority would create an infatuation of Tyria toward Wuornos. Shortly thereafter the two would marry living from motel to motel. The staple to male-oriented pornography is steamy sex among bisexual women. Among mainstream Hollywood such a relationship possesses a softer focus under an assumption a quest for Mr. Right may continue (Greenberg, 2004).

The motives of Wuornos are nothing less than psychopathic or psychoses driven. Wuornos who would claim guilt would seek innocence by reason of insanity. Wuornos would claim herself to be the victim of male aggression an avenging angel of a wretched and unjust system. The killing would begin according to Wuornos when her first victim Richard Mallory would threaten to kill and rape her. After her trial the fact Mallory had served 10 years for another violent rape would surface. Her lover Tyria Moore would confess to Wuornos' crimes in return for her freedom. No longer able to tolerate confinement, Wuornos on death row after twelve years of imprisonment would admit to her crimes. Her psychoses would become quite severe as at one time she would claim a spaceship to take her to Jesus. On the day of her execution she

Carley, S. G. (2013). *Serial killers, mass murders, & disorders.*
Boston: SGC Production.

would appear quite sane, at least sane enough to be killed for her actions.

No one could ever satisfactorily explain the origins of Wuornos' behavior. Some speculation exists the reason to be a horrific childhood, still others may contend a genetic predisposition toward violence, or the disassociated state of escaping death from her first victim. It may be a sadistic romance gone astray. In either case the majority of women with these same circumstances do not kill. A psychiatrist would claim there to be no real way of knowing exactly why Wuornos or other serial fashion murderers decide to kill. Separating the x-factor of those who kill from those who do not kill is a difficult task. Wuornos may not have been as diabolic as serial killers such as Ted Bundy or Ed Gein but make no mistake, Aileen Wuornos is the worst (Greenberg, 2004).

Carley, S. G. (2013). *Serial killers, mass murders, & disorders*.
Boston: SGC Production.

Belle Gunness

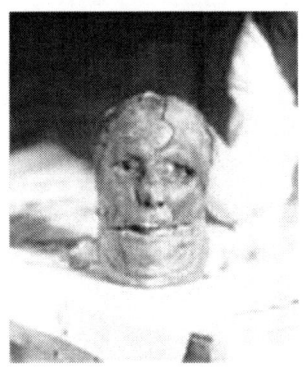

Belle Gunness

The Indiana Farmhouse of Belle Gunness would be gutted by a fire on April 28, 1908. It would seem the Norwegian American widow to be inside with her two sons and daughter as among the charred ruins would lie four corpses. Upon first glance no one would doubt the corpse to be Belle despite the headless corpse to appear slightly smaller than the six-foot pig farmer. It would turn the fire to be arson, and the prime suspect Ray Lamphere would be arrested. Investigators would perform a more in-depth search of the property specifically for Andrew Helgelein who would go missing for three months. He would respond to letters from Belle to sell everything and to go to her, he would never be seen from again. An investigation would ensue per the request of Andrew's brother. Authorities would come across a freshly filled hole and turn up a stinking gunny sack after shoveling away some dirt. The missing man would be inside the sack in dismembered pieces. His arms would be disarticulated and legs sawed off above the knee. He would be decapitated and how he came to this state would remain a mystery. Nearby would be yet another soft spot with the remains of a girl and more digging would turn up the decayed remains of two children and a man. A massive crime scene would be present and at the end of the search would lie 13 victims mostly male. Lamphere would deny involvement and many would wonder whether a woman, Belle Gunness, could possibly be the vicious killer to enforce these brutal acts.

Belle's background would possess a number of startling deaths as her husband Mads Sorensen would die in 1900. He would be insured for $8,500 just as her insured adopted children too would die from poisoning. The insured establishments of Belle would be burned to the ground. Peter Gunness, Belle's second husband would not last a year. Belle's report of Peter's death would be accidental as a jar of scalding water and a meat grinder would fall upon his head. Belle would place matrimonial newspaper advertisements to lure men who upon a short stay on her farm would disappear. According to Lamphere, Belle was still alive claiming to take her to the train before her house would burn down. Belle as of recent would bring a woman into her home whose physical dimensions would match the headless corpse. It would appear perhaps Belle had pulled a fast one and upon warning of a visit from the brother of Andrew Helgelein would fake her death. Supporting this possibility would be her nearly empty bank account totaling in the vicinity of $50,000, the funds she would extort from her many visitors.

It may be women are worse than males among the deviant types. Murdering an enemy is one thing, but enjoying death and suffering is another. Belle Gunness one may view as a true female degenerate, lacking maternal instinct, finding pleasure in the torture of others, and in this case even her own children. It would seem in this case for male accomplices to be involved as the act of digging holes and dismembering bodies is difficult work. It would seem Belle to reward them with sex. It is not uncommon for female criminals to

Carley, S. G. (2013). *Serial killers, mass murders, & disorders.*
Boston: SGC Production.

mix crime with eroticism using sexuality and the temptations of personal gain in luring her accomplices. It could be quite possible Belle to experience hysteria or epilepsy. Lamphere would be found guilty of arson but sufficient evidence could not be provided of his role in the murders. Sightings would occur around the country of Gunness, and it would be suspected she was going under the alias of Esther Carlson. She would be arrested for fraud and murder in 1931 in Los Angeles, California. She would die before her trial and nothing would be proven (Ramsland, 2009).

Carley, S. G. (2013). *Serial killers, mass murders, & disorders*. Boston: SGC Production.

Lavinia Fisher

Lavinia Fisher

Lavinia Fisher may very well be the first serial killer the United States has ever seen. She was born in 1793 and would take her married name from her husband John Fisher. They would live in the Charleston, South Carolina, region and would manage the Six Mile Wayfarer House during the early 1800s. It would be around this time men would begin to mysteriously disappear. As the reports of missing men would compile the authorities would make the deduction these men's last presence to be at the Six Mile Wayfarer House. The Fisher's involvement in these disappearances could not be determined by evidence. The lack of evidence and the couple's popularity would lead to the charges being dropped. Adding to her popularity among the community and business within the hotel would be Lavinia's beauty and charm as a woman. It would be these very characteristics Lavinia would make use to help her husband rob and kill these male travelers frequenting the hotel. Rumors would begin to spread as more and more men would go missing. Eventually the town would be in an uproar and a group of vigilantes would go to the Fisher's in February of 1819 to stop the killings. They would be satisfied with leaving a watchman on the premise, one David Ross to monitor the happenings of the Fishers. Ross would be attacked by two men and

Carley, S. G. (2013). *Serial killers, mass murders, & disorders.* Boston: SGC Production.

dragged among a group of other men as Ross would look to Lavinia for help. She would choke Ross smashing his head through a window. Somehow Ross would escape his fate and alert others to the happenings in the hotel. John Peeples at this same time would travel to Charleston from Georgia and would stop at the Six Mile Wayfarer House to rest after a long trip. The beautiful Lavinia would warmly greet the stranger and the two would chat. She would offer Peeples a cup of tea and pour it out when she was not looking. She would alert him a room had opened up and Lavinia would show Peeples to his room. He would possess the sense of being a victim to robbery and would sleep on a chair instead of on the bed. As he was dosing off he was alerted by a loud shrewd noise. The bed he should have been sleeping on suddenly spikes would arise through the buttons of the mattress. Scared for his life Peeples would jump out of the window and alert the authorities. Four people would be arrested including Lavinia, John, and two men who were in on the operation with them.

The grounds of the Six Mile Wayfarer House would be dug up and thoroughly searched. They would find dozens of items which could be traced to the missing travelers among the hidden passages of the hotel. They would also find sedatives in the tea bags, a mechanism to rise spears out of the mattress, and the sets of hundreds of remains in the basement. Upon the plea of not guilty by the Fisher's, they would be forced to remain in jail while their co-conspirators would be released on bail. The Fisher's would be found guilty of robbery and murder at their trial and sentenced to death by hanging. Given time to appeal their conviction, they would make a bold but daring attempt at escaping from the prison confines. A rope would be made of linen and John would lower himself to the ground but the rope would break. Not wanting to leave Lavinia behind, he would return to jail and the two would be kept under maximum security detail. The Constitutional Court in February of 1820 would reject the Fisher's appeal and schedule their execution for later that month.

Carley, S. G. (2013). *Serial killers, mass murders, & disorders.* Boston: SGC Production.

The Reverend Richard Furman would offer counseling to the Fishers. Lavinia would want no part, but John would beg for his sole to be spared. The Fisher's would be taken from the Charleston jail on February 18, 1820, and sent to the gallows behind the building to be hanged. John would pray with the minister asking him to read a letter. The letter would be read to a group of over 2000 people asking for mercy from a wrongful judicial process. He would plea his case verbally to the crowd and beg for mercy before finally being hung. Lavinia quite contrary did not go so quietly. She would refuse to walk the gallows and requested to wear her wedding dress. Lavinia would rant and rave as they would carry her to the platform. She would scream to the crowd whom she would in part blame for her conviction. Before tightening the noose around her neck she would scream to the crowd, "If you have a message you want sent to hell, give it to me, I'll carry it." Lavinia would jump off the scaffold herself and dangle downward into the crowd. People would speak of the wicked stare on Lavinia's face as the life would be squeezed out of her. Sources say the Fisher's remains to be in the cemetery between King and Archdale streets, the Unitarian Church graveyard. This is highly unlikely though and most likely they did not receive a proper burial as unclaimed by family members were most likely buried alongside a field next to the jail.

Other Notable Female Serial Killers

Delphine Lalaurie would be born in or around the year 1875. She would live with her husband and two daughters in New Orleans in the mid-1820s. This wealthy high class family could be viewed as despicable for their treatment of slaves. No evidence would exist of abuse until 1834 when the Lalaurie mansion would catch fire. Rescue workers much to their dismay would find a 70 year old woman chained to the stove. It would be the chained woman who would initiate the blaze in a suicide attempt in avoidance of the punishments by Madame Lalaurie. The residents of New Orleans

Carley, S. G. (2013). *Serial killers, mass murders, & disorders.* Boston: SGC Production.

would begin to question the treatment of the slaves in the Lalaurie mansion. Authorities would come across a dozen starving and maimed slaves with reports of amputations at the limbs, macabre experiments, and sewing mouths closed. Lalaurie would escape justice and later die in Paris (Castillo, 1999).

Amy Archer Gilligan would be born in 1868 spending her life as adult caretaker/murderer of the elderly claiming anywhere from five to 50 victims. It would be Amy along with her husband James who would first open the Archer Home for the Elderly and Infirm in Connecticut. Archer would be left with large insurance payouts when her first and second husbands would die under what one may consider mysterious circumstances. Archer-Gilligan would continue her operation of caring for the elderly running what would become a murder house. The Archer home would act as the final resting spot for 60 individuals between the years of 1907 and 1917. The mounting death toll would increase and arouse suspicion among family members and upon exhuming bodies, strychnine and arsenic would be found in their systems. Archer-Gilligan in 1919 would be found guilty of second degree murder and sentenced accordingly to life in prison. She would die in 1962 in the Connecticut Hospital for the Insane.

The birth of Bertha Gifford would occur in 1872. One should not be fooled by her gentle appearance as the sick relatives and neighbors she cared for were. Gifford's victims' bodies would be exhumed finding her to poison them with arsenic. In her 1928 trial she would be found guilty by reason of insanity and spend the duration of her life in the Missouri State Hospital. She would die in 1851 having claimed the lives of as few as three and as many as 17 victims.

Nanny Doss was born in 1905 who would claim 11 victims. She would possess a line of dead husbands and relatives. Her first marriage was at the young age of 16 producing four children of which she would murder two of her daughters. She would remarry in 1929 to Robert Harrelson and during their 16 year marriage, she would murder her two grandsons for insurance money. She would be raped by her husband in 1945 and respond by poisoning him. Doss' third husband would die, and after a suspicious fire would burn her house down, she would once again collect insurance money. Doss would marry her fourth husband in the early 1950s Richard Morton, and in the short span of a few months would kill her husband and mother. It would be after the death of her fifth husband she would be apprehended when attempting to collect on two insurance policies. Doss would plea guilty to murder in 1955, and sentenced to life imprisonment where she would die in Oklahoma State Penitentiary in 1965.

Dorothea Punte was born in 1929 who would run a boarding house for the elderly during the mid-1980s. She would steal from her boarders and eventually murder them through use of poison. In all she would claim from three to nine victims. Punte would have a handyman dispose of a box of junk in 1985 which in reality was a decomposing human body. A fisherman would find the decomposing body along a river bank. The missing tenants and Punte would be investigated. Seven bodies were found buried directly on the property yet Punte would profess their deaths to be of natural causes. Punte would be sentenced to life imprisonment at her trial in 1992 where she would die in 2011 at the Central California Women's Facility.

Gwendolyn Graham and Cathy Wood were born in 1963 and 1962 responsible for five deaths. These women were employed as nursing home nurses during the mid-1980s. These women are a bit different than the other women on the list as there acts would be sexually sadistic. They would kill five patients in months at the Alpine Manor in Grand Rapids, Michigan. The duo would even

Carley, S. G. (2013). *Serial killers, mass murders, & disorders.*
Boston: SGC Production.

brag about their murders of which no one would believe. The two women would be apprehended when Wood's ex-husband would go to the police with the story in 1988. A plea bargain would get Wood a reduced sentence, yet Graham would receive the maximum punishment of the law and receive five consecutive life sentences. She is currently incarcerated at the Federal Correctional Institution in Tallahassee, Florida where she will be spending the next 20 to 40 years of her life.

Carley, S. G. (2013). *Serial killers, mass murders, & disorders*. Boston: SGC Production.

Dr. Harold Shipman (Dr. Death)

Harold Shipman

In consideration of Harold Frederic Shipman the belief by many is systematic reform is, in fact, not necessary because there will never be another like Shipman. These same people will shrug off the incident as a killer who happened to be a doctor, many of these people of which compose the doctoral community. I would take a very different view of the matter in contesting it was the very fact Shipman to be a doctor, which would permit him to kill and continue his path undiscovered. The opportunity to kill would be awarded by the profession, and the controls and safeguards of his status and duty would avoid Shipman of the suspicion of wrongdoing. The conviction of Harold Frederic Shipman would occur on January 31, 2000 for the murder of 15 patients while a British general practitioner in the northwest of England. Shipman's methods would be through the administration of lethal doses of diamorphine (diacetylmorphine), he would use to kill the patients. Upon his conviction Shipman would be charged with 15 consecutive life sentences being found guilty on each count. While in custody Shipman would commit suicide on January 13, 2004. The initiation of a public inquiry would occur in February 2001 as so many

Carley, S. G. (2013). *Serial killers, mass murders, & disorders.* Boston: SGC Production.

important issues were raised by his conviction. The chairperson of this inquiry would be Dame Janet Smith, a senior high court judge who would appoint as her medical advisor Aneez Esmail.

Investigated within this inquiry would be the number of deaths in which responsibility would fall onto the hands of Shipman. The dates under investigation would cover a broad time range from the time of August 1970 to July 1998. Shipman would certify over 1,000 deaths of which would amount to the largest forensic investigation in the history of the U. K. Smith would conclude of these certified deaths 218 to be unlawful acts of murder by the hands of Shipman. Smith would further conclude the possibility of Shipman's involvement in 62 other patient's deaths yet sufficient evidence would disallow her from making this decision. This statistic would make Shipman the most prolific serial killer in the history of the U.K. and perhaps the whole world. Of this statistic 47 were men and 171 were women. Shipman would typically prey on the elderly, especially those who lived by themselves. Shipman's visits to these patients could be as a call from the patient, a routine visit, or a solicited call. Shipman's visits would be initiated by patient ailment, to provide a prescription, or take a blood sample. It would be during the course of these visits Shipman would administer the lethal dose of morphine or diamorphine (Esmail, 2005).

The motives behind Shipman's actions consists of much speculation. Who would embark on a career of killing their patients after taking the Hippocratic oath and working so diligently in becoming a doctor? Shipman would continue his refusal to speak to anyone regarding his role in the killings, as he would persistently deny any involvement even after his questioning and arrest. No useful information exists of Shipman's relationships or family background and no complete psychiatric or psychological assessments. The inquiry would obtain certain evidence in the form of evidence from the Shipman trial, medical and prison reports, and videotape of police questioning. A panel of forensic psychiatrists were given access to this inquiry in addition to post conviction reports pertaining to Shipman's abuse of pethidine (meperidine) in 1976. Shipman's motivations for the killings and his character would remain unknown through this rather extensive investigation of the inquiry and other pertinent knowledge. The only logical explanation for Shipman's motives are that there are no motives for him to commit such heinous crimes. Viewing motive as the rational explanation in the decision-making process of committing a crime. Motivating Shipman to go into medicine may be the death of his mother from cancer when he was an adolescent. It would be early in the career of Shipman he would become addicted to pethidine and according to psychiatric reports he would be experiencing depression. The problem or problems driving Shipman to addiction would never be resolved, and the drug addiction would seem to compound the manifestation of an addictive personality. It may be Shipman to become an addict of killing as the power and control given to him through association with death, he would seem to derive pleasure.

Within Shipman's community he was widely popular, and well respected by both his patients and fellow health care professionals. He would remain isolated professionally and possess very few friends. The earliest victims of Shipman would be of very poor health and even terminally ill. The risk was minimal for Shipman to provide these patients opiates, whose death would be expected in any case leading to both little chance of suspicion or detection. Besides Shipman perhaps convinced himself watching these individuals slowly die to be as immoral an act as killing the person. This justification would be only within the mind of Shipman, and his response of killing the victims was surely and clearly to suffice personal needs, and the process of selection by Shipman was a means of avoiding detection. In consideration of Shipman's crimes,

Carley, S. G. (2013). *Serial killers, mass murders, & disorders.* Boston: SGC Production.

it is impossible not to consider also the length of time Shipman would go unsuspected, and the context of which the killings would occur. The inquiry would issue numerous recommendations after a long and costly examination of four years and over $40 million (Esmail, 2005). The recommendations from the evidence would cover the regulation and monitoring of the work of general practitioners, the regulation of controlled drugs among the community, the investigation of deaths by coroners, and the system of death certification. Enabling Shipman to kill and go undiscovered for many years would be fundamental weaknesses within the existing systems according to the inquiry. Despite regulations to prevent the stockpiling of pharmaceuticals, Shipman was able to compile large quantities of diamorphine. He would avoid reporting the deaths to the coroner certifying a cause of death among his patients. On cremation certificates Shipman's records would contain no effective check on the information. No one would notice the large number of death certificates signed by Shipman as no system would be in place of monitoring this information. Facing revelations pertaining to Shipman, doctors within the United Kingdom would argue against system reform claiming another Shipman is not going to exist. That Shipman was a killer who would happen to be a doctor, again I would take the view it was Shipman's position as a doctor enabling him to kill at will and remain undiscovered. Absence of safeguards and controls would permit Shipman to operate without suspicion, and it was his profession affording him this opportunity to kill. Great trust is invested upon doctors by society giving them immense power. Shipman's abuse of this trust would expose the power among the profession and the lack of power of the patient. It would seem professional organizations should be in place to better equalize the imbalance of power among the doctor-patient relationship as Shipman would clearly abuse this trust. The best safeguards against the next Shipman include more of a questioning attitude toward doctors monitoring their work with the implementation of better systems, especially in regard to the care of their most vulnerable patients. Should this mean among the medical profession the presence of greater regulation, so be it, this is the lesson after all with the case of Harold Shipman.

Other Physician Serial Killers

The political killers engaging in biological warfare are the Nazi and Japanese doctors. The BWA chairman himself finds the Harold Shipman record to be a unique case, yet I contend the medical profession to possess more serial killers than any other if not all the other combined. A close second may be the profession of nursing. Dentists have had their notorious characters, yet veterinarians seem to not be prone to homicide. The 1888 unsolved murders in London by the so called Jack the Ripper is thought to be of a member of the medical profession. Prime suspects would include the physician to Queen Victoria Sir William Gull along with Dr. Thomas Barnado. Still other suspects would include a barrister, Montage John Druitt who would be of a respected medical family and would pass himself off as a doctor. Dr. Stanley, Dr. George Chapman (Severin Klosowski), and Russian Dr. Alexander Pedachenko all suspects in the Jack the Ripper case of five murders. While on the subject a psychotic who had studied medicine Gaylord Sundheim would not have conclusive evidence of being the "mad butcher" in the 1930s in Cleveland, Ohio (Kinnell, 2000).

The number of recorded instances of multiple murders by doctors is significant to lay the claim those of a pathological interest in controlling life and death are attracted to the profession. Kenneth Bianchi one may consider a would be doctor possessing homicidal tendencies as one of the 1978 "Hillside Stranglers" representing one half of the murderous duo, the other his own cousin. He would present himself under a false identity as a psychological counselor always wanting to be a psychiatrist. The Demon in the Belfry murders would be committed by a San Franciscan medical student, Theodore Durrant, who would murder two women in church nine days apart in 1895. Durrant would be hanged three years after his crimes. A Los Angeles nurse Robert Diaz would pretend to be a doctor as he had always hoped to be, and would provide unauthorized injections on patients. He would like to be called Dr. Diaz even as just a nursing student. Upon his 1984 conviction, Diaz would receive the death penalty (gas chamber) for murdering 12 patients through the use of lignocaine (lidocaine).

One may say many of these individuals are not even real doctors Diaz, Druitt, Sundheim, Bianchi, Durrant. Here are a few stories of actual practicing physicians committing serial acts of murder. Dr. Edward William Pritchard would insure a servant girl and then kill her. He would also kill his own daughter, mother in law, and wife. Pritchard would have the unhonorable distinction as the last public hanging in Glasgow (1865). American, Dr. Bennett Clarke Hyde would fight over a family inheritance by killing his in-laws through use of strychnine, cyanide, and bleeding. The typhoid that would kill his three in-laws would also cause his sister in-law to become ill. The doctor to provide evidence against Hyde in the 1910 court trial would die before the trial would ever begin (Wilson & Seaman, 1992). The late wife of Dr. John Hill would die of bacteriogenic shock. She would be embalmed before any toxicology tests could be performed on the order of her father. Hill would marry his ex-mistress, who would make the claim Dr. Hill too tried to kill her, and would admit to her to killing a friend, his father, and brother, all with morphine. In 1972, Hill would be assassinated on his front doorstep. The Green Beret Killer, Dr. Jeffrey MacDonald of the U. S. army, would be convicted for the murder of his pregnant wife and children in 1970. In 1849 the mother in law to practitioner William Palmer would die of apoplexy followed by the deaths of his insured wife and brother. He would also poison a betting crony with strychnine as a serial forger. Doctors responding to this instance

Carley, S. G. (2013). *Serial killers, mass murders, & disorders.* Boston: SGC Production.

would accept Palmer's explanation of a natural death. Dr. George Henry Lamson would record the first lethal injection of aconitine in poisoning his brother in laws for their estates in 1881. In 1863 Dr. De La Pommerais would kill his mistress for her insurance money, and his mother in law for her estate through the use of digitalis. Dr. Sam Sheppard made famous by the movie The Fugitive would in 1954 kill his wife by striking her with 35 blows to the head. He would be sued after two surgical deaths. His mother in law and mother too would die. Dr. Sheppard would have a restraining order put on him for his threats to kill his second wife (Smyth, 1992). The three heavily insured wives of Dr. J Milton Bowers would die of suspicious circumstances, two in the 1880s and the other in 1865. Dr. Bowers would be accused of forging a confession exonerating him for the poisoning death of his brother in law. Dr. Warder of Brighton through the use of aconite would kill his three wives. He would offer expert testimony in the trial of Dr. William Palmer mentioned earlier who would take cyanide to avoid execution. One of the Jack the Ripper suspects Dr. George Chapman would commit the serial poisoning of three of his partners and be hanged. A fellow of the Royal College of Surgeons Dr. Robert George Clements in 1947 would make use of morphine in killing his wife for money. Signing his previous three wives death certificates is suspected of killing them also. A doctor examining his dying fourth wife would diagnose her with leukemia as would Dr. Clements. The on call doctor would kill himself later. Through use of a muscle relaxant Dr. Carl Coppolino would murder his wife, who was also a doctor. Dr. Coppolino would order his mistress to inject her husband with the muscle relaxant who would die of coronary thrombosis. Dr. Coppolino would be the attending physician. He would be tried and eventually convicted in 1967 (Game & O'Dell, 1989). Dr. Buck Ruxton in 1935 would commit the jigsaw murders as he would dissect his wife and maid and scatter the body parts among the borders of Scotland. Dr. Hawley Harvey Crippen would be hanged in 1910 for killing his two wives and along with Dr. Buck Roxton

Carley, S. G. (2013). *Serial killers, mass murders, & disorders.*
Boston: SGC Production.

both reside within Madame Tussaud's Chamber of Horrors. Dr. Henry Lovell William Clark during the 1930s would be part of an elaborate murder scheme to kill his mistress' husband with arsenic and gelsemine, and then his wife by four paid assassins. Double filicide has been committed by two American doctors from the time of 1985 to 2000. One from St. Louis murdering his two sons several years apart for insurance money. An alcoholic oncologist by the name of Dr. Debra Green would kill her two children by arson and confess to the attempted murders of both her third child and husband, also a doctor (Murder Detectives, 2000).

Killers of Strangers and Patients

The London Prostitution Poisoner would go by the name of Dr. Thomas Neill Cream who would have the distinction as the first male hanged in Britain in the year 1892. He would kill three women in America. One of America's most prolific serial killers "Dr. Poison" would be Dr. Michael Swango who would also kill people in Africa during the 1990s. The medical establishment would not recognize the ability of a medical professional to engage in such monstrous behavior. In September of 2000 he would be sentenced to life in prison. France's worst ever serial killer would be a doctor, Dr. Marcel Petiot who during the second world war would murder up to a hundred people for their possessions, as a condition for their escape. Thirty Italian immigrants of lower socioeconomic status during the 1930s were killed by an American Dr. Morris Bolber as part of an elaborate insurance scam. Bolber would obtain the names of potential victims from the Philadelphia Witch who would poison her husband to death. The deaths would be made to look either by natural means or accidental as without leaving a mark cerebral hemorrhaging would be caused through the use of a sand filled canvas bag (Game & O'Dell, 1989).

Carley, S. G. (2013). *Serial killers, mass murders, & disorders.* Boston: SGC Production.

A former mental patient Dr. Ronald E Clark from Detroit, Michigan, in 1967 would assault his patients sexually and kill them with sodium pentothal. In New Jersey a decade later Dr. Mario D Jascalevich through use of curare would murder five of his patients. Through acts of sexual sadism a Norwegian doctor during the late 1970s, Arnfinn Nesset, would kill as many as 138 patients also using curare. The jury would find Dr. Nesset guilty on all 21 counts, he would be tried for murder, despite his defenses of insanity and then euthanasia (Game & O'Dell, 1989). An Eastbourne general practitioner by the name of Dr. John Bodkin Adams at his trial would admit to easing up to 400 older women into their deaths. It is Dr. Adams, a forger of prescriptions, who would act as the role model to Harold Shipman. French Doctor, Edme Castaing in 1823, forger of wills would be one of the first to use morphine as a lethal poison killing two of his patients in this manner. American Dr. Thomas Thatcher Graves would convince a patient of his, who was a rich widow, to hand power of attorney to him. To return this act Graves would mail a bottle of poisoned whiskey killing her and a friend. Graves would poison himself from his cell in 1893. The Torture Doctor, Doctor Henry Howard Holmes is reported to kill over 200 women between the years of 1892 and 1896 from his murder castle in Chicago. Holmes would be the first serial killer hanged in America (Hickey, 1997). The biological warfare and ethnic cleansing of the Japanese and Nazi doctors could deem them mass killers or political serial killers. One name standing out is the bloodthirsty intellectual behind the French Revolution, Dr Jean-Paul Marat, in his association to political serial killing. One of the writings of Marat would state along the lines of "to maintain public tranquility, 200,000 heads must be cut off." His writings of assassination plots of good citizens while in bed would lead to the massacre of over 1,000 aristocrats and inmates of mental asylums, prison hospitals, and jails. The public would view Marat as a martyr upon his 1793 assassination. Other notable political serial killers include Dr. Dadovan Karadzic a Serbian psychiatrist whose crimes

Carley, S. G. (2013). *Serial killers, mass murders, & disorders*.
Boston: SGC Production.

against humanity would make him wanted for genocide. The Argentinian doctors who in 1992 would murder patients for organs may fit this description. The mass purges and executions during the 1960s would be viewed as the act of an evil dictator in Papa Doc Duvalier the Haitian dictator. Duvalier would kill 300 people annually, yet continue a persona as a humanitarian in tropical medicine. Repeat killings such as in the cases of Nesset or Shipman may be remote. Yet the two major investigations of a serial euthanasia/mass murder in 2000 in France and England would show although an increased awareness exists within the authorities, that history tends to repeat itself (Gee, 2000).

Carley, S. G. (2013). *Serial killers, mass murders, & disorders.* Boston: SGC Production.

Dean Corll (The Candyman)

Dean Arnold Corll

Dean Corll would be born on December 24, 1939 in the state of Indiana growing-up in a combative home where his parents were always quarreling. While Corll was still an infant his parents would divorce and remarry after the second World War, yet Dean's father would provide no stabilizing influence punishing his children harshly to even the smallest of infractions and regarding his children as insufficient. Corll and his brothers would be left with a series of sitters upon his parents' second separation. Dean would be left with a heart condition the result of rheumatic fever resulting in his frequent absences from school. When his mother would remarry he would seem to welcome the change as the family would move to the state of Texas. The candy business starting as a part-time job would turn to their livelihood as Corll seeking to gain new friends would be generous with candy samples. Despite his heart condition, in 1964 Corll would be drafted into the military displaying his first flagrant signs of homosexuality. In December of 1969 Corll would turn 30 and his personality would become glum and hypersensitive. Corll would start hanging around teenage boys including Elmer Wayne Henley and David Owen

Carley, S. G. (2013). *Serial killers, mass murders, & disorders.* Boston: SGC Production.

Brooks where he would pass out candy and host glue sniffing parties at his Pasadena apartment in a suburb of Houston. Corll could be considered sadistic in his sexual relationships with boys and young men leaning toward bondage. During 1970 on one occasion Brooks would find Corll nude upon entering the apartment as a homemade torture rack would have two naked boys strapped to it. Corll would release his playmates and feel embarrassed of the situation offering Brooks a vehicle in return for his silence of what he witnessed. Corll's passion would turn to a lust for blood and using Henley and Brooks as procurers, he would offer them $200 for each person they would lure to his apartment.

The date of Corll's first murder would occur on September 25, 1970. In all Corll and his accomplices would kill a minimum of 28 persons between the years of 1970 – 1973. His victims were all male ranging in ages of 13 – 20. The first victim would be Jeffrey Konan a college student who was out hitchhiking. Corll's victims would often be drawn from a Houston area known as the Heights where police would ignore disappearances accounting them as runaways. Henley would bring two of his friends and neighbors to Corll who at times would kill two at once. In a single sitting in December of 1970, he would murder 15 year old David Yates and 14 year old James Glass. Joining the missing list one month later would be brothers Jerry and Donald Waldrop, and in October of 1972 Richard Embry and Wally Simineaux would join the slaughter. Killed at separate times would be another pair of brothers Mike and Billy Baulch in May of 1972 and July of 1973. Residing across the street from Corll's apartment would be his youngest victim a nine year old. Elmer Henley would summon Pasadena police officers to Corll's apartment on August 8, 1973. There the candy man Dean Corll would be found dead Henley claiming to have unloaded his revolver in defense (White et al., 2011; Stone, 2010).

Carley, S. G. (2013). *Serial killers, mass murders, & disorders.* Boston: SGC Production.

End to Corll's Reign of Terror

Henley would bring a girl to a Corll paint sniffing orgy and the homosexual killer would go into a rage. Corll would taunt and threaten Henley with a gun when Henley would manage to disarm him. Henley would insist to be frightened for his life and fire the six shots into the shoulder and back of Corll to save himself. Henley would take this opportunity and guide the police to a southwest Houston boatshed being rented where seventeen victims would be found buried. Four more graves would turn-up upon driving to Lake Sam Rayburn and six more at High Island Beach. A total of 27 bodies would be found. Henley would insist two more bodies to be at High Island and two more in the boat shed, but police would call off the search. Brooks and Henley would confess to luring the victims to Corll over the years as Brooks would finger Henley as responsible for at least one of the slayings. Brooks would state most of the murders to occur when Henley to be involved, it would be the three of them working together. Henley would be sentenced to life imprisonment convicted of multiple murder in August of 1974, and in March of 1975 Brooks would receive an identical term. Other local pedophiles would be linked to Corll's murder ring, yet no prosecutions would arise. In December of 1978 an appeal would overturn the conviction of Elmer Henley, the result of pre-trial publicity. In June of 1979 Henley would be convicted and sentenced for a second time.

Carley, S. G. (2013). *Serial killers, mass murders, & disorders.*
Boston: SGC Production.

Elmer Henley

Elmer Wayne Henley

Elmer Wayne Henley Jr. is a convicted serial killer born on May 9, 1956. On July 16, 1974 he would receive six consecutive life sentences for his role in the abduction, rape, and murder of a minimum of 28 boys by Dean Corll in and between the years of 1970 – 1973. Many victims would be lured to Corll's apartment by Henley or his accomplice David Brooks. The 17 year old Henley would shoot Corll dead on August 8, 1973. At the time of the murders the act would represent the deadliest serial killings in American history. Henley would be the eldest of four sons born to Mary Henley and Elmer Wayne Sr. His father was a brutal alcoholic who would beat his wife and children with some regularity. His mother a good Christian would always attempt to instill a good ethic in her children so they would grow-up to be responsible members of the good society. When Henley was 15, his parents would divorce in 1970, and his mother would retain custody of the four children. In school Henley was always a superior student. Although when his parents would divorce, he would take on a series of menial jobs causing his grades to falter. Eventually at the age of 15 Henley would drop out altogether.

Carley, S. G. (2013). *Serial killers, mass murders, & disorders.* Boston: SGC Production.

Henley Meets Brooks and Corll

Before leaving school the 16 year old Brooks and Henley would become good friends. The two would skip school together and Brooks would introduce Henley to Corll, his adult friend. In time Henley would spend much of his free time with Corll, despite the suspicion regarding Corll's sexual preference. Initially the trio would work as organized thieves burglarizing those in the surrounding neighborhoods. Corll testing Henley's loyalty would ask if he were willing to kill if deemed necessary. Henley would claim to be more than willing to kill should the opportunity present itself. Henley would be aware of the disappearances in his neighborhood, a total of eight teenage boys among the ages of 13 and 17. Henley would actually be part of the recovery search for two of the missing boys, Malley Winkle and David Hilligeist, who would disappear on May 29, 1971. They were friends of Henley's from the neighborhood.

At the age of 15 Henley would be introduced to Corll in the winter of 1971 while the killing spree would already be in full force. At this point it may be a wonder Henley did not become a victim himself. In any case, Brooks would take Henley to meet Corll claiming a deal could be made in which Henley could make some quick cash. Corll would tell Henley that he was part of an underground homosexual slavery ring in Dallas, Texas, recruiting young boys much like yourself. Henley would receive the same offer he gave Brooks his accomplice at the time, $200 for each boy brought to the apartment. Initially Henley would ignore Corll's offer, yet in 1972 a result of financial hardship Henley would convince himself to take Corll's offer. Corll and Henley would devise a plan upon luring the boy back to his lair of which first he would cuff his hands behind his back, and upon releasing himself con the victim into cuffing himself. The pair would cruise the Houston Heights until persuading a youth to enter Corll's GTX.

Carley, S. G. (2013). *Serial killers, mass murders, & disorders.*
Boston: SGC Production.

They would use the smoking of marijuana as the lure, and the unsuspecting youth would traverse to Corll's apartment. All would go as planned as Henley would con the victim into cuffing himself, at which time Corll would pounce on the victim tying his feet and taping his mouth. Henley would leave Corll alone, believing the individual to be sold into the homosexual slavery ring (Stone, 2010). The next day Henley would receive his $200 bounty. Speculation exists to the identity of the first victim of Henley and Corll, but it is believed to be 17 year old William Karmon Branch who would be found buried in Corll's boat shed. The boy would go missing in February of 1972.

Henley while in the company of Corll and Brooks on March 24 would persuade 18 year old Frank Aguire a friend of his to accompany them back at Corll's apartment. Aguire would smoke a large amount of marijuana back at Corll's and be conned into cuffing himself just as their prior victim. Corll would drag Aguire to his torture board and rape him before strangling him and burying the body at High Island Beach. Henley would claim to try to talk Corll out of the rape and killing of Aguire of which Corll would refuse. Corll would tell Henley the other boy he helped abduct was raped and killed and that Aguire would be meeting a similar fate (Stone, 2010). Both Corll and Brooks would inform Henley his friend David Hilligeist to be buried in a boat shed with Malley Winkle. The grim reality of death would not deter Henley as he would vow to assist in further killings. Within a month Henley and Brooks would be at it again persuading 17 year old Mark Scott to join them for a party at Corll's. Scott would be raped, murdered, and buried at the High Island Beach in a similar manner than the other victims. On May 21 two more victims would be buried at High Island, Johnny Ray Delone and Bill Baulch.

Killing Goes Into Full Force

Carley, S. G. (2013). *Serial killers, mass murders, & disorders.*
Boston: SGC Production.

In June of 1972 Corll would move to the Westcott Towers where a 17 year old Steven Sickman would be killed in less than a month at the new residence. Henley would assist Corll in the abduction and murder of two more boys on October 3, Richard Hembree and Wally Simoneaux. According to Brooks, Henley would accidentally shoot Hembree in the mouth when entering the room the two boys were bound. Apparently while waving around the .22 caliber revolver, it would go off and happen to enter Hembree's jaw. Hembree would be buried in the boat shed and both were murdered in cold blood. Phoning his fiancée, Richard Kepner would be abducted one month later. The 19 year old would be buried at High Island as at this point Henley would already be part of a minimum of nine abductions and murders. When Henley would move to Mt. Pleasant in the early part of 1973, Corll would work solo abducting 17 year old Joseph Lyles. Henley would enlist in the U. S. Navy, but on account of his education he would be rejected. In the short span of two months in June and July in 1973, Brooks, Corll, and Henley would claim eight more victims ranging in ages from 15 – 20. Henley would participate in at least six of these abductions or the murder itself. Billy Lawrence a 15 year old friend of Henley would be abducted on June 4 spending three days of torture and abuse at Corll's new Pasadena apartment before being strangled with a ligature and buried at the Sam Rayburn Lake. Raymond Blackburn would be hitchhiking less than two weeks later when he would be abducted, strangled, and buried at the lake. Other victims during this short time span include Charles Cobble and Marty Jones, Michael Baulch and John Sellers, and Homer Garcia. Without the assistance of Henley, Brooks and Corll on August 3 would kill James Dreymala a 13 year old, who would call his mother and tell her he was at a party.

Kerley and Williams Somehow Escape

Carley, S. G. (2013). *Serial killers, mass murders, & disorders*. Boston: SGC Production.

Timothy Kerley age 19 would be promised a party on August 8, 1973 at Corll's home. The pair would voyage out to purchase sandwiches and return to Corll's home with 15 year old Rhonda Williams. Henley would infuriate Corll by bringing a female to his apartment. Corll would remain calm hiding his anger, and when the two teenagers and Henley would pass-out from alcohol and marijuana abuse, Corll would gag and bind them. Corll would be placing handcuffs on Henley's wrists when he would awake and Williams and Kerley would be bound and gagged lying on the floor aside him. Henley would be dragged into the kitchen by Corll having a .22 caliber pointed at his stomach while his hands would be cuffed. Henley would promise to participate in the torture and murder of Williams and Kerley if Corll would release him, which he did. Williams and Kerley would be tied to the torture board. Corll would hand Henley a long hunting knife and order him to cut away at Williams' clothing and rape her as he would rape Kerley. As Henley began to cut her clothing, Corll put his weapon down and would undress and climb atop Kerley (Stone, 2010).

Corll would begin his assault of Kerley, and Henley would cut away at Williams' clothes. Williams would talk with Henley asking if this was real and if he was going to do anything. Henley would reach for the .22 caliber and point the weapon at Corll and like a hero would scream, "You've gone far enough Dean!" Corll was not visibly shaken walking toward Henley stating "Kill me Wayne! You won't do it!" Henley would continue by pressing down on the trigger and expelling a single bullet from the barrel of the .22 caliber hitting the forehead of Corll. Corll would continue his advance in the direction of Henley which would prompt him to expel two more bullets from the barrel of the gun both striking Corll with great force in his shoulder causing Corll to go into a retreat mode staggering out of the room the teenagers were being held. Henley would continue his attack which could now best be described as relentless expelling three more rounds each entering Corll's body into the rear right shoulder and lower back region. Corll would not survive the attack and would become a rare statistic in which the serial killing perpetrator is killed in the act of committing the crime (White et al., 2011). Kerley and Williams would be released as Henley would confess to his role in the Houston mass murders after phoning the police regarding the incident upon the request and suggestion of Kerley and Williams.

Henley's Confession

Henley's confession on August 8 would be that for a period of three years with the assistance of David Brooks the duo would procure teenage youths for Dean Corll. Some of these youths would be their very own friends and companions. Henley would admit his role in the abductions since the winter of 1971 which would turn into murder within each abduction. Henley would go on to state Brooks to be an accomplice for an even longer period than he. Henley would state, he and Brooks to receive a $200 bounty for each victim lured to Corll's apartment and that the majority of the victims to be buried in three locations, the High Island Beach, Sam Rayburn Lake, and a southwest Houston boatshed. Henley would assist in the recovery efforts of the victims allowing police to escort him to these three sites. Twenty-seven youths would be found between the ages of $13 - 20$ on the dates ranging from August 8 – August 13. It would be each Corll, Henley, and Brooks each burying the victims. In 1983 an additional victim would be discovered. In the boat shed would be found 17 of the victims, six in High Island Beach, and four at Sam Rayburn Lake. The body of Mark Scott remains undiscovered at High Island Beach. In August of 1983 a 29th victim would be found buried at Jefferson County Beach. The victims all male would be found sexually assaulted and tortured. Autopsy reports would claim the cause of death to be either shooting, strangulation, or a combination of both. In the 1974 trial of Elmer Henley dispute would arise of whether one of the victims found buried at High

Carley, S. G. (2013). *Serial killers, mass murders, & disorders.* Boston: SGC Production.

Island, 17 year old John Sellars, was actually a victim of Corll. Sellars would vanish on July 12, 1973 yet unlike the other victims killed by a .22 or strangulation would be shot by a rifle including four gunshot wounds. Still Henley and Brooks could lead police to the body on August 13, 1973 buried in a similar manner to Corll's other victims.

In June of 1974 Henley would stand trial in San Antonio, Texas, charged with the murders of six teenage boys who he would lure to Corll's apartment from March of 1972 to July of 1973. Henley would be sentenced to six consecutive life terms after being found guilty on July 16, 1974. Henley and his attorney's would file an appeal on July 25 contending the news media to prejudice the trial, a motion to move the trial from San Antonio would be denied, Henley's denial of an evidentiary hearing, and that the jury had not been sequestered. On December 20, 1978 Henley's conviction would be overturned. Henley would be tried for a second time in June of 1979. Henley would again be convicted and sentenced to six consecutive life sentences on June 27.

Carley, S. G. (2013). *Serial killers, mass murders, & disorders.*
Boston: SGC Production.

Jane Toppan and Erzsebet Bathory (Sexual Sadism)

Defining Sexual Sadism

The ambiguous definition for the term sexual sadism according to the DSM includes the acting out of sadistic and sexual fantasies resulting in harm or death. Fantasies not involving action would not classify sexual sadism. Despite the case consisting of two females the majority of sexual sadists are male. Sexual sadism as an evil concept overlaps the behaviors constituting a psychiatric diagnosis. Evil may be the only word to describe the actions of the sexual sadist. Such repugnant and horrifying actions create the impulse in deeming such actions evil. Such a response is often the result of torture and violent sexual crimes toward a victim. A classic example of the sexual sadist is the serial killer who experiences orgasm upon murdering a victim. Adolescence is a time when sexual sadistic fantasies may first occur. Adolescents experiencing callous unemotional personality may use these fantasies as a rehearsal for future sadistic acts. An early treatment option for these individuals is dynamic psychotherapy. No form of therapy can convincingly cure the individual of sexual sadistic fantasy.

Carley, S. G. (2013). *Serial killers, mass murders, & disorders.* Boston: SGC Production.

The first appearance of the term sadism would occur in the 1835 Dictionnaire Universel of Boiste, yet would not be a popular used term until the publication of the 1886 monograph of Krafft-Ebing (Coward, 1992). According to Krafft-Ebing in existence are eight sexual sadism varieties: sadistic acts with animals, sadism with objects such as whips, ideational sadism restricting to thoughts, symbolic sadism, defilement of a woman, comparable means, flagellation, stabbing injury, mutilation of corpse, and lustful murder (Hucker, 1997). It may be the development of sexual perversion to be a product of adolescent experience such as in the case of Donatien Alphonse François *Marquis de Sade* (1740-1814). De Sade would be sent to live with a clergyman uncle of his by his father as he would first become active in a varied sex life. He would next be sent to boarding school with the Jesuits when his father would learn of this. It would seem the corrective measures of the Jesuits which would initiate the perverse sexual ambitions of de Sade. This would include sex-tinged humiliations such as floggings and beatings upon the buttocks. The fantasies of de Sade would fortunately for his victims not become a reality (de Sade, 1995). De Sade would pay prostitutes to stuff communion wafers in their vagina as well as whip him and conversely him whipping them. De Sade's active imagination would involve much more in the direction of zoophilia and cutting among other acts of sodomy.

For the contemporary definition for sexual sadism one may look toward the DSM-IV-TR. A description of sexual sadism on p. 530 involves psychological and physical suffering of a victim of which is sexually exciting to a person. Sexual fantasies and urges are intense. In addition these sexual fantasies impair important areas of functioning. The criterion of the DSM does not require sadistic acts instead only the thoughts are necessary to diagnose sexual sadism. This may fall along the lines of Krafft-Ebing who find ideational sadism to be a variety of sadism. Still this would challenge the common implication of the term of the involvement of pathological behavior. How can one call someone a sadist who has never engaged in sadistic acts. One may challenge the DSM in requiring certain behaviors as defining features of the disorder. The definition just seems overinclusive and ambiguous as it seems a distinction should be made among those who fantasize and those who act out their fantasies. There may be a problem with the second criterion in determining sexual sadism as well in significant stress or impairment from sexual behaviors or urges. The individual who fantasizes of sadistic acts may seek counseling, whereas the individual you read about in the news continues their path of destruction without emotional distress or significant impairment. The majority of these men are psychopaths and the success rate in treating such individuals with psychoanalysis one can assume is a very low percentage.

Evil Within Sexual Sadism

In finding an act or a person evil is to make a judgment upon another. Despite this the word seems to be thrown around with some regularity by the media, journalists, lawyers, and judges to describe the horrific act (Stone, 2009). It is these acts as the maximum display of defiance toward rules. Torture of a victim may be an evil act and may not need require of a sexual nature such as one throwing acid in the face when a girl breaks up with him. Perhaps an act sexual in nature should not evoke sexual excitement among a perpetrator such as the cutting of a woman's breast. Without the accompaniment of sexual arousal an absence of sexual sadism exists. Violent acts such as murder and especially rape despite the erection or orgasm of a perpetrator does not constitute sexual sadism. This would not devoid the act as evil yet sexual sadism remains ambiguous within violent crimes possessing a sexual motive. One such example involves 19 year old Jason Massey who would kill two 13 year olds, one male and the other female. The girl had her hands and feet cut off along with being decapitated. It could not be determined if the girl was raped as considerable decomposition would occur before finding the body. The killer's diary would show his desire to be the most prolific serial killer of all time killing as many beautiful girls as possible. Before the act Massey would kill many cats and dogs, and would claim never to have raped the victim. It is unclear if the killer experienced any sexual gratification in committing the "evil" act. Despite the evil nature of these crimes they may not fit the definition of sexual sadism.

Surrounding sexual ideas is the aura of intimacy and privacy. Nothing can be more a violation of the sacred, than violent and torturous acts of a victim's sexual parts. Especially regarding the preconscious of the sexual organs. Adding to the violation of such acts is the possibility of a pregnancy of a woman by a man she otherwise would not permit to father her children. Rape is a more evil crime than robbery and sexual sadism the even more evil. Such acts of sexual sadism may permanently scar a woman making her undesirable or amount to castration so she could not become pregnant. Sexual crimes last many years, unlike robberies leading to at times genetic death despite a surviving victim. A defining feature of sexual sadists are ritualistic behaviors. It is not uncommon for them to seek attachment to a willing partner. Upon an interview of 20 partners to sexual sadists seven of which would murder some of their partner's victims, 13 did not. These relationships were consensual and in nine of the 20 cases the women would experience incest as a child. Such early experiences would create a desire among the women of sadistic treatment from their partner. Partners of sexual sadists through a series of stages may be initiated into sadistic practices. During the candy and flowers stage, he would behave with gentlemanliness giving gifts and praise before proceeding to the next stage in expanding her sexual repertoire. This can take the form of choking, anal intercourse, or bondage. The man attempts to gain full control of the woman cutting her off from family and friends to make her his sexual slave. Often the pattern

Carley, S. G. (2013). *Serial killers, mass murders, & disorders.*
Boston: SGC Production.

will continue no further, yet can continue to end with her death. Sexual sadists may lead a double life exacting pain on their partner, but concurrently seeking women to torture and murder. Some women partners may even be forced into taking part in the murders involuntarily. These compliant women would want desperately out of the relationship toward the end, yet would be threatened with torture and death. There was no continuum of treatment of the sexual sadist in regard of treatment to victims as compared to treatment of their partner, they were just merciless toward victims. They would be mildly sadistic with a partner engaging what one may consider sexually sadistic or at least deviant behavior (Warren, J. & Hazelwood, R., 2002).

An example of this phenomenon can be seen with Karen Homolka who would marry Toronto serial killer Paul Bernado. Karen would come from a dysfunctional Canadian family and not much else is known of her early life. Apart from her father's bout with alcoholism. She would cut her wrists during bouts of depression during adolescence. Her first sexual experience would occur when visiting a boyfriend in Kansas as they would use cocaine and she would permit him to practice bondage on her. He would humiliate her through sadomasochistic practices calling her ugly. At a later time she would marry Paul Berndado who through a brief candy and flower stage would humiliate her with total subjugation. Karen was a respected anesthesiologist for a veterinarian. Paul would persuade her in 1990 through use of halothane and triazolam to subdue her younger sister. Tammy would inhale her vomit and die accidentally. Paul would next rape and murder two teenage girls with the assistance of Karen. To keep Karen from going to the authorities Paul would take pictures of her having lesbian sex with the victims to use as blackmail. After continued beatings resulting in black eyes and severe facial swelling Karen would go to the police. She would be found a willing accomplice and sentenced to 12 years and would be released from prison in 2007. The sociopathic and amoral Karen who would grow accustom to violent and sadistic men would plan on marrying a murderer she would meet while both incarcerated (Burnside & Cairns, 1995).

On a spectrum of sexual sadism perhaps the Bernado-Homolka marriage would lie upon only an intermediate position. The progression of the infliction of suffering by Bernado would progress to the point of humiliating and beating his wife in a degrading manner. Karen's pet iguana would bite his hand when he would put it in the cage of which Paul would proceed to decapitate the hand. Paul would then have Karen skin and cook the hand of which Paul would eat. As studies would show pertaining to Paul, 75% of sexual sadists prefer anal sex (Hazelwood & Michaud, 2001; Hazelwood, Dietz, & Warren, 1992). It would be in some cases these were not acts of homosexuality instead the exacting of pain and degradation. Within certain serial killers the preference is strictly an erotic homosexual interest as is displayed by the cases of Dean Corll, Wesley Dodd, and William Bonin. It is common among sexual sadists to demonstrate a wide range of paraphilias including transvestitism and bondage. Other serial killers would describe themselves of a heterosexual orientation, yet would possess bisexual erotic interests. This is a group including the likes of John Gacy, Albert Fish, and Arthur Shawcross. In a study of 150 serial killers committing serial sexual homicide, 13.3% of this group identify as homosexuals. Some sexual sadists are more mild possessing an attachment to their partner, who only mildly humiliate their partner to achieve sexual excitation. As a prelude to sex such a man may pinch or lightly slap the woman while calling her a whore or cunt. Such a relationship may survive for years with no progression to dangerous behaviors. One such marriage would last 26 years. More toward the middle of the spectrum is the man introducing his wife to anal intercourse only to abuse her physically and mentally, and have her assist in the murder of other women. In the middle portion of the spectrum is the Marquis de Sade himself. His female victims he would inflict moderate degrees of humiliation and pain. Even the Marquis would not indulge in extreme torture and especially not engage in sexual homicide. The actions of the serial killers of our era far exceed the actions of the Marquis and notably any of his fantasies. Even more disturbing is the extreme spectrum of sexually sadistic crime.

Men committing serial sexual homicides frequently engage in sexual sadism. When sexually sadistic paraphilias require the death of a victim this describes a lust murder or erotophonophilia (Money, 1990). The characteristics of sadistic personality disorder are present within the sexual sadist. Serial killers consisting of the traits of sexual sadism is nearly 50% as one may suspect of a group committing multiple sexual murders. The proportion may still be higher dependent on whether or not the killer would experience some form of sexual pleasure from the act of killing. A distinction should be made among the rapist and the serial killer. Men committing rape, a defining feature is sexual sadism. Yet there search for sexual gratification does not involve killing the victim. The serial killer's search for sexual gratification involves the act of killing. Serial killers are but a small subset of the number of rapists. Ninety-percent of serial killing sexual sadists possess additional paraphilias such as exhibitionism, bondage, and even cannibalism. A prelude to serial sexual homicide is sexual sadism. Sexual sadists may rehearse fantasies during their teenage years to enact in their twenties and thirties.

Erzsebet Bathory & Jane Toppan

The phenomenon of sexual sadism as mentioned earlier tends to be a strictly male trait. Only a very small percentage of women derive sexual arousal or orgasm upon the death and suffering of another. With the motive of revenge few women have enjoyed killing their former abusers such as is the case of Aileen Wuornos (Russell,

2002). Her mother would entrust her relatives to care for Aileen who would be molested. She would embark on the career of hitchhiking and killing Floridian truck drivers. Upon shooting these men to death, there is no evidence she would experience sexual arousal at the time of their deaths. Erzsebet Bathory would live as the countess of Hungary from 1560 to 1614. She would live in a castle in Hungary with her uncle King Stefan Bathory. Her close relatives would consist of many mentally ill and eccentric persons. The countess would become preoccupied with the preservation of her beauty when she would approach the age of 40. She would conceive the notion bathing in the blood of virgins would perpetuate her good looks. Her servants would lure young girls walking along castle side roads. Inside the sanctity of the castle, the girls would be suspended from the ceiling by hooks to have their bellies cut. The blood would be collected for the countess in a tub. The countess would press her body against the young girls during the act of cutting and achieve an orgasm at this very moment. There is no exact death toll of Countess Erzsebet's victims, yet it is believed she killed more than 600 in this manner. She would be caught and arrested, but by virtue of her membership to the aristocracy she would avoid execution. She would be immured among her own castle and fed through a hole in the wall in which she would be imprisoned (Penrose, 1996).

Jane Toppan was a nurse in Boston, Massachusetts, who would live the years of 1854 – 1938. Jane's original name would be Honora Kelly her father an alcoholic who would die insane, and her mother who would die while she was still young from tuberculosis. She would become an indentured servant to the well to do Toppan family upon the death of her mother. She would change both her first and last name to Jane Toppan although she was never formally adopted. Toppan would meet all the criteria of psychopathy as an imposter and liar. Despite her hate toward her foster family, she would remain with them for ten years beyond her indentured servitude until the age of 18. She would earn the reputation as a malicious gossip and thief while attending nursing school. She would work as a private nurse despite never finishing her training. She would experiment with morphine and atropine by poisoning her patients, and would expand her operation beyond the hospital setting, to include entire families who would hire her, along with her landlord and stepsister. When Jane would reach her 40s, she would begin to burn down the homes of those who would hire her. As it would turn, she would achieve orgasms from her patients dying of poisons. This was according to reports after her arrest at the age of 44. Found not guilty by reason of insanity, she would die in the asylum she was committed in Taunton, Massachusetts. Upon sentencing, she did not appear mentally ill, yet over the years would become increasingly paranoid believing people to have poisoned her food. She would once comment to one of the nurses, "to get the morphine and you and I will watch them all die" (Schechter, 2003).

It is only very few women within the forensic literature whose sadism is recognizable. One for such is Cindy Hendy accomplice to David Parker Ray who while women were strapped to the Toy Box would whip them. She would loathe the victims viewing them as packages. It would seem though she did not derive pleasure from her abuse of others just as Teresa Knorr or Jessica Schwarz. Jessica Schwarz would torture and kill her stepson and Teresa Knorr would torture and kill her own two daughters (Stone, 2009). Schwarz would treat her biological children with kindness, yet display much opposite behavior toward her 10 year old stepson. She would force her stepson to wear a t-shirt stating, "I am a piece of s*#%, don't talk to me." A babysitter would tell him to take the t-shirt off of which he would state himself to be too scared at the risk of receiving even worse beatings. Until Jessica's return the babysitter would place a sweatshirt over the t-shirt. He would be forced to swallow a roach if he did not properly clean the kitchen floor. Knorr would become increasingly jealous of her three adolescent daughters. As a result she would take one of her daughters to the California countryside where her son would be forced to be an accomplice burning his sister alive through use of accelerants. She would starve another one of her daughters by chaining her to a pipe in a closet. These lethal acts would follow lesser instances of abuse and various kinds of tortures.

Carley, S. G. (2013). *Serial killers, mass murders, & disorders*.
Boston: SGC Production.

Hermann Mudgett (Dr. Henry Holmes)

Life of Dr. Henry Holmes

It would seem the public to possess insatiable interest of the serial killer. Who it would appear has always existed and may always continue to exist. As an example over the course of the twentieth century worldwide would be in existence 310 serial killers. Of this number 112 would occur within the United States, and many would coexist at the same time. On occasion this would cause difficulties within law enforcement distinguishing which serial killer was committing which murder. As technology should change the interest in serial killers seemingly remains the same. A consensus definition of the term serial killer involves a premeditation to kill, three or more victims of the killer, and a break between the occurrence of one murder to the next. The frontier days of the United States up to the Civil War during the chaos, one may suspect individuals fitting the definition of a serial killer would exist. Hermann Mudgett would represent the first documented case of a serial killer within the United States, an individual so terrifying he could make Hannibal Lector seem no comparison.

Carley, S. G. (2013). *Serial killers, mass murders, & disorders.* Boston: SGC Production.

The birth of Hermann Webster Mudgett would occur on May 16, 1860, to a strict Methodist family in an isolated village of New Hampshire's Lake District. Herman was a bright lad with a strict father who would beat Hermann with brutal regularity (Schechter, 2003, p. 180). These beatings would be accompanied by confinement to an attic with no food or interaction of any sort. Hermann would also experience bullying from his classmates at school. He was once dragged into the doctor's office when he was out on a visit, and the group would force little Hermann's face onto the hand of the skeleton the doctor would keep in his office for demonstration purposes. The traumatic experience may have led Hermann into an interest in anatomy. By the age of eleven Hermann's experiments would involve the dissection of live animals, the bones of which he would keep for his collection. While Hermann and his only known close friend were playing together in an abandoned building, his friend would be killed from a suspicious fall. Hermann would be standing directly behind his friend when he would fall.

Hermann would graduate from high school at the age of sixteen and marry one year later to wealthy Clara Lovering. Herman would abandon her after making use of her money. In 1887 on January 28 Herman would remarry to Myrta Z Belknap in Minneapolis, Minnesota. Mudgett happened to continue his marriage with Lovering and technically he was committing bigotry. Mudgett and Belknap would have a daughter Lucy Theodate Holmes born in Englewood, Illinois on July 4, 1889. The three would reside in Wilmette a Chicago suburb, Mudgett/Holmes would spend the majority of his time tending to business in the city. After marrying his second wife in Mudgett's defense, he would file for a divorce, which as it turns would never be finalized. Mudgett would take a third wife Georgiana Yoke and the two would marry on January 9, 1894. An employee of Mudgett's Ned Connor, he would also possess a relationship with his wife. As it would turn Julia would become a victim of Mudgett.

Hermann would make the decision to become a physician. His college career would start in Burlington, Vermont, but Hermann would find interest in the University of Michigan who would take a part in the then controversial practice of dissecting cadavers. Mudgett would develop an insurance scam while at the University of Michigan purchasing insurance policies on a fake individual. Mudgett would steal a corpse and claim the settlement when the family members could not identify the body, the result of disfiguring deaths. Mudgett would graduate from the University of Michigan with a medical degree and would move around. He would run a business as keeper of an insane asylum and next as a pharmacist. Through Mudgett's travels an unusual number of unexplained deaths would occur in his immediate area of which he would not be suspected. Mudgett would settle in Chicago at the age of 26 and register himself as Henry Howard Holmes. Upon his passing of the pharmacist exam, he would take the name Holmes on his license. Holmes would work in the Holton Pharmacy in Chicago and would eventually buy the business from Mr. Holton's widow. Holmes would stop making payments and Holton would take him to court. Holmes would claim Holton to move out west and she would never again be heard from.

The Holmes Castle

Holmes would build a castle on the land across the street employing over 500 workers who would have no idea of its purpose. The castle would consist of soundproof chambers, hidden peepholes, surgery rooms, guest rooms with gas jets, a 3' x 3' x 8' glass bending oven firing to 3,000 degrees Fahrenheit, and body sized chutes leading to the cellar consisting of steel lined acid vats and a lime pit. He would keep these workers from reporting to the police by changing builders during the initial construction. It would be in this sense only Holmes would possess a true construction of the building. The original use of the castle would be as a hotel. The ground floor of Holmes castle would consist of a jewelry shop and his relocated drug store. The upper two floors in addition to consisting of his personal office would be a maze of over one-hundred windowless rooms consisting of doorways opening to brick walls and stairways to nowhere. Doors could only be opened from the outside and other strange constructions were present as well. For a time of three years the victims of Mudgett would be female employees of his, lovers, and guests of the hotel. His employees would be part of his elaborate insurance scam as the condition of employment would require his employees to take out life insurance policies of which Holmes would pay the premiums and also be the beneficiary of the policy. Most of the victims which Holmes would obtain were young females he would lure to his castle through advertisements or other means and killing them upon their visit. This would include a list of at least 50 visitors to the 1893 World Fair or Colombian Exposition. At one time or another Holmes would kill most of the people who would get close to him.

There is no exact body count of the victims of Holmes but estimates are in the vicinity he would kill 200 people. Much of these murders were part of Holmes elaborate insurance scam. Others would have their skeletons reassembled and sold to medical schools, and still others simply discarded after the killing of which Holmes would admit was simply for the pleasure of killing. Holmes would use different means in killing his victims locking them in soundproof rooms asphyxiating them through the gas lines fitted in the rooms. Holmes at times would lock his victims in his office bank vault listening to them scream, panic, and eventually suffocate from lack of oxygen in the sound proof vault. He would very meticulously dispose of the bodies down a secret basement chute dissecting some, stripping the flesh, and crafting skeletal models to sell to medical

Carley, S. G. (2013). *Serial killers, mass murders, & disorders*.
Boston: SGC Production.

schools. Holmes would place other bodies in lime pits for destruction after cremation. Holmes would possess two giant furnaces in addition to bottles of poisons, pits of acid, and a stretching rack. His medical school connections would permit Holmes to easily sell his collected organs and skeletons. With one of the most remote rooms of the castle Holmes would perform illegal abortions, and the patients who would die during the procedure, he would process their corpse and sell their skeletons. The victims' bodies went by a secret chute to the basement, where some were meticulously dissected, stripped of flesh, crafted into skeleton models, and then sold to medical schools. Holmes also cremated some of the bodies or placed them in lime pits for destruction. Holmes had two giant furnaces as well as pits of acid, bottles of various poisons, and even a stretching rack. Through the connections he had gained in medical school, he was able to sell skeletons and organs with little difficulty. Holmes picked one of the most remote rooms in the Castle to perform his hundreds of illegal abortions.

Holmes Get Caught

The scams of Holmes and his inability to pay his bills would catch up with him in time. In 1893 a collection agent would arrange a meeting with Holmes along with over 20 of his other creditors. The charming and responsive Holmes would leave Chicago the next day moving city to city until his arrest in 1894 in Boston, Massachusetts. As Holmes would move about he would kill along the way including Benjamin Pitezal the one closest to him. He would work alongside Pitezal in an insurance scam claiming Pitezal to fake his own death. He would burn Pitezal alive pouring gasoline over his entire body. To make the incident look like an accident caustic solvent would be poured onto the face of Pitezal and he would be left out in the sun. Over time Holmes would kill Pitezal's three children. It was not long after Holmes would be arrested not for murder instead for insurance fraud. He would render a guilty plea on May 28, 1895, facing only a few short months in jail. As it would turn the whole ordeal may have been avoided, only a short time earlier Holmes would be part of another elaborate insurance scam which unfortunately for Pitezal would fail. Holmes plan in this scandal was to take a policy on himself and bill the insurance company $20,000. To do so Holmes would have to fake his own death. He would look for the assistance of Marion Hedgepath who Holmes would come across when he was incarcerated for the first time. This was for a horse swindle in Missouri. Holmes would meet bail but until this time he would strike a conversation with convicted train robber Marion Hedgepath who would be serving a 25 year sentence. Holmes would promise Hedgepath a $500 commission in exchange for the name of a trusting lawyer. Hedgepath would direct Holmes to Colonel Jeptha Howe who would find Holmes plan altogether remarkable. Holmes elaborate plan however would fail when the suspicious insurance company would refuse to make the payout. Holmes would not press the claim and instead turn to his scheme with Pitezel leading to the murder of Pitezel by Holmes.

During this time Frank Geyer a Philadelphia police detective would continue the case of Pitezal's missing children. He would visit the very cities Holmes would pass through Toronto, Indianapolis, Philadelphia, Cincinnati, and Fort Worth, including some smaller cities. Evidence would point to the Pitezal children being killed in different cities, and basing upon this evidence the castle of Holmes would be subject to a search and seizure. The horror known as the Holmes castle would include torture devices such as the Elasticity Determinator stretching the human body to twice its natural size. Holmes would be forced into a confession of 27 deaths but as mentioned is suspected for over 200 (Schechter, 2003). Holmes would be killed on May 7, 1896 by way of hanging for the murder of Benjamin Pitezal. Holmes would joke with the hangman as he prepared the noose for his hanging. Holmes death from hanging

Carley, S. G. (2013). *Serial killers, mass murders, & disorders*. Boston: SGC Production.

would not come quick. His neck would not snap instantly as is often the case, instead he would dangle from the noose suspending his body in mid-air. Holmes would twitch for over 15 minutes until pronounced dead 20 minutes after the springing of the trap.

It is only until recently in which attempts have been made for the scientific collection of data on these individuals (Schechter, 2003). The traditional categorization of serial killers according to the FBI has been as organized or disorganized. These categorizations may appear simplistic considering existing problems in obtaining sufficient data. The phenomenon is a low base data, and these individuals are often deceptive leaving significant data to be tainted (Boyd, et al., 2007).

Penalty by Death

Discussion of the death penalty is always most applicable when it comes to serial killers, and is almost always considered in states permitting the death penalty. A modern time critical case pertaining to the death penalty would be the 1972 Supreme Court case Furman vs. Georgia. The Supreme Court would rule the death penalty as unconstitutional in its manner of imposition, yet giving discretion to entities other than judges and jurors to impose the penalty may be constitutional. The presentation of childhood circumstances and the circumstances of the crime should be permitted as the death penalty should never be mandatory. Without the loss of life the death penalty for kidknapping or rape may be severe according to the cruel and unusual clause as stated in the eighth amendment. In Gregg v. Georgia the Supreme Court would find the death penalty to be constitutional. Relating to aggravated circumstances the Supreme Court in the Payne v. Tennessee case would permit statements of victim impact during the penalty phase of the trial rather than just the guilt or innocence phase. This during a death penalty trial. Controversy exists of whether or not children may be executed for their crimes. Children as young as 12 years would be executed for their crimes during the colonial times. More modern rulings such as Thompson v. Oklahoma would find the death penalty to pertain only to those over the age of 16 at the time of the crime. The assumption is those over the age of 18 can be executed although the Supreme Court in Stanford v. Kentucky would claim those ages 16 – 18 could be subject to the penalty of death by execution. Upon revisiting the issue the Supreme Court would reverse this ruling in Roper v. Tennessee stating ages 16 – 18 could not be executed. This decision would come in reference to Trope v. Dulles stating judges to make their decisions on evolving standards of decency marked by the progress of a maturing society. Relating to this decision is Ford v. Wainwright 1986 where the Supreme Court would hold a person must be competent to be executed.

The central theme to the death penalty controversy is the taking of a life. What such alternatives could be given to an individual of a horrific disposition such as Dr. Henry Holmes. Data would suggest the presence of two options possessing even greater deterrent value than the death penalty or life in prison. Banishment involves total solitary confinement in which a person is permitted no human contact minus legal or medical purpose. No visits, letter, television, or Internet use. Another more economical option is permanent coma either revocable or irrevocable. A second advantage is a life does not have to be taken. Inmates could be kept in drawers such as in the morgue as a technician monitors physiological signs of the inmates. No treatment or staff would be necessary or lights and standard meals for that matter. Each could be housed on an inexpensive site in a small building. The majority would find banishment the greatest deterrent with permanent coma a close second well ahead of penalty by way of death. The legal issues accounting to these alternatives may make it difficult to make a reality but not insurmountable.

Carley, S. G. (2013). *Serial killers, mass murders, & disorders.*
Boston: SGC Production.

Theodore (Ted) Bundy

Childhood and Adolescence

The birth of Ted Bundy would occur in 1946 on November 24 in Burlington Vermont. Ted Bundy never would know his father yet spending time in Philadelphia for three years he would admire and adore his grandfather. Ted Bundy and his family at the age of four would move to Tacoma, Washington, to live with other members of their family. Leaving his grandfather behind would cause Ted distress at his young age. His mother would come across a local cook who would work at the military base Johnnie Bundy. It was Johnnie's quiet demeanor and southern style which would draw her to him. The two would meet at a church activity. Ted would become jealous of his mother's romance which is a normal reaction of a child at this young age. Johnnie and Ted's mother would marry and have their first child in 1952 followed by three more children.

Bundy would idolize his teacher in first grade and would upset little Ted when she left to have a baby. Ted would react much differently to his second grade teacher who he would despise. Who could

Carley, S. G. (2013). *Serial killers, mass murders, & disorders.* Boston: SGC Production.

blame little Ted after all she did break a ruler over his hand. That's what Ted gets for punching a schoolmate in the face during lunch hour. This would begin the feelings of unease which would grow inside Ted Bundy growing into the murderous entity he was to become. Bundy was always an excellent student in school, maybe because his mom used to help him and he liked the extra attention. In terms of sexual relations, Ted and his mother would not discuss the issue. Ted would always view his mother as one who did not like to socialize and she would never discuss her own childhood. She would right after high school get pregnant and Bundy would become an illegitimate child, which would haunt Bundy and leave his mother with resentment for little Ted.

Right through high school Bundy would go to Sunday school every week. He would study the Bible but not do well in retaining the information. Bundy was political minded and would speak to his mother of religious hypocrisy. His parents did not smoke or drink alcohol, and Johnnie despite being a quiet fellow would consist of a violent temper. Bundy would often choose to be alone and enjoyed listening to the radio. Bundy would have trouble socializing and when just a child would investigate trash cans in search of pornographic pictures of women. Bundy who was undersized would take part in very few endeavors pertaining to organized sports. His mother disliked sports because it would cost her money and Ted's stepfather never went to his games. Bundy may have experienced trauma when he could not make the basketball or baseball teams. Ted would adapt and become the proficient skier and would even create a forgery system permitting him free access to the slopes. In a material world Bundy would be obsessed by material possession fantasizing of being adopted by the stars like Roy Rogers or Dale Evans. Ted would experience feelings of humiliation when driving in his family's economy car. Bundy did not necessarily experience physical or emotional abuse only to say his childhood would be empty.

Carley, S. G. (2013). *Serial killers, mass murders, & disorders.* Boston: SGC Production.

Bundy would have trouble acquiring adequate social skills during middle school despite having a few friends here or there and attending the occasional party. In high school Bundy would regress becoming more shy and introverted. He did not enjoy drinking alcohol and one may view Ted as a serious student. Bundy would never be in any trouble in high school and some may be view him as an arrogant person. Bundy had only one date with a female in high school. The limited income of Bundy's family would lead to feelings of inferiority as he would compare himself to those with more material possession. During Bundy's senior year in high school he would volunteer his services for a local political race. A few years down the road he would drive the Republican candidate for lieutenant governor and would assist in the election attempt of a governor. The political affiliations Bundy would make would permit friends for him to be a sociable person.

Bundy The Murderer

Bundy would describe himself as the malignant being. This is to say he was an entity not separate from the self, compelling him to kill. The desire Bundy would experience during the act of killing another was not necessarily from the violence, but instead the desire to take full possession of the victim. Bundy would give the victims as painless a death as possible and the sex was not extreme. After each deviant act the entity within Bundy would continually grow stronger. Bundy's first murder would occur in Seattle, Washington, in January of 1974. He would smash Sharon Clarke's head while she was in bed with a rod. Sharon would survive the event after a lengthy coma and awake with no memory of the events which would occur. There was never an explanation of the attack as Sharon was a stranger to Bundy. Weeks later a college student living only blocks from Sharon, Lynda Ann Healy would disappear. Over the next seven months women would be disappearing with regularity.

Carley, S. G. (2013). *Serial killers, mass murders, & disorders.*
Boston: SGC Production.

In 1974 from March to June while attending a concert or movie, traveling across campus, or leaving a bar, four female college students would disappear. Bundy would put his arm in a sling on July 14, 1974 and ask women to help him put his sailboat atop his car. He would tell them he needed to drive them to the boat of which the women would refuse. All but one Janice Ott and she would never be seen or heard from again. A woman at the same lake in the washroom would disappear this same day. The remains of these women would be in the forest by the lake. Bundy's killing spree would continue in full force through October of 1974, his victims mostly attractive college aged white women. One month later Bundy posing as a police officer would convince a young woman to enter his vehicle. He would place a handcuff on her and she would scream and exit the vehicle forcefully. Bundy would hit her with a crowbar in an attempt to crush her skull and she would leap in front of an oncoming car. The car would pick her up and she would escape. On this same day another woman would turn him down yet another would be abducted and killed. In January of the following year Bundy would start killing in Colorado taking one woman from her bed while sleeping. Another woman meeting her girlfriend at the local bar would disappear. A victim would be found fully clothed with her pants down. Women were consistently disappearing from a gas station, a mine shaft. It would occur on August 16, 1975 when Bundy's suspicious driving in the middle of the night would alarm police. Bundy would not stop when a patrol car tried to pull him over. A hair would be found in Bundy's car matching the hair of one of Bundy's victims. Witnesses would claim Bundy to be in the area when a victim would disappear. In Aspen Colorado Bundy would be tried for murder.

Bundy could convince those around him he was special with his good looks, humor, intelligence, and charming personality. Bundy would be cooperative with his captors who in turn would be courteous toward Bundy. This would involve a healthy diet and no

Carley, S. G. (2013). *Serial killers, mass murders, & disorders.*
Boston: SGC Production.

restraints when in the court room. Bundy would make the request to defend himself and would require the use of law books. Within the Aspen law library Bundy could wander freely during pretrial hearings. He would escape jumping out of the library window only to be captured a short eight days later. Bundy would contest there to be no solid evidence he would commit any crime and that he in fact was the victim of the matter. Bundy would state many men to fit his physical description. Bundy would file many motions making use of his legal skills to delay the case. He would lose some weight during this time and with a hacksaw carve a whole in a light fixture within his prison cell. Through a small 12 inch opening Bundy would escape and move around to Chicago, Michigan, Atlanta, and finally would settle down in Tallahassee, Florida, in the vicinity of the sorority houses of Florida State University (FSU). In 1978 on January 15, five women would receive a severe beating in a sorority of which two would die as they were bludgeoned and at least two raped. Only a short one month later a 12 year old girl would disappear while leaving school. Her sex organs would be mutilated as she was found strangled to death. Bundy would live under the alias of Chris Hagen and would survive off of his stolen car and credit cards. In 1978 on February 15, Bundy's slow driving would get the attention of a suspicious police officer, and at 1:30 AM the police officer would follow Bundy. The officer would check to see if the car was stolen, and as he turned on the blue pursue light Bundy would accelerate. The officer and Bundy would struggle but the officer was able to subdue Bundy. Bundy was arrested and would identify himself as Ken Misnor, but it would be a short time to discover this to be Ted Bundy suspected murderer from Colorado. Bundy would claim innocence despite severe incriminating evidence. One of his victims had a bite mark on her buttocks matching that of Ted Bundy. Bundy's charm and intelligence would be displayed when he was tried for two murders in Florida. It would seem Bundy would have made a good lawyer under different circumstances. Bundy would be found guilty and sentenced to

Carley, S. G. (2013). *Serial killers, mass murders, & disorders.* Boston: SGC Production.

consecutive life sentences. Bundy's closest friends said of Bundy as a child to be a quiet, bright, and serious minded fellow. Bundy would be flooded with interest of his demeanor as a child. Bundy would use appeals over the next ten years to stay alive and admit to 23 more murders. While in prison Bundy would receive offers of marriage and even father a child during this time. Bundy would get the electric chair on January 24, 1989 in the state of Florida. The crowd would cheer with news of his death.

Bundy would fit the profile of a Factor 1 psychopath. The atypical nature of Bundy's psychopathy would be his high intelligence and no signs of such behavior during childhood. Perhaps his mother would hide Ted's early behaviors and Bundy would possess enough intelligence to hide his erratic childhood behavior also. Evidence exists Bundy may have masturbated while watching women through peep holes as a child. An eight year old girl in Bundy's neighborhood would disappear when he was just 15 years of age. Bundy would deliver newspapers to this family's home and he knew the girl. Bundy would deny his involvement in this disappearance.

Inheritance and Biology of Psychopathy

Caesare Lombroso during the 19th century would advance a theory criminals may possess of distinct physical characteristics, for one a low forehead. As a discredited theory much new research on the claim supports the idea genetics and biology promote criminal behavior, antisocial personality disorder, and psychopathy (Bartol & Bartol, 2008). Alertness and exploration of newborns can increase with the presence of the novelty seeking gene influencing within adults sensation seeking behaviors. The DRD4 gene among newborns would increase the likelihood of certain behaviors in a study such as response to the human face, following a red ball with their eyes, and attentiveness to the sounds of a rattle. The controversy within the novelty seeking gene is a failure to sufficiently link the gene to personality despite the indications of a connection to hyperactivity, addiction, and antisocial behaviors. It may be unclear how certain biological factors can translate to certain behavior. Some explanations involve intelligence deficits, neurohormonal disorders, or brain dysfunction. Psychopaths may possess language deficits at the hormonal level (Hare, Hart, & Harpur, 1991). The result is poor processing of words and difficulty obtaining its emotional meaning. Still others view the primary factors as psychological in the form of parenting patterns. The theoretical differences among psychopathy is one is born with defective traits, and the other stating it is normal traits increasing the predisposition to psychopathy. The normal characteristics which can attribute to psychopathy can be explained with the acronym FUMES: fearless, unresponsive to pain, muscular, empathy deficient, and stimulation seeking.

These normal characteristics require parental skills to develop the skills and prosocial habits to be a success in the classroom and avoid using power as a tool of manipulation. The environmental models for aggression and physical and sexual abuse may set the flavor for the psychopath as such a direction is set. The two main components of psychopathy include affective cognitive instability and behavioral social deviance (Hare, Hart, & Harpur, 1991). This view is facilitated by the Hare's Psychopathy Checklist Revised (PCL-R). This means, makes use of a self-report and observational data from an interview in a 20 item assessment. Some debate whether or not three or four factors may create a more valid assessment. In any standard factor 1 is most reflective of psychopathy. Contributing to factor 1 are failure to accept responsibility, lack of empathy, shallow effect, lack of remorse, manipulative behaviors, pathological lying, grandiosity, and glibness. The components of factor 2 involve a history of supervisory violations, adjudication of delinquency, irresponsibility, impulsivity, unrealistic goals, early behavioral problems, poor behavioral control, parasitic lifestyle, and increased need for stimulation.

Research on psychopathy would indicate decreases in criminal activity for psychopaths to decrease at the ages of 40 - 45 primarily holding for non-violent crimes. The decrease for violent crimes is more slight. Between the ages of 35 – 45 factor 2 of psychopathy diminishes more so than factor 1. Factor 2 can act as a good predictor of criminality and poor predictor of IQ or socioeconomic status. In predicting violence factor 1 is a better predictor possessing no correlation to IQ or socioeconomic status. Treatment does not tend to effect the psychopath, especially those high in factor 1 traits as is the case with Ted Bundy. Treatment may even contribute to psychopathic delinquency. Psychopaths can learn little of themselves in therapy, yet learn more of others and use this information boldly. The reason is their weakness in language, missing the emotional components of language, the individual is devoid of empathy or remorse. Socioeconomic status and family background can be good predictors of criminal behavior, yet not in the case of psychopathy, especially in relation to factor 1 traits. Those high in factor 1 traits, one can expect to be listening to deceit within reports.

Common Development of Psychopathy

Psychopathic antisocial personality disorder consists of preexisting risk factors. One such risk factor is biological disruption in the form of early childhood, birth, prenatal, or genetics. Another factor is low socioeconomic status along with a family history of social interpersonal dysfunction and family history of psychopathy. General characteristics of the FUMES child are risk factors for psychopathy. From birth to school age four factors contributing to the development of psychopathy include child temperament factors, parental factors, parent/child interaction, and environmental factors.

Carley, S. G. (2013). *Serial killers, mass murders, & disorders.*
Boston: SGC Production.

Child temperament factors involve a lack of emotional responsiveness along with a lack of social interest resulting in rejecting parental responses. Parental factors involve the child's failure to learn behavioral contingencies, a result of inconsistent parenting. A child's defensive style, hostility, aggression, expectation of punishing responses is the result of punitive parenting. The parent child interaction can promote psychopathy through unreliable parenting and defective expressing of emotion resulting in insecure attachment. The unreliable or abusive parent creates a child who does not want to face rejection or disappointment and decides to go it alone. Environmental factors include high exposure to the media or models of violence and deviant behavior leading to imitation or disinhibition. Antisocial aggressive patterns can also be the result of exposure to toxic levels of heavy metals. Inhibitory behaviors can also be the result of brain disorder or frontal lobe damage during an early age.

From school age to adolescence the predisposing personality factors associating with the development of psychopathy involve a low baseline level of brain stem arousal contributing to stimulation seeking, undercontrolled, and impulsive behavior. Another factor is distortion combinations of repressive psychodynamics, physiological arousal, and habitual numbness to social contingencies resulting in an inability of a child to be conditioned to the events of the environment. As the child does not profit from experience, he or she does not relate to the experience of others. Energetic and mesomorphic or muscular components lead to an increasing manipulation and control of others along with stimulation seeking and an increase in risk taking. Behavioral problems may be exacerbated by neurological disorder such as attention deficit hyperactivity disorder (ADHD). Personality development can be a preexisting risk factor to psychopathy during school age to adolescence through peer and teacher labeling resulting in the effects of a self-fulfilling prophecy. The self fulfilling prophecy is the result of inaccurate expectations leading to actions that cause those expectations to come true. Social and academic failure can result in feelings of inferiority and interpersonal hostility or demonstrations of antisociality such as setting fires, theft, and interpersonal violence. Such displays evidence warranting a diagnosis for conduct disorder.

During adolescence the factors contributing to the development of psychopathy involve a youthful psychopath attempting to hone an exploitive style expressing hostility, in the attempts to conquer feelings of inferiority through the humiliation of parents, peers, or teachers. The continuance of antisocial behavior results in trouble with the law. Increases in psychological and physical aggression take place to control others. An inability to profit from experience occurs along with physiological impulsivity. Repeated legal offenses become highly probable through antagonism and interpersonal hostility and a disordered cognitive attention style. A criminal education occurs through the contact with other antisocials increasing the results of criminality. Such antisocial behavior becomes a lifestyle the psychopath can excel.

The escalation of antisocial behavior should occur during adulthood through the late twenties of the psychopath. Hostility increases through incarceration, rejection, and failure. The inability to profit from experience results in a lack of insight and empathy and an inability to form therapeutic bonds. The psychopath rationalizes behavior, feeling his desires justify any actions. The psychopath may devalue the worth of others finding their needs and attitudes do not affect them. "If they are hurt, I should not feel responsible." The psychopath may find the inherent goodness in their decision-making, and feel no undesirable consequences should occur for this reason, or if they should occur, it would not really matter. The psychopath thinks of themselves first and feels entitled to both wants and needs. To obtain goals they may need to make use of force.

Psychopaths may experience rule avoidance finding rules are no more than a means and entity keeping them from fulfilling their needs. Uneven burn-out of antisocial behavior occurs in the mid-thirties the result perhaps of lengthy incarcerations or age related metabolic factors contributing to sensation seeking and impulsive behavior. Persistent criminal endeavors can perhaps be the result of a reduction in strength and stamina.

Carley, S. G. (2013). *Serial killers, mass murders, & disorders.* Boston: SGC Production.

Ted Kaczynski: The Unabomber

The Unabomber

It would occur on April 3rd, of 1996 the end of a 17 year manhunt with the apprehension of Theodore John (Ted) Kaczynski. The charge of being the elusive Unabomber named such for the tendency of the bomber to direct his attacks to university related places and personnel. Over the span of 17 years Ted Kaczynski would orchestrate 16 attacks resulting in 23 wounded and maimed and three deaths. The first incident would occur on May 25, 1978 with a package left in the parking lot of the University of Illinois in Chicago. The return address on the package would be Northwestern University where it would be returned. The package would explode the following day injuring one person. The occurrence of the last known attack was on April 24, 1995 with the delivery of a mail bomb to the Sacramento Headquarters of the California Forestry Association. The package would kill Gilbert Murray president of the association when he would attempt to open the package. In avoidance of the death penalty Kaczynski would eventually plea guilty to four consecutive life terms in a plea bargain. In all the 17 year manhunt for Kaczynski would involve the storage of 12 million bytes of information by the FBI, ATS, and Postal Service agents

Carley, S. G. (2013). *Serial killers, mass murders, & disorders*. Boston: SGC Production.

consisting of an 80 person squad. The efforts of this group along with extensive psychological profiling and eyewitness accounts would lead to Kaczynski's apprehension when Kaczynski's sister in law would begin to suspect Ted to be the Unabomber. Ted's brother David, the husband of Ted's sister in law Linda, would recognize publishings in the New York Times and Washington Post. They would come across the 35,000 word manifesto while at their mother's house. It would be David who would turn in his own brother to the authorities. Even before this time developing concerns would arise of Ted's mental health among David and Linda. It would be in a 60 Minutes interview on September 15, 1996 they would state they took two of Ted's letters to a psychiatrist as they felt the material to be of a violent disposition. Consideration would occur for a civil commitment of Ted which would never take place.

Childhood to Emerging Adulthood

The birth of Ted Kaczynski would occur on May 22 in the year 1942. The quiet and reclusive childhood of Kaczynski was altogether unremarkable. He would have loving parents though. Ted and his mother would spend time together with her reading the Scientific American to Ted when he was quite young. Kaczynski and parents were a socially withdrawn group. His mother once voiced concerns of Kaczynski not playing with the other children, but instead playing next to the other children. Consideration was given to placing Kaczynski in a program for autistic children. Her advice from Dr. Spock would keep her from making this decision as she would decide otherwise. Neighbors would comment about each of the Kaczynski children stating they didn't mingle much with their neighbors, especially Ted who would not even respond to a hello.

Kaczynski would graduate high school in three years from Evergreen Park High School in a suburb of Chicago. He was not a memorable person despite his membership to the German, math, and biology clubs. What people do recall of Kaczynski, explain him as a quiet and reclusive individual. Still others recall Kaczynski as possessing an interest for pyrotechnics and explosives in high school. Despite enjoying to blow things up, Ted was never viewed as someone that could hurt anybody, just to say he was quiet and reclusive, shy and immature. Kaczynski would receive a scholarship to Harvard University at the age of 16 as a National Merit Scholarship finalist. Kaczynski would graduate from Harvard University before his 21st birthday with average grades and would take part in no activities. His living quarters for three years at Harvard would be a seven man suite in the Eliot House, a dormitory of Harvard. Kaczynski would take graduate courses at Northwestern University and the University of Chicago receiving a Master's degree in 1964 in mathematics and a Ph.D. from the University of Michigan in 1967. The title of Kaczynski's dissertation would be Boundary Functions. He would be remembered by his professors as an intelligent, serious, and quiet individual. Before his graduation he would publish journal articles some may find outstanding. It would occur in 1966 Kaczynski would visit the psychiatrist to discuss a sex change. His feelings of humiliation while in the waiting room would lead him to talk to the psychiatrist of other issues. Kaczynski would not be, so to speak, a true transsexual yet was possessing serious difficulty with his sexuality. This could have been the result of his lack of intimacy with anyone. Kaczynski would write in his diary after this meeting "Why not kill this psychiatrist and anyone else I hate?" It would seem this chronic anger fueling the actions of Kaczynski. Kaczynski would contact mental health professionals sporadically for different issues such as depression, concerns pertaining to women, and insomnia.

Kaczynski Lives in Isolation

Kaczynski would seem to possess a brilliant future accepting a position of an assistant professorship of mathematics at the University of California at Berkeley for the school year of 1967 and 1968. Two factors would force Kaczynski into a major life change. Kaczynski was basically unsuccessful in his role as professor. He was not a good teacher receiving poor evaluations along the lines of ignoring his students' questions. Kaczynski was a loner and few recollections exist of his demeanor. The tremendous level of political activism during the 1960s would be a second factor effecting Kaczynski. Kaczynski would witness numerous riots and protests such as the People's Park riot of May 1969 occurring only one short month before his official resignation at Berkeley on June 30, 1969. Kaczynski would live in the vicinity of the People's Park, the conflict generating from environmental-social concerns. These radical concerns did not seem to exist in Kaczynski prior to his tenure at Berkeley. Much like the Berkeley activists who would give up moving back to the proverbial land, Kaczynski too would seem to give-up on society moving to Montana. Kaczynski was not agreeing with political views and would focus his attacks on computers, airplanes, and engineering.

The reasons for Kaczynski's resignation were never clear. Kaczynski would live in Utah and Montana in the 70s and 80s. His twentieth anniversary report at his Harvard University reunion would list his address as 788 Bauchat Pass Khadar Khel, Afghanistan. This was in 1982 and this place does not exist. His location at this time is somewhat sketchy. Kaczynski would work odd jobs and menial labor living a simple lifestyle. His father of the same name Theodore Kaczynski would commit suicide in 1990 after a diagnosis of cancer. The effect on Ted is unclear, but it would seem it could not have much more negative impact on Ted considering since 1978 he was mailing out explosive letters to university faculty and staff. In time Kaczynski would settle in a mountainside cabin in Lincoln, Montana, on 1.4 acres purchased by him and his brother in 1971. The 10 x 12 foot cabin would possess no electricity, plumbing, or phone but may continue to be adequate consisting of a woodburning stove, a narrow bunk, two chairs, and a table. Kaczynski would grow some of his own food and hunt squirrel, rabbit, and porcupine for food. Kaczynski would spend five dollars weekly for provisions at the Lincoln Blackfoot Market. His mode of transport would be a dilapidated one speed bicycle. He would ride up to 50 miles to Helena, Montana. Kaczynski would read for leisure and would never drink or smoke. He would frequent the Lincoln bookstores and library. When Kaczynski would speak, which was rarely, he would be polite. Kaczynski's mother would visit him occasionally and he would receive partial financial support from his brother.

Before Kaczynski's apprehension his life would fragment, with bouts of depression demonstrated by his unwashed and dirty clothing. Kaczynski would miss payment on his November 30, 1995 property tax deadline owing presently in the arena of $114.27. Kaczynski would try to get a job at the Blackfoot Market but was refused. In terms of formal employment Kaczynski would not work from the time of 1981. Kaczynski would be found competent to stand trial in January of 1998. He would render a guilty plea nearly immediately after this time on January 22, 1998 to all federal charges pertaining to the bombings. The conditions were he never be released from prison and not profit from his crimes. The attorneys of Kaczynski said he would not be capable of enduring a trial where he would be viewed and depicted as a sicko. Kaczynski's sentence would be more than harsh consisting of four life sentences in addition to 30 years, and would be sent immediately to Supermax, the Alcatraz of the Rockies situated in Florence, Colorado. Kaczynski would join the company of Oklahoma City bomber Timothy McVeigh, mastermind of the 1993 World Trade Center bombing Ramzi Yousef, and the hitman Charles Harrelson father of actor Woody Harrelson.

Carley, S. G. (2013). *Serial killers, mass murders, & disorders.*
Boston: SGC Production.

Causes of Kaczynski's Behavior

Kaczynski would seem to suffer from a lifelong case of schizoid personality disorder (SPD). It would seem many different diagnoses could apply to Kaczynski. Of all personality disorders it may be SPD to be the most determined by genetic factors. The traits of introversion and shyness Kaczynski would demonstrate possess a high genetic determinant (DiLalla, 2004). Schizoid tendencies seem to be present within other members of the Kaczynski's. David as an example would spend large amounts of time living in a tent outdoors, and would for a time live in an even more remote part of Montana than Ted. To compound these genetic factors are Ted's mother's decision to facilitate isolating behaviors. Ted's Unabomber manifesto would speak of the unnaturalness to being absorbed in study at a desk all the time. Three instances in Ted's life may also have contributed to his fondness for isolation. When Ted was just nine months old, he would experience a severe allergy resulting in hives and be hospitalized for a week permitted next to no contact with his family. After the experience he would become increasingly withdrawn. At the age of seven Ted's brother was born causing a reaction to the loss of attention from his parents. After David's birth, as an example, Ted would never again snuggle up with his aunt. It would be David, Ted's brother, receiving the million dollar reward for the information leading to his arrest. Ted would refer to David as Judas the traitor to Jesus. Ted's promotion from the fifth grade directly to the seventh grade would further distance him from interacting with his peers. Ted would skip another grade a few years later continuing this process. Ted would never really develop emotionally in the area of heterosexual relationships. He would not date or socialize for that matter girls in middle school or high school. After Ted's high school graduation he would go on one or two dates with a girl, but end the relationship soon thereafter to cater to his religious beliefs. Ted would have next to no heterosexual interaction until 1974 when he would show interest toward a 19 year old waitress he would work with at the Kibbey Corner Truck Stop in Lincoln, Montana. She would possess no indications Ted was interested in her until after she left the job and was enrolled in school. Ted through a letter would invite her to move in with him in Canada and second letter would contain a dating resume. Kaczynski's most successful romantic relationship would be at the age of 36 in 1978 a short four months after the first Unabomber attack. Kaczynski would approach his supervisor at his job while he noticed her pumping gas at a gas station. He would visit her apartment and play cards with her, her sister, and sister's boyfriend. They would go on two dates together before she would tell Ted she wasn't interested. David reported that Ted would become quite upset from this ordeal. His depression, and one would assume the emotion to be anger, would cause him to act in a juvenile manner. He would write insults about her on the lavatory walls near the factory the two would work together. David who was working with Ted would be forced to fire him for writing disparaging remarks on a wall in front of him about the woman he dated briefly. As for Ted's social life this is about the highlight of it.

Characteristic of those experiencing SPD Kaczynski was never directly confrontational. The majority show not even passive aggression a result of the display of minimal levels of interpersonal conflict. Kaczynski would show patterns of impersonal aggression outside of the Unabomber activity including paranoid concerns. An example is a note Kaczynski would write to the retired owner Joe Visocan at the Kibbey Corner Truck Stop on October 1, 1974.

"Dear, sweet Joe:

You fat con-man. You probably think I treated you badly by quitting without notice, but it's your own fault. You gave me this big cock-and-bull story about how much money I could make selling tires and

Carley, S. G. (2013). *Serial killers, mass murders, & disorders.*
Boston: SGC Production.

all that crap. "The sky's the limit" and so forth. If you had been honest with me I would not have taken the job in the first place; but if I hadn't taken it, I wouldn't have quit without giving you a couple of weeks notice. Anyhow, I have a check coming. I am enclosing a stamped, self-addressed envelope in which you can send it. I had better get that check, because I know what authorities to complain to if I don't get it. If I have to complain about the check, then while I'm at it, I might as well complain about the fact that you don't have a proper cage for putting air in split-rim tires, which, if I am not mistaken, is illegal.

Love and Kisses,

Ted Kaczynski"

The behavior of SPDs is affected by certain characteristics according to the cognitive perspective. Disruptions of the emotional routine and feelings people no longer care about the individual. Beliefs he or she can survive alone and feelings of necessity for independence of freedom each characterize the disorder. From what we know of Kaczynski, he could fit the classification of many a disorder within the DSM-IV-TR such as paranoid personality disorder or avoidant personality disorder. Kaczynski's depression would lead him to a suicide attempt in January 1998 making use of his underwear as a self made noose. The federal prison psychiatrist at the time Dr. Sally Field finding Kaczynski competent to stand trial would diagnose him with paranoid schizophrenia. The diagnosis of SPD according to the DSM-IV-TR clearly applies to Ted Kaczynski. As true with Kaczynski according to the DSM-IV-TR he would possess few friends and demonstrate very few communication disturbances. The requirements of a diagnosis of SPD involve detachment from social relationships, introversion, and constriction of emotion in the social setting. The result being vocational or social disruption. This disruption may be the result of

Carley, S. G. (2013). *Serial killers, mass murders, & disorders.* Boston: SGC Production.

no desire for close relationships, the seeking of solitary pursuits, little interest in sexual experiences, obtains pleasure from few activities, lack of close friends, indifference to criticism, and detachment. Kaczynski it would seem possesses of each of the disruptions classifying SPD.

Kaczynski one may mistake for the lead character in Joseph Conrad's The Secret Agent, a bomb wielding professor. Kaczynski would seem brilliant to many, but at the same time would lead a troubled life fleeing academia for the hermitage of the Montana mountains. The unkept Kaczynski would live in his cabin living off turnips, he himself would grow much like the anarchist in Conrad's novel living off raw carrots. Kaczynski would seem no stranger to Conrad's novel as he would use the name Conrad as an alias on three occasions when mailing bombs in Sacramento, California. Josef Conrad's full birth name would be Teodore Jozef Konrad Korzeniowski very similar to Ted's full name Theodore John Kaczynski. Kaczynski would make use of the initials FC on numerous bombs and letters sent to news organizations which would stand for Freedom Club. Anarchists in The Secret Agent would use the initials FP, Future of the Proletariat. In Kaczynski's family home would be the complete work of Conrad. Kaczynski would spend 26 years in the wilderness, apparently Conrad's works were a fixture in his cabin. He once wrote in a 1984 letter to his family that "he was reading Conrad for like the twelfth time." This according to counsel for Kaczynski's brother and mother attorney Anthony Bisceglie. Kaczynski was not the first killer to find his inspiration from literature or film. The individual who killed Beatles singer John Lennon, Mark David Chapman had an unhealthy obsession with the novel A Catcher in the Rye. Timothy McVeigh's fascination with the Turner Diaries would lead to the Oklahoma City Bombing. John Hinckley Jr.'s consummation to the movie Taxi Driver would lead him to the assassination attempt and shooting of the at time President of the United States Ronald Reagan.

Carley, S. G. (2013). *Serial killers, mass murders, & disorders.* Boston: SGC Production.

Lack of Treatment of Ted Kaczynski

Ted's family though concerned for his social development would not do more than consult with school counselors. The absence of any formal or sophisticated examinations could be a factor in Kaczynski's personality as an adult. If Ted were to receive any formal examinations there is certainly no record. This is common with schizoid personality disorder in avoidance of the therapeutic relationship. If a therapist should meet with one possessing a diagnosis of SPD, it is important to build trust and avoid confrontation. Similar to psychopathy are the benefits of early intervention (Strupp, Lambert, & Horowitz, 1997). Disruptions of the socialization process such as shyness or introversion may require positive and better than average parenting to avoid future dysfunctions. Ted Kaczynski's parents may have failed, although well-intentioned, in helping a young introverted Ted Kaczynski. Guidelines parents may use in assisting their shy or introverted child can include gentle rather than pushy encouragement. The family should try to avoid a persona as perfectionists. Discuss a child's shyness with them making them aware your bouts with shyness if they should exist. Role playing can be helpful in coping with real life situations. A parent should encourage the child to act out positive role playing patterns even if he or she cannot perform the patterns in real life. Communicate with the child asking them what goes on in their head when he or she are feeling shy. It tends to be a negative statement such as "they'll laugh at me" or "I can't." Encourage the child to say positive things out loud making use of positive reinforcement if necessary. Take part in the development of your child's friendships offering rides and providing a place to play. Avoid negative comparisons and criticisms, and shaming should be avoided as a disciplinary technique. Children should learn the concepts of empathy and how to demonstrate empathy on others. The self-centeredness as part of introversion can diminish with this technique. Deal with shyness in a positive manner not by just simply discussing the issue with a teachr. Talk to your child about reflection and sensitivity. Let your child know the strengths of good listening. Make wise comparisons, do not compare your child to others who are more extroverted. Trying to get a child to work harder can backfire and result in even less exertion of effort by a child. An intimidated child can become even more inhibited with a sense of inferiority a parent may instill. Take inventory of your child's basic social skills making sure they are adequate. These taken for granted skills are important in how he or she interacts with others. Keep a close eye on situations which may increase a child's shyness. Children are not shy with everyone and certain situations can bring about shyness more than others. Handling shy situations with role playing can be excellent advice.

Carley, S. G. (2013). *Serial killers, mass murders, & disorders*. Boston: SGC Production.

Jeffrey Dahmer

Alright freak, what do you want for your last meal?

people...

Childhood and Adolescence

The birth of Jeffrey Dahmer would occur on May 21, 1960. Jeffrey would grow-up on a wealthy estate in a suburb of Akron, Ohio. His father was a success as a research chemist and as such would blame Jeffrey's behavior on medication his wife Jeffrey's mother would take during her pregnancy. During the first grade Jeffrey's teacher would write a note to his parents stating Jeffrey was experiencing feelings of neglect. This neglect was not in the form of physical or sexual abuse yet instead the constant tension from his parents' fighting and bickering among one another. Jeffrey's parents would even fight over the custody of Jeffrey's remains after his death. His mother's experience of postpartum depression after his birth would leave him with feelings of guilt he was ever born.

Dahmer would commit peculiar acts during his childhood which would seem even the more peculiar after his arrest for his adulthood crimes. For one according to Jeffrey's neighbors he would possess a fascination for dead animals and insects and would listen to the heart beats of his friends placing his head on their chests. Dahmer would collect roadkill cutting off their heads placing the decapitated extremity onto a pole or stick. He would also dry out and remove

Carley, S. G. (2013). *Serial killers, mass murders, & disorders.* Boston: SGC Production.

the skin of these dead animals. Dahmer's early life experiences demonstrate he may derive pleasure from the sufferings of others. At the age of five years Dahmer would convince his friend to put his hand in what he would claim to be a nest of ladybugs. In reality his friend would be placing his hand in a hornet's nest. Dahmer gave his grade school teacher some tadpoles who in turn would give the tadpoles to another student. Dahmer's feelings of rejection would cause him to punish his friend. Jeffrey would handle the situation by pouring motor oil in the tadpole tank killing them. During Dahmer's teenage years he would hunt out dogs and run them over with his car. In the eighth grade Dahmer would admit to masturbating daily and fantasizing about other boys. Dahmer's first experience sexual in nature would occur in the ninth grade with his male neighbor as the two would fondle and touch each other. They would take part in this action a few times and stop at the risk of being caught. Dahmer's dissection of a pig in biology class would end with him taking the head home, removing the skin, and keeping the skull. This was a time when Dahmer would possess thoughts of necrophilia having sexual thoughts of corpses. Dahmer would drink frequently during high-school even during school hours. Despite taking part in normal high-school activities and maintaining decent grades Dahmer could be viewed as a loner. Dahmer would only be seen with a woman at his prom and he would neither dance with nor kiss his date.

Adult Years

At the age of 18 Dahmer's parents would be in the middle of a divorce and fighting for custody of Dahmer's younger brother. In 1978 Dahmer would fantasize of a teenage jogger who would frequent the area and would go into the woods with a baseball bat. The boy would not show on this day but this is yet another example of the patterns of thought and violence running through Dahmer. It would be in 1978 Dahmer would first kill, his victim being 19 year old Steve Hicks. Dahmer who lived by himself and had a car would be drinking and driving and make the decision to pick-up a hitchhiker. Hicks would go to Dahmer's parents house where the two would smoke marijuana and drink beer. The two may have had sex or an attempt could have been made by Dahmer. In any case Steven would try to leave and when Dahmer would try to stop him a struggle would ensue. Hicks would be hit over the head with a barbell and strangled to death. Dahmer would proceed to take off Hicks clothing and ejaculate and masturbate onto his dead body. Dahmer would bring the body to a crawlspace beneath the home of the parents cutting the body into pieces and placing the body parts into plastic bags. Dahmer would become a drifter after his first murder resisting urges to kill again over the next few years. Dahmer would attend the Univerity of Ohio, spend some time in the Army, and for a short time live on a beach in Florida. Dahmer would get a job at a blood plasma center in Wisconsin where he would live with his grandmother. After being fired a year later for poor performance he would get a job at a chocolate factory. For a period of nine years after his murder of Hicks he would continue to possess fantasies of capturing people yet would commit no acts of homicide.

Upon Dahmer's return from the army he would retrieve the body pieces of his first victim and upon smashing them to fragments would scatter the remains in the woods. Dahmer would begin a pursuit for a relationship in public establishments. Dahmer would be a homosexual date rapist going to gay barhouses and putting drugs in their drinks. He would then take the drugged man to a hotel room. While in a sleeplike state Dahmer would perform anal intercourse on the man. Dahmer would leave the man, he would awake with very little recollection of the occurring events. In Dahmer's attempts to not kill, he once visited a young man who had died in the funeral home. Dahmer was interested in digging up the body so he could have sex with the dead corpse. Dahmer once stole

Carley, S. G. (2013). *Serial killers, mass murders, & disorders.*
Boston: SGC Production.

a mannequin and had sex with it. All this time Dahmer's abuse of alcohol would increase.

Dahmer would be arrested in 1986 the charge lewd and lascivious behavior for masturbating in the presence of two 12 year old boys. Dahmer would be forced into therapy for his actions and be described as cooperative and willing to change. Dahmer would not commit any murders from the time of 1978 to 1987 yet in 1989 after killing three men he would render a guilty plea to second degree assault and the enticement of a child for immoral purposes. Dahmer would try to lure a 13 year old boy to his apartment bribing him with $50 to see his new camera. Dahmer would persuade the boy to unclothe kissing his stomach, unzipping his pants, and pulling out his penis. Dahmer explaining it would make the boy look sexier in the pictures would touch the boy's penis. At this time the boy would drink coffee Dahmer had placed alcohol and tranquilizers into. Upon the boys return home his parents would notice the peculiar behaviors, and when he would describe the experience his parents would press charges on Dahmer. The arrest and conviction of Dahmer would do nothing in the direction of discovering Dahmer as the murderer he had become.

Dahmer would undergo more therapy and a parole psychologist would inform the judge Dahmer was showing signs of improvement. This would occur while Dahmer was carrying the skull of his most latest victim. A victim whose skull he would paint to resemble store sold items. Awaiting sentencing Dahmer would kill his fifth victim, and a different psychologist would deem Dahmer as an uncooperative and unwilling fellow to work out his problems. Dahmer would receive five years probation and ordered to take therapy which would never occur. Upon Dahmer's release he would purchase a black table and make a temple of it of bleached and painted skulls. The temple would collect the skeletons of his victims which would be used as an area of worship to permit Dahmer to gain more control of his life. Dahmer's excessive absenteeism would get him fired from his latest job in 1990 and from this time his pace of killing would greatly increase. He would kill twelve more times up to the following summer.

Dahmer's Treatment of Victims

Dahmer's primary interest would be sex with unconscious men. He would attempt to make them zombies so they would forget their very identity and stay with Dahmer. This would occur by drugging the victim and drilling holes in their heads to pour muriatic acid in the hole. Dahmer would attempt to keep the men alive so as to continue to have sex with the victim. One victim would be in this condition for three days before finally passing on. Dahmer would store and package their bodies to eat them so he and the victim would become one. Each of Dahmer's 17 victims he would have sex with their dead body. Fourteen of the victims he would cut them open at the abdomen placing his penis in the cavity and ejaculating in the body. With six of the victims he would perform oral intercourse on the beheaded victim ejaculating. He would also engage in anal intercourse with five or six victims after their death. Dahmer would claim to enjoy masturbating in front of and on their dead bodies.

Dahmer's Last Years

In May of 1991 Dahmer's 13th victim would receive a drugged drink, have a hole drilled into his skull, and muriatic acid poured into his skull. As the young man was sleeping Dahmer would go out to get a beer and return to find the naked man sitting on the roadside. A firetruck, two women, and the police would all be on the scene. Dahmer would explain to the group his friend simply had too much to drink. The police would cover the man in a blanket and enter Dahmer's apartment where they would lay the man on the sofa. The police would not discover the dead body lying in Dahmer's bedroom. Dahmer would show the officers pictures of him with the young man and they would take his story for the truth. Upon leaving Dahmer would finish the man off with a lethal injection. Dahmer would take pictures of the dead body and continue to perform sexual acts on the dead body committing sodomy and masturbating on the body. The flesh and skeleton would be acidified and the skull saved for Dahmer's temple. During a three week span in July of 1991 Dahmer would claim four more victims. Dahmer would offer Tracy Edwards age 32 the same offer as his previous victims, money in exchange for taking Dahmer's picture. While watching The Exorcist in Dahmer's bedroom Edwards' hand would be cuffed by Dahmer and a knife placed at his chest. As Dahmer would rub one of his skulls he would say Edwards' skull too would be staying with him. Edwards would kick Dahmer in the chest and escape and as he would attempt to report the incident to police they would have a difficult time believing such a bizarre story. Eventually two officers with some extra time would visit Dahmer about the incident.

It would seem over time Dahmer to experience a deterioration resulting in psychotic and dissociative episodes. This may be seen with the escape of his last victim on July 22, 1991 as he would make no attempt to apprehend the victim or otherwise leave his apartment. Dahmer's disconnection from reality would lead him to shout incantations as the victim would flee the apartment. Upon the arrival of the police he did not request a search warrant or resist in any manner simply permitting them to enter the apartment. Upon entering Dahmer's bedroom could be found various body parts lying around and a refrigerator full of human heads. Dahmer would struggle when the officers would attempt to detain Dahmer yet eventually would surrender. Dahmer would confess and provide a detailed description of the course of events which would take place. In all Dahmer would face two charges of murder and 13 counts of first degree intentional homicide. Left with no options Dahmer would plea insanity. The unimpressed jury would find Dahmer sane

Carley, S. G. (2013). *Serial killers, mass murders, & disorders.*
Boston: SGC Production.

and sentenced to 15 consecutive life sentences equivalent to a total of 957 years. Dahmer would express remorse after his capture expressing the opinion he did not in any way believe himself to deserve to live. Dahmer would refuse efforts to protect him while a prisoner from other inmates. In 1994 on November 28 while washing the bathroom prison floor Dahmer would be beaten to death along with another inmate by a 20-inch bar used for the prison exercise machine. Christopher Scarver would take Dahmer's life on this day claiming "God told me to do it." The nature of Dahmer's crimes may lead one to believe in fact Scarver was not experiencing delusions. During the November autopsy of Dahmer, reports would state Dahmer would remain shackled during the entire procedure.

Etiology and Treatments

In extreme situations such as in the case of Jeffrey Dahmer a single diagnosis may be unusual. Dahmer at one time or another would demonstrate various diagnoses including pedophilia, alcohol dependence, psychosis, marijuana abuse, mixed personality disorder, borderline personality disorder, sadistic personality disorder, and antisocial personality disorder. Upon a period of resisting killing Dahmer would experience a cognitive shift after killing his second victim. This is to say Dahmer would feel it his destiny to kill from the absence of a God and the influence of evil forces or the devil. This would be a time he would exert no forces in the direction not to kill and as the killings would become easier so too would the pace at which the killings would occur.

It is not obvious Dahmer is a primary psychopath despite the assumptions within crimes of such a nature (Boyd et al., 2007). Dahmer's experience of guilt-related anxiety is present and despite his deception of the police in May 1991 Dahmer should not be viewed as pathological. After his time of capture Dahmer would be surprisingly open about his behaviors and motives up to his time of capture. Dahmer's remorse and shift toward spirituality in prison according to spectators was believable. Dahmer's most pronounced diagnosis is that as a paraphilia and paraphilia not otherwise specified. Dahmer's unique variation to necrophilia would possess no reference. Dahmer would express all of the hallmarks of paraphilia such as pervasiveness, compulsivity, persistency, and exclusivity. The drive and pattern for this behavior often occurs as midadolescent fantasy. These sexual fantasies of sex with corpses would first arise in Dahmer when he was just a teenager pursuing dead animals resulting in the explosion to necrophilia (LoPiccolo, 1993). Sex hormones and neurotransmitter abnormalities according to research cannot be viewed as the primary factor for paraphilic behavior (Laws & O'Donohue, 2008). Instead the behavior of paraphilia should attribute to conditioned arousal to objects which are inappropriate. Other factors include the inability to possess a positive moral system, choice of short-term pleasure over long-term consequence, distorted sexual thinking, lack of sexual outlets, lack of victim empathy, alcohol and drug disinhibitions, and the assorted combinations of these factors. This is to say Dahmer's behavior is more an environmental determinant than a genetic determinant. Dahmer's genetics could however have played a secondary role in his behaviors the result of sexual hormone and neurotransmitter abnormalities. As mentioned this could be the result as Dahmer's father would claim of medication his wife would take during her pregnancy with Dahmer. Evidence does not support necessarily one of these factors would apply to Dahmer or that he was not provided ample opportunity to explore normal sexual outlets. Dahmer however meets many of these environmental descriptions as explanations for paraphilic behavior such as his inability to place long-term consequences over short-term pleasures and the effects alcohol would possess on Dahmer's process of decision-making.

Dahmer's disorder would never seek significant treatment which is a pattern among paraphiliacs. Paraphilic disorders range from sexual masochism to the coercive aggression present within pedophilia. The treatment options will vary as well. The creative diversity of sexual preference makes working in this field a constant challenge. Antisex crusaders may take part in other means of sexual gratification such as one who has an enema for sexual lust known as klismaphilia. Paraphilias can be difficult to treat and success is often short-lived and relapse a commonality (LoPiccolo, 1993). One such time honored treatment would be castration a means in other past cultures of purifying both woman and races. Physical castration is not always an effective means of treating sexual disorders (Marvasti, 2004). Certain methods of castration involve chemocastrators and neurosurgical castration. The best form of treating paraphilia however is within a treatment program or sexual offender program as they are often referred. The optimization of such a program occurs through several factors. The deliverance of the program should be contextually psychotherapeutic building a degree of trust within a counseling relationship. A therapist should be weary of false sincerity by a client as is present within the case of Dahmer. One should be especially suspicious when a client is quick to state he or she no longer possess any interest in such deviant activities. Concurrently stating he or she are most interested in natural sexual outlets. The common components of a typical sex offender treatment program involve offender assessment, any acute measures if necessary, individual or group therapy, behavioral techniques, aversive conditioning, masturbatory satiation, aversive behavioral rehearsal, sexual education programs, support groups, and finally ancillary surveillance.

An example of offender assessment is phallometry measuring the responses to various stimuli. This can be helpful in identifying any deviant sexual fantasies which can be key in treating aberrant behaviors. This can be done physically with a cooperative subject using a penile tumescence encircling the penis. A less intrusive measure is the Abel Assessment for Sexual Interest measuring the time a subject views sexual stimuli sets. A thermography measuring penis temperature can also be a valid measure. Acute measures such as short-term chemocastration may be necessary making the use of medications. Group and individual therapy can help clarify individual level of deviancy. Behavioral techniques such as covert sensitization may be implored where the individual imagines the deviant act and then imagines a negative reaction such as vomiting. Masturbatory satiation therapy may be implored where an offender will masturbate to appropriate sexual fantasies verbalizing the fantasy aloud. The offender should masturbate for 45 minutes to two hours afterward verbalizing deviant sexual fantasies. This should all be recorded. Aversive behavior rehearsal decreases deviant arousal and behaviors by making the behavior publically observable. The offender should explain the offenses committed using a mannequin to reenact any offenses. A narration should occur of the offender's thoughts heightening the aversive effect by having family members witness the display. Sexual education programs can offer assertiveness training and support groups such as sexaholics anonymous can be effective. A report group of family, friends, and neighbors should be made aware of the situation so as to being able to report any suspicious behaviors.

Carley, S. G. (2013). *Serial killers, mass murders, & disorders*. Boston: SGC Production.

Gary Leon Ridgway (Green River Killer)

Childhood and Adulthood of Gary Leon Ridgway

Gary Leon Ridgway otherwise known as the Green River Killer would be the most prolific serial killer the United States would ever experience. Ridgway convicted on 48 counts of murder would be suspected of killing over 90 women ranging in ages from 15 to 38. The term Green River Killer would arise as many of the bodies would be dumped in the Green River in the Seattle and Tacoma, Washington area (Karloff, 2002). The women were mostly runaways and prostitutes he would pick up along the Pacific Highway South. He would take these women's life mostly by strangulation using his arms, yet at other times through the use of ligatures dumping their bodies in various sections of the wooded King County. DNA evidence would eventually link Ridgway to the murders and on November, 30, 2001 he would be arrested at the Kenworth Truck Factory where he would work. Ridgway would be spared the death penalty with his confessions to the whereabouts of other missing women. The plea bargain would permit Ridgway to live the remainder of his life in prison without any chance of parole.

Gary Leon Ridgway would be born on February 18, 1949, to his father Thomas Newton Ridgway and his mother Mary Rita

Carley, S. G. (2013). *Serial killers, mass murders, & disorders.*
Boston: SGC Production.

Steinman in Salt Lake City, Utah. He would be raised in Seatac, Washington. Ridgway would lead what some may consider to be a troubled homelife witnessing violent arguments among his parents. Ridgway would wet the bed as a young boy and teenager, and his mother would discover the accidents bathing him immediately. His domineering mother would belittle Gary in front of family members as he would possess mixed emotions of anger and sexual attraction. Ridgway would be of low intelligence possessing an IQ of 82. He would be kept back twice in the same grade in high school, and his classmates at Tyee high school would find the forgettable Ridgway to be altogether unremarkable. The troubled teenage years of Ridgway would take full center with his attack on a six year old boy in the woods stabbing him in the ribs through the liver. The boy would survive the attack stating as Ridgway would walk away to comment, "I always wondered what it would be like to kill someone."

Ridgway would join the Navy at the age of 18 while still in high school. He would marry his high school girlfriend Claudia Barrows after graduating and would be sent to Vietnam. It was at this time Ridgway would start spending much of his time with prostitutes contracting gonorrhea for a second time. He would continue to have unprotected sex with these women despite feelings of anger over the incident. Gary's wife Claudia would begin dating again and within a year the marriage would fail. Those who knew Ridgway would describe him as mostly a friendly person who was somewhat peculiar concurrently. Infidelity by both partners during Ridgway's two marriages would lead to divorce. Marcia Winslow Ridgway's second wife would claim Gary to one time place her in a chokehold. It would be during the time of Ridgway's second marriage he would take an interest in religion. This interest would lead Ridgway to spread the gospel door to door. Ridgway would read the Bible aloud at work and at home converting his wife Marcia to the strict teachings of the pastor. Ridgway could be known to cry reading the

Carley, S. G. (2013). *Serial killers, mass murders, & disorders.*
Boston: SGC Production.

Bible, most often after sermons. Ridgway would continue to be involved in prostitution while married to Marcia, and attempt to have sex with Marcia in public and other inappropriate places. At times these places would involve the same areas Ridgway's victims would be found. Ridgway would seem to be a sex addict possessing perhaps some sort of psychosexual disorder. Such disturbances sexual in nature relate to emotional or mental causes. In Ridgway's case, he would seem to have sexual perversions marked by his obsession and need for control over women. This may be the reason Ridgway would look for these women as part of his sexual perversion. This pattern could be seen with his own wife as mentioned attempting to have sex in inappropriate surroundings. It may be Ridgway could not fully enjoy sexual intercourse and would resort to sexual activities with prostitutes (Meyer, Chapman, & Weaver, 2009). Ridgway was also demanding of sex from his three ex-wives demanding sex multiple times daily. Ridgway would complain of the presence of the prostitutes in his neighborhood only to make use of their services on a regular basis. Ridgway's lust would seem to conflict with his religious beliefs. Ridgway's son Matthew would be born in 1975.

Green River Killings

In a 2001 interview with Sheriff Reichert, Ridgway would be believed to commit 71 murders in the Seattle and Tacoma, Washington, area during the 1980s and 1990s. Between the years of 1982 and 1984 the majority of these murders would occur. These women would be strangled to death believed to be runaways and prostitutes picked up alongside the Pacific Highway South. Other than four victims found in the Portland, Oregon area, the majority of the bodies would be dumped around the Green River, a heavily wooded area. The bodies would be left posing nude at times in clusters. Ridgway at times would return to the bodies and perform acts of necrophilia. This form of paraphilia involves a fascination and erotic attraction to corpses. Four victims would remain unidentified as only the skeletons would remain of many of Ridgway's victims. In an act of confusing the police, Ridgway would contaminate dumping sites with written materials, cigarettes, and gum of others. At times Ridgway would transport bodies across state lines.

The process of Ridgway murdering a victim would begin by him picking a woman up in his car, most often a prostitute. To gain trust Ridgway would often show them a picture of his son. After engaging in sexual intercourse Ridgway would strangle the woman to death from behind. Ridgway would start making use of ligatures to strangle his victims to avoid the wounds and bruises inflicted upon him by manual strangling. Ridgway would kill victims in his home, truck, or secluded areas. In investigation of the murders, the creation of the Green River Task Force would occur by the King County Sheriff's Office during the 1980s. Robert Keppel and Dave Reichert, the most notable members of the task force, would interview the serial killer Ted Bundy to gain a better understanding of the operation of Ridgway. This is eerily similar to the CSI television program where serial killer Nate Haskell is used to investigate a murder. This is most likely in reference to the use of Ted Bundy in the Green River Killer investigations. Although the meetings with Bundy were mostly unsuccessful in the Green River case, they were able to get Bundy to admit to other unsolved cases. John E Douglas would also contribute to the Green River Killer investigation.

In 1982 and 2001 Ridgway would be arrested for prostitution. Ridgway would become a suspect in 1983 for the Green River killings, and pass a lie detector test in 1987, at which time police would take hair and saliva samples from Ridgway. Judith Mawson and Ridgway would begin dating in 1985, and she would be his third wife in 1988 when the two would marry. Mawson would claim there to be no carpet when she moved in according to a 2010 Mawson statement. According to detectives the reason for this is most likely Ridgway had wrapped a body in the carpet and disposed of the body. Mawson would state, Ridgway supposedly for overtime pay, would leave during early morning hours. Mawson would speculate some of the murders would have to of occurred during these times Ridgway would claim to be working overtime. Mawson would have no knowledge of a Green River Killer, and not suspect Ridgway in any manner, until he was contacted by authorities in 1987. Ridgway would claim his marriage to Mawson would reduce his urges to kill, and he would commit far less murders than he otherwise would have. Ridgway truly would love Mawson, who would claim a feeling of saving lives by being his wife and making him happy.

DNA analysis would occur of 1987 samples providing the necessary evidence for an arrest warrant. A spray painter at the Kenworth Truck Factory, this is where Ridgway would be arrested. The charge would be the suspected murder of four different women, 20 years after Ridgway's first identification as a potential suspect. The DNA left in a victim would match the DNA found in Ridgway's saliva. Spray paint spheres found on three other murder sites would link Ridgway to three more of the murders.

Green River Killer Pleas Guilty

Ridgway would be moved from his maximum security jail cell in the King County Jail to an undisclosed location in August of 2003. Reports would state Ridgway would be spared a sentencing by death for his confession to the involvement of other Green River murders. As part of a plea bargain on November 5, 2003, Ridgway would plea guilty to 48 counts of aggravated first degree murder part of a plea bargain sparing him the death penalty. Part of the stipulation would be to assist in finding the remains of the victims. Accompanying the Ridgway guilty plea would be his statement all of the killings would occur in King County and the bodies found in Oregon were in the attempt of throwing off police. Prosecuting attorney Jeffrey Baird would note the 41 unsolved murders would leave lingering doubt as to the content of these crimes. Although the truth would be attained, Gary Ridgway in no way deserved mercy, the mercy would be for the families of the victims. King County Superior Court Judge Richard Jones would sentence Ridgway on December 18, 2003, to 48 consecutive life sentences with no chance of parole. For the tampering of evidence in each of the cases, he would receive an additional 10 years to each life sentence, a total of 480 years.

Of any American serial killer Ridgway would confess to the most confirmed murders confessing to 48 murders of which 42 would be suspected by the police as Green River killings. Ridgway would confess to the killing of 65 women on February 9, 2004, yet on December 31, 2003 would confess to his role in the death of 71 women. Not revealed until after his sentencing would be the women were prostitutes, and he would have sex with the women before killing them. He would also claim to return to the bodies and have sex with the dead bodies. His later victims he had to bury in order to fight necrophilic urges. Before committing the murders he would make the victims feel comfortable by talking with them. Ridgway would make a career of killing these women, and to date remains incarcerated at the Washington State Penitentiary in Walla Walla, Washington.

Carley, S. G. (2013). *Serial killers, mass murders, & disorders.* Boston: SGC Production.

John Wayne Gacy (The Killer Clown)

John Wayne Gacy

John Wayne Gacy would be the third most prolific serial killer in the history of the United States committing 33 known murders and suspected of killing 34 or more in total. Gacy would be phrased the "Killer Clown" as the child entertainer Pogo the Clown. The killing spree of John Wayne Gacy would continue from 1972 until the time of his arrest in 1978 involving the murder of 33 boys and young males. Of this death toll 29 of the bodies would be found in a crawl space under the floor of Gacy's home, and the remaining bodies would be found in nearby rivers. He would be sentenced and convicted to death, and on May 10, 1994, Gacy would be executed by lethal injection.

The birth of John Wayne Gacy would occur in Chicago, Illinois, on March 17, 1942. Gacy would be the second of three children born to John Wayne Gacy Sr. and Marion Elaine Robinson. His father was an alcoholic who would constantly abuse him, yet was close with his mother and sisters. At the age of 16, Gacy would start to experience blackouts, the result of head trauma from a swing striking him on the forehead at the age of 11. Gacy would attend four high schools dropping out before completing his senior year.

Carley, S. G. (2013). *Serial killers, mass murders, & disorders.* Boston: SGC Production.

Gacy would leave his family and move out west. Gacy would run out of money in Las Vegas, Nevada, and make the decision to travel back home to Chicago. Without any high school certification to speak of, Gacy would enroll in and eventually graduate from Northwestern Business College. Shortly after Gacy's graduation he would receive a management trainee position at the Nunn-Bush Shoe Company. In 1964 he would be transferred to Springfield, Illinois. It would be here Gacy would meet his first wife Marlynn Myers and the two would marry in September, 1964. He would join the Jaycee's, a local Springfield organization, and rise to vice-president of their Springfield chapter by 1965. Marlynn's parents would purchase Kentucky Fried Chicken Franchises offering Gacy a position as manager. The Gacy's would make the decision to move to Waterloo, Iowa.

The Gacy's would have a son and daughter and settle in Waterloo. Gacy was working diligently for the KFC franchise, yet would find time to join the Jaycees. Gacy would be named outstanding VP of the Waterloo Jaycees in 1967, this is despite the spreading rumor of his homosexuality. Gacy would become much involved in the steamier side of Jaycee life involving drugs, pornography, and prostitution. Gacy would cheat on his wife on a regular basis. At this time Gacy would create a club in his basement for young boys permitting them to drink alcohol. This would permit Gacy the opportunity of making sexual advances toward these young males. Gacy the middle class idol would find his life come crashing down upon him with two sexual assault accusations from a 15 and 16 year old boy. Through this Gacy would profess his innocence and would only be caught when hiring another boy to assault his accusers. Gacy would be arrested when the assaulter would be caught, confessing to Gacy's involvement in the circumstance. This would occur in August of 1968, five months after the accusations would first take place. Gacy would receive a conviction on a count of sodomy and receive a 10 year prison sentence to the Iowa State

Carley, S. G. (2013). *Serial killers, mass murders, & disorders.*
Boston: SGC Production.

Penitentiary. His wife would abruptly file for divorce, and he would never see his children again. His father would die of cirrhosis during this imprisonment on Christmas day of 1969. After serving 18 months Gacy would be paroled, and upon his release he would move back in with his mother in Illinois. His criminal activity would be successfully hidden until police would investigate Gacy for the murders.

Upon moving in with his mother, Gacy would get a job at a Chicago restaurant as chef. He would buy a house in 1971 with his mother's assistance at 8213 West Summerdale Avenue in Cooke County, Chicago. Under the floor would be a four foot deep crawl space. Gacy would receive a charge of disorderly conduct on February 12, 1971 with a claim from a teenage boy he would try to pick him up and have sex with him. The boy would not appear in court and the case was dropped. Gacy would be discharged of parole in October of 1971 as the Iowa Board of Parole would learn nothing of this occurrence. Gacy would again be arrested on June 22, 1972 charged with battery. This time a young man would state Gacy to flash a sheriff's badge, and upon luring him into the car would force him into sex. Once again the charges would be dropped. During this same month, Gacy would marry again to Carole Hoff, whom he would be acquainted with during his high school years. Hoff would move in with Gacy into his Summerdale Avenue home along with her two daughters. Gacy would start a construction company, and his marriage to Carole would begin to deteriorate. Gacy would start going out late and staying out all night as the sex life of the marriage among Gacy and Carole would come to a halt. Carole would find the wallets of young men lying around with picture IDs inside. Gacy would engage in gay pornography within his home, and not long after his second marriage would come to an end in March of 1976. Within the local democratic party, Gacy would be an active member initially volunteering to clean the party offices. He would later serve on the Norwood Park Township streetlight committee in 1975 and

Carley, S. G. (2013). *Serial killers, mass murders, & disorders.*
Boston: SGC Production.

1976. In time he would become the precinct captain, and would even be photographed with First Lady Rosalynn Carter on May 6, 1978, at the annual Polish Constitution Day Parade. Gacy for the third year in a row would be directing the parade. Gacy would receive an autographed picture of himself with Carter with an S pin, indicating security clearance by the United States Secret Service. The Secret Service would receive embarrassment when this photo would arise within a search of Gacy's home.

John Gacy Murders and Trial

An employee of Gacy, John Butkovich, would disappear in July of 1975. Butkovich would engage in an argument with Gacy over backpay owed to him. The parents of Butkovich would urge police to investigate Gacy. Nothing would link Gacy to the disappearance and the case would go unsolved. Over a year later in December of 1976 another Gacy employee would disappear, Gregory Godzik, and once again the parents would urge an investigation of Gacy. In both cases the police would not investigate Gacy or discover his past criminal history. The following month in January of 1977 an acquaintance of Butkovich, Godzik and Gacy, John Szyc, would disappear. Gacy who would be driving the missing Szyc's vehicle would claim Szyc to sell him the car before leaving town. Finding this a believable story the police would not further pursue the matter. Gacy would become tired of the constant digging of holes in the crawlspace, and would desire more available space at all times. To make more space Gacy would hire an employee of his David Cram who would stay in a spare bedroom of the house. One night Gacy would be drunk and in his clown costume, and Cram coming home from work would join him for a couple of drinks. Gacy through trickery would place Cram in handcuffs and spinning him around the room wildly began screaming, "I am going to rape you." Cram would fight his way out grabbing the key to the cuffs and returning to his room.

Carley, S. G. (2013). *Serial killers, mass murders, & disorders.*
Boston: SGC Production.

A victim of Gacy's who would not die would lead to his arrest and capture. Jeffrey Rignall would be lured into Gacy's car in March of 1978. Gacy would take Ringall back to his home making use of chloroform where he would rape and torture the young man before dumping his body in Lincoln Park. Ringall could remember very little in his chloroform haze, yet could continue to recall a black Oldsmobile, some side streets, and the Kennedy Expressway. The Expressway exit was staked out until the finding of the black Oldsmobile owned by Gacy, and he would be followed to his 8213 West Summerdale address. Gacy would be issued a warrant and arrested on July 15. Facing a battery charge for the Rignall incident, he would be arrested for the murders in December. This could have been avoided when a 19 year old in December of 1977 would complain of being forced to have sex with Gacy at gunpoint, the police however would take no action. On December 11, 1978, while still awaiting trial for the Ringall incident a 15 year old boy, Robert Piest, would disappear from the Des Plaines pharmacy where he would work. Piest would tell a coworker he was going to a contractors house down the street about a job. The owner recalls speaking with Gacy at the pharmacy that night about a remodeling job. Des Plaines police would talk to Gacy about his conversation with Piest of which Gacy would deny the existence of any communication among the two. Des Plaines police would take part in an extensive criminal background check of Gacy discovering he would be a convicted sodomist.

Gacy's home would be searched on December 13 turning up some suspicious items including a receipt from the pharmacy Piest worked, clothing too small for Gacy, a two by four with drilled holes on each end, drivers' licenses belonging to others, and a 1975 high school class ring. Most peculiar would be the offensive odor ruminating from the crawlspace beneath the house. Upon further investigation the disappearance of Godzik would be revealed. They

Carley, S. G. (2013). *Serial killers, mass murders, & disorders.*
Boston: SGC Production.

would trace the high school class ring to Azyc, and they would learn of Butkovich from Gacy's second wife. Gacy would confess to over 30 murders on Decemeber 21, 1978 to his employees who would inform police. Gacy would be arrested for marijuana possession shortly thereafter as police would take out a second warrant. Upon their return to the Summerdale home the human remains would be found in the crawlspace. When Gacy was told he would be facing murder charges, he would confess to 25 to 30 murders. He would state the majority of the remains to be in the crawlspace of his home, but the last five bodies he would throw into the Des Plaines River. Gacy would draw a diagram for the police explaining the location of the bodies.

Gacy would claim he would pick up the male prostitutes or runaways off the street. He would take them back to his house through promises of sex for money and strictly through the use of force. When they were back at his house he would handcuff them, and muffle their screams by sticking clothing in their mouths. As he would sexually assault them, he would choke them with a rope. Gacy would remain with the bodies until decomposition would otherwise allow him. The police would return to the crawlspace for more remains, and for the next four months to follow, more and more remains would emerge from the Gacy residence. Between December of 1978 and March of 1979 29 bodies would emerge from Gacy's crawlspace. The youngest of Gacy's victims would be only fourteen years of age the oldest being 21 years. Eight of the victims could not be identified because of such extreme decomposition. On April 9 Robert Piest's body would be discovered on the banks of the Des Plaines River.

Gacy's trial would begin in Chicago on February 6, 1980. He would plea not guilty by reason of insanity. A plea which would be outright rejected. Gacy's lawyer would state Gacy to have flashes of temporary insanity during each murder before regaining his sanity in luring another victim to his home. Gacy would joke of being guilty only of running a cemetery without a license. Gacy would try to claim all 33 deaths were accidental the result of erotic asphyxia. This claim was denied and on March 13 he would be found guilty and sentenced to death. Gacy would be executed at the Stateville Execution Center in Crest Hill, Illinois on May 10, 1994 by way of lethal injection. The execution of Gacy would be a media sensation as large crowds would gather outside the penitentiary where numerous arrests would occur for disorderly conduct, open container violations, and public intoxication. Gacy t-shirts would be sold and at the moment of Gacy's death the crowd would cheer as one.

Gacy was never remorseful for his actions and would feel his death would not bring anyone back to life. As the execution was to begin, the IV into Gacy's arm would become clogged, and it would take 10 minutes to replace the clogged tube causing the disturbance, to be replaced. Upon resuming the execution, it would take 18 minutes to complete. The error according to anthesiologists would be the inexperience of prison officals, leading to the adoption of a new execution method within the state of Illinois. They would remove Gacy's brain upon his death to better understand potential biological abnormalities which may attribute to psychopathological behavior. Unfortunately no abnormalities would be found upon inspection of Gacy's brain (Dunea, 1994).

Carley, S. G. (2013). *Serial killers, mass murders, & disorders.* Boston: SGC Production.

DISORDERS

John Hinckley (Borderline Personality Disorder)

Criminal Responsibility and Competency to Stand Trial

Today seems to be a world in which people are living in fear for the welfare of both family and friends as citizens strive to accept judicial decisions in a time violent crime plagues the United States society. The insanity defense or the concept of criminal responsibility raises many moral ambiguities perhaps more than any other legal concept (Meyer & Weaver, 2006). For both society and the accused the portrayal of the insanity defense is as a choice among security and liberty whether right or wrong. This boundary continues to shift under the pressures of society socially, economically, and politically despite the behavioral sciences' best efforts to draw a firm line in distinguishing among badness and madness. Each juror must determine culpability when an insanity defense is raised upon an individual being charged with a crime. Making such a determination is difficult because of the broad ethical questions the legal concept of criminal responsibility raises pertaining to the limitations of one individual's responsibility to another and because of the ramifications for family members, victims, defendants, among others (Bartol & Bartol, 2008). Criminal responsibility in judicial application is nearly always interwoven with the concept of a defendant's competency to stand

Carley, S. G. (2013). *Serial killers, mass murders, & disorders.* Boston: SGC Production.

trial. Mental health experts involved in the judicial process may often confuse the issues of competency to stand trial and criminal responsibility. The term criminal responsibility includes concepts such as automatism, insanity, and diminished capacity referencing the state of the defendant's mind at the time of the crime. Competency to stand trial references the defendant's psychological state at the time of the trial. In the assessment of these issues such a temporal distinction is of crucial importance. Psychologists are frequently called upon to address the issue of mental competence in a variety of areas (Meyer & Weaver, 2006). In the legal arena competence also references the ability to be executed, to be a witness, to manage day-to-day tasks, and to make a will. The contributions of psychologists to the assessment of competency is not appreciated by everyone. In fact, New Mexico legislature would pass a bill limiting psychologist's testimony regarding competency in 1995. Despite the House convincingly passing the bill by a 46 – 14 vote, the state Governor would veto the bill.

Two independent but related factors must be present for a punishable criminal act to occur. First the individual must possess the general intent to do so, mens rea, and second legally defined illegal behavior must occur, actus rea. Both a guilty mind and an illegal act must be present before the occurrence of a punishable act, minus a few criminal statutes. For at least the last 2,000 years of recorded history consideration for both the intent and act has occurred. Historically encompassing a variety of criminal responsibility standards is the United States judicial process. One such example borrowed from English case law is the McNaughten rule stating, if a person is deemed at the time of the crime to be insane to provide a good defense. Until the volition test or the irresistible impulse was added, the criminal responsibility standard would continue. The question would arise of whether mental disease or defect had robbed the individual of his or her free will to control behavior despite the knowledge the behavior was wrong.

Carley, S. G. (2013). *Serial killers, mass murders, & disorders.* Boston: SGC Production.

The Durham rule would be set forth in 1954 widening the standard. The Durham rule of Judge David Bazelon would be rejected in the adoption of the American Law Institute's (ALI) Model Penal Code. The assertion of the ALI is criminal responsibility does not exist if the person lacks the capacity to conform his or her behaviors to the standards of the law or lacks the capacity to find wrongfulness in his or her conduct. The standard of the ALI would not be as restrictive as the McNaughten rule, yet continue to narrow the Durham rule. Changes in the federal law would be the next big change in criminal responsibility a result of the Hinckley trial.

The defendant's current state of psychological functioning deals with the issue of competency to stand trial, whereas the defendant's state of mind at the time of the crime deals with criminal responsibility. The principle of competency to stand trial firmly bases upon the Sixth Amendment to the United States Constitution and criminal responsibility to English case law. For the determination of competency to stand trial, case law provides specific guidelines of which generally fulfill three broad criteria. One, with a reasonable degree of understanding the individual should be able to consult with an attorney. The individual should possess factual understanding of the judicial process secondly. Third, the individual should possess rational understanding of the proceedings. The final decision regarding competency is a judicial process and forensic opinions are just that, opinions of a clinical nature. A defendant found incompetent to stand trial may not be confined for further treatment for a determined time period (Jackson v. Indiana, 1972).

The Life of Hinckley and the Attack

Shortly before 2:30 PM on March 30, 1981 a gunman would fire six bullets from a .22 caliber revolver. Of the six shots fired four of the Devastator bullets would find human targets. The most damage

Carley, S. G. (2013). *Serial killers, mass murders, & disorders.*
Boston: SGC Production.

would be incurred by presidential press secretary James Brady when the exploding bullet would cause extensive neurological damage. Brady would live yet never fully recover. Washington DC police officer Thomas Delahanty would be shot in the back and survive. The third bullet would hit the Washington Hilton across the street. Secret service agent Timothy McCarthy would be struck with the fourth bullet in the chest and would survive. The final two bullets would strike the presidential limousine one of which would ricochet and enter the chest of President Ronald Reagan who too would survive. The attack would last but a few short seconds as a secret service agent would describe feelings of desperation in trying to stop the attack. Hinckley would be described as continuing to fire shots as the secret service would take him to the ground. The senseless and violent brutality of John Hinckley's actions would raise many questions of the stability, history, and psychological motivation of gunman John Hinckley. Hinckley would state his motivations behind his actions during the seven week trial to be a means of capturing the love of Yale University student and movie star Jodie Foster. Hinckley's attempt at capturing the heart of Jodie Foster would fail, yet his behavior would lay the foundation to major revisions at the state and federal levels in criminal responsibility statutes.

The birth of John Hinckley would occur in 1955 in the state of Oklahoma. Hinckley would possess a normal childhood moving to Dallas, Texas, at the age of four. Hinckley would play basketball in high school and even quarterback his elementary school football team. Hinckley would be a fan of the Beatles since the age of nine. Hinckley would continue to be a John Lennon and music fan into adulthood. Hinckley and his family would move to a prominent Dallas neighborhood when he was 12, and he would lose all social status immediately. Hinckley would no longer be the kingpin so to speak. Hinckley would move to Evergreen, Colorado, in 1973 after graduating high school. Around this same time or soon thereafter he would make the decision to attend Texas Tech University in Lubbock, Texas. Hinckley's efforts in obtaining a degree in Lubbock over the next five or six years would be in vain. Hinckley would quit school in 1974 and move to Dallas. Hinckley's interest was more in the area of music or politics, he just wanted to be on his own (Caplan, 1984). In 1976 Hinckley would move to Hollywood with a dream to be a star which would never transpire into any success. Hinckley did however watch the movie Taxi Driver 15 times. Hinckley would return to Lubbock in 1977. It would be at this point Hinckley's emotional adjustment and overall adaption would decline (Roesch, 1979). He would receive medical treatment for minor ailments over the following year. Hinckley's interest of the National Socialist Party would grow in October of 1978 with their involvement to the American Nazi movement. In September of 1979 Hinckley would begin to publish the American Front Newsletter and one month prior would purchase his first firearm. Upon fabricating membership lists from 37 states, Hinckley would appoint himself national director of the American front. Since high school Hinckley would have moved 37 times.

Hinckley would experience his first anxiety attack in 1980 after gaining 60 pounds since high school. Hinckley would purchase another firearm, and People magazine in May of 1980 would announce Jodie Foster's attendance to Yale University. Jodie Foster is the star of the movie Taxi Driver Hinckley would see 15 times during a single summer in 1976. Hinckley would fuel his belief of being able to win the heart of Jodie Foster. Hinckley would have a phone conversation with Jodie Foster on September 20, 1980 of which Hinckley would write of his disappointment in his diary (Caplan, 1984). Hinckley would purchase six more guns and the Devastator bullets used in the attack on the President and his entourage. Hinckley would begin traveling around the country including Tennessee, Nebraska, Ohio, DC, Colorado, and Washington state. Hinckley would start following around President

Reagan and President Carter. Hinckley would fail to share his thoughts, fantasies, or planned activities during psychiatric treatment between October of 1980 and February of 1981 with Dr. John Hooper. The plan formulated by Hinckley's family and Dr. Hooper would encourage Hinckley's emotional stability and independence. These efforts were apparently for nothing as Hinckley would arrive in Washington, DC from Los Angeles by bus on March 29, 1981. On the morning of March 30 after breakfast Hinckley would write his final love letter to Jodie Foster, and upon learning of President Reagan's schedule, he would make his way to the Washington Hilton Hotel loading his Devastator bullets into his gun. It would only take seconds for Hinckley to enact his plan to gain the love of Jodie Foster and obtain glory.

The Hinckley Trial

The John Hinckley trial would be well publicized. The attempted assassination of the president would be but one of the 13 charges brought against Hinckley. Little would differ among the defense and prosecution's depiction of the circumstances of the event. In terms of the defendant's psychological condition at the time of the crime, much debate and difference would exist. The trial would last over seven weeks the result of the insanity defense. The costs of the trial were impressive as the prosecution would pay over $300,000 for the testimony of mental health experts. The experts for the defense would receive funds in excess of $150,000. Attorneys for the defense would accumulate between $500,000 and $1,000,000 not including salaries of ancillary staff, public relations, and court officials (Caplan, 1984). The jury would deliberate for two to three days, and on each of the 13 counts John Hinckley would be found not guilty by reason of insanity. Upon the decision by the court, Hinckley would automatically be committed to the St. Elizabeth's Hospital in DC to be treated until such time Hinckley would pose no threat to himself or others on account of his mental illness.

Carley, S. G. (2013). *Serial killers, mass murders, & disorders.* Boston: SGC Production.

The federal statute covering the insanity defense would be modified over the following weeks including 26 different bills. Two important changes would take place pertaining to criminal responsibility at the federal level. The irresistible impulse concept would be removed from the original McNaughten model. This is the model stating the basis for a successful insanity defense is a defendant's inability the result of defect or mental disease to appreciate the criminality of conduct. The second important change would involve the burden of proof switching from the prosecution to the defense. A reduction would occur in the level of proof the prosecution would require to clear and convincing evidence from beyond a reasonable doubt. The certainty level required by the jury would change from an estimated 90 to 95% to somewhere below this level. The significance of these changes to the federal level would serve as models to the state court consisting of far more insanity defenses. In evaluating insanity, part of the difficulty of professionals is assessments occur long after the act is committed when the most relevant data sets involve the objective information of individual functioning at or near the time of the crime. The person's mental health history before the time of the crime is another relevant data set. The mental state at the time of the evaluation would act as the least relevant data set. The availability of the final data set which is the least relevant is often the one mental health professionals will most focus upon. Certain factors can contaminate these data sets such as coaching from other inmates if a person spends time in jail, coaching from attorneys, false data to support insanity plea, emotional reaction to the damage of the crime, time in jail could affect mental state, and psychotropic medication use. Hinckley's defense attorneys would offer to their client in May and November of 1981 to plea guilty in exchange for penalties to run concurrently and not consecutively. Hinckley would be eligible for parole in 15 years under this agreement. The prosecution would

Carley, S. G. (2013). *Serial killers, mass murders, & disorders.*
Boston: SGC Production.

decline because making a plea bargain in a presidential assassination would seem improper.

As of 2009 Hinckley would continue to receive treatment at the St. Elizabeth's hospital some 28 years after the incident. With the approval of a presiding judge Hinckley may be released upon the recommendation of the hospital. This would only occur if Hinckley could be viewed as no longer a threat to himself or society. Such a dilemma can be amplified by the political issues of when to release such an individual who is proven to be dangerous in the past, and although does not represent any present imminent danger may very well be dangerous in the future. One can notice the inherent complexity in determining whether to make such a recommendation considering Hinckley's symptoms may be diminished through his use of psychotropic medication among other interventions. The behavior of John Hinckley as of recent years is without blemish. This compared to his earlier years providing much material to retain his presence in the hospital. Hinckley would once in 1986 exchange letters with the notorious serial killer Ted Bundy according to a psychiatrist expressing his sorrow for his difficult position. Hinckley's obsession of Jodie Foster would continue into 1988 requesting a mail order company to send a nude drawing of her. A room search within the hospital would come across 57 pictures of the actress. A federal court appeal in 1999 would permit Hinckley to make supervised trips off hospital grounds, and in 2004 would be permitted unsupervised overnight visits with his family. Hinckley's father John Sr. in 1984 would sell the Vanderbilt Energy Corporation, his oil and gas prospecting company for $26 million. During the 1980s John and his wife would spend $1 million to increase public awareness of the insanity defense and mental disorders through a national advertising campaign.

Borderline Personality Disorder

Carley, S. G. (2013). *Serial killers, mass murders, & disorders.* Boston: SGC Production.

At the Hinckley trial several different diagnoses would be offered, yet the consensus of the experts of the one diagnosis applicable to Hinckley would be that of borderline personality disorder (BPD). The first incorporation of the BPD diagnosis would be in the DSM-III in 1980, which would time and again prove a useful category (Strupp, Lambert, & Horowitz, 1997). A much favored old term by clinicians, emotionally unstable personality, would seem to resurrect itself through BPD, despite the DSM-IV-TR making no mention of this. Common within those experiencing BPD are soft neurological signs, anxiety and irritability, avoidance of solitude in the escape of psychological boredom, emotional instability, unpredictable behavior, and antisocialness (Atkinson & Goldberg, 2004). It would seem these individuals to grow increasingly narcissistic as their behaviors become more predictable and as individuals improve. A common feature of bipolars is pseudologia phantastica as in the attempt to increase self-esteem the individual lies. This is not in the same manner of the malingering con-game as seen in antisocial personality disorder. The DSM-IV-TR describes BPD as beginning during early adulthood as a pervasive pattern of mood, impulse control, and self-image. This is evident within such behaviors as severe dissociation, efforts to avoid abandonment, lack of anger control, unstable interpersonal relationship pattern, chronic feelings of emptiness, disturbed identity, mood instability, and self-damaging behavior.

Typical among bipolars is some form of abuse where love equates with loss of control and pain. The early life of bipolars is often soap opera like and chaotic. Receiving random reinforcement at best are the attempts at self-definition. The keys to obtaining nurturance is through sickness and abandonment. The chaos known as BPD requires variable treatment responses as a polyglot syndrome (Kroll, 1993). Not uncommon are multiple hospitalizations, and the use of SSRIs may be necessary to stabilize extreme response patterns. Appropriating relaxation training and biofeedback are the presence

Carley, S. G. (2013). *Serial killers, mass murders, & disorders.* Boston: SGC Production.

of disordered autonomic-emotional functioning. Should the individual permit the development of trust group therapy can be useful. As is the case, many clients are emotionally unpredictable and difficult to work with, unwilling to share the attention of the therapist. Inclusion of such individuals can be costly pertaining to group progression. The challenging and correction of the following beliefs as part of dialectical behavior therapy should occur in treating BPD: my uniqueness is misery, I deserve for bad things to happen to me, people are always bad or good and there is no middle ground, I'll be alone forever, I'll be unhappy unless in a relationship, and people will hurt me, so I must protect myself.

Efficiency and Effectiveness of the Legal System

Highlighting several overall perspectives on the legal system would be the case of John Hinckley (Meyer & Weaver, 2006). Effectiveness and efficiency are the two main criteria of which the legal system should be judged. The question may arise of whether or not our legal system is, in fact, effective. Perhaps no one knows, as there appears no manner of attaining this truth unlike the clear conclusions one may derive from the medical or financial systems. Restricting certain pieces of useful information from reaching the jury seems the aim of many legal maneuvers. The method of interactive assessment to maximize effectiveness the legal system permits little affordance. Jurors could not simply have the questions answered they would need when they would want these answers restricting efficiency and effectiveness. The shared belief the legal system is not particularly effective is most likely accurate. A concept foreign to the legal system seems to be cost accountability. As an example the O. J. Simpson case would cost taxpayers over $9,000,000. Profiting from this ineffectiveness would be the attorneys. Any other profession would certainly have to answer to others outside their profession if they were in such control of the system and making substantial profits from less than effective

Carley, S. G. (2013). *Serial killers, mass murders, & disorders.*
Boston: SGC Production.

endeavors. These people would have to turn to the legal system. Attorneys just go before other attorneys and a judicial system housed by attorneys. The legislatures and law making bodies too are dominated by attorneys. Reform is ultimately going to require the actions of attorneys reviewed by board members of non-attorneys and who do not particularly favor attorneys. Upon the assumption of jury system retention reform should include: system redesign not treating jurors as gullible, level playing field among sides involving time and money, permit juror notes and questions, permit jurors to have defendant's costs paid by plaintiff, provide a legal category of frivolous suits, except for capital cases abandon unanimous requirements, stringent criteria for the admission of expert testimony, greater powers of judges in permitting testimony, simplify legal system language, penalties for not responding to jury summons, excuse fewer people from jury duty, increase competency requirements to be a juror, reduce the availability of peremptory challenges, and expansion of trials not requiring a jury verdict. The Vikings would reference the United States jury system as an antiquated legacy. In arriving at a good system it would seem experts to come up with more than pulling 12 people off the streets to decide innocence and guilt. Many countries would abandon the jury system such as Japan and India. Britain's retention of the system supporters would point toward. Of criminal trials only 5% are heard by juries and less than 2% of civil trials. Relying on lay jurors or judges are the nations of continental Europe and the United States military.

Carley, S. G. (2013). *Serial killers, mass murders, & disorders.* Boston: SGC Production.

Marilyn Monroe & Tim (Sexual Dysfunctions)

Norma Jeane

In cases of female psychosexual dysfunction less significant personality pathology exists. A component of female sexual dysfunction vaginismus involves intense involuntary spasms of the vaginal musculature primarily occurring within the leviator ani and bulbocavernosus muscles. Sufficing to elicit muscle spasms can be the various types of vaginal contact or the anticipation of intercourse. The result is extreme pain during intercourse (dyspareunia) where intercourse can become impossible. In certain cases yet not a defining feature of vaginismus are orgastic problems or sexual inhibitions.

Gladys Pearl Monroe Baker would give birth to her third child on June 1, 1926 at the Los Angeles general hospital. She would name her child Norma Jeane Mortenson. Her mother's second husband would be listed as the father Edward Mortenson. Speculation exists the biological father to be a co-worker of Gladys whom she would have a brief affair, Stanley Gifford. Whoever her father was she would never know him. Norma Jeane would spend the first seven years of her life in foster homes due to her mother's instability.

Norma Jeane would go under the care of very strict foster parents who were devout Christian Scientists. She would move back in with her mother at the age of seven. Gladys' mental health would deteriorate to the point of a hospitalization and diagnosis for paranoid schizophrenia. Gladys would seem to possess a predisposition for the disorder a result of the genetic component to the disorder. The death of Gladys' great-grandfather would in part attribute to an unknown psychotic disorder and her maternal grandmother would be institutionalized. Her parents would both fit the description of a manic-depressive. Eventually the half-brother to Norma Jean would receive a schizophrenia diagnosis (DePaulo, 2005).

Grace a friend of the family would take in Norma Jeane and encourage her to be a movie star. Norma Jeane would be shuffled among seven foster families the result of financial hardships over the next four years until 1941 when she would be reunified with Grace and her husband. Norma Jeane would be sexually assaulted in one of her foster homes by an actor who would rent a room there. Norma Jeane would attempt to make the issue public, but her foster mother at the time would refuse to believe her and she would never again make mention of the issue. Grace and her husband were forced to move in 1941 the result of financial troubles. Norma Jeane would be 16 years of age at the time, and the couple would be unable to take her with them. Grace would encourage Norma Jeane to marry Jim Dougherty, the 21 year old son of her neighbors. They would marry on June 19, 1942, and Marilyn would later claim despite the marriage being somewhat boring, it was neither unhappy nor painful. Jim would join the Merchant Marines in 1943, and would be shipped to fight in World War II one year later. It was at this time Norma Jeane would work at a parachute-inspecting plant and aircraft. In escape of loneliness and insecurities she would turn to alcohol.

Carley, S. G. (2013). *Serial killers, mass murders, & disorders.* Boston: SGC Production.

David Conover an army photographer working for the Yank magazine in 1944 would be photographing the women working in the factories in their support toward the war effort. Noticing Norma Jean's natural beauty, he would take pictures of her in different locations hiring her to travel with him around California. Within a year she would be on the cover of 33 national magazines when the Blue Book Modeling Agency would take notice of Norma Jean. Norma Jean would file for divorce in 1946 after engaging in several extramarital affairs. Just turning 20 a 20th Century Fox casting director Ben Lyon would give her what would be her first interview in the movie industry. 20th Century Fox would hire Marilyn for $75 per week on August 26, 1946 under the stipulation she change her name. Lyon's suggestion would be the name Marilyn, and Norma Jeane would choose the name Monroe, her mother's maiden name. Marilyn Monroe would be born (DePaulo, 2005).

Marilyn Monroe

Marilyn would not immediately be thrust into stardom. She would start by playing smaller roles as in the musical performance of Ladies of the Chorus and the movie The Shocking Miss Pilgrim. She would agree to pose nude in a calendar in 1949, which would create some deal of controversy when she would later become an iconic figure. In this same year her lover and mentor would be Johnny Hyde. Marilyn would report to a psychologist years later that Hyde would watch her giving herself an enema, which she frequently did to alleviate chronic constipation, exclaiming it to turn him on. For the first time the two would engage in anal sex. This would become the focus of their sexual encounters from then on as Marilyn would do what she could to please Hyde. Johnny would even drink her urine.

During her adult life Marilyn's casual stance toward sex would continue engaging in numerous affairs. Curiosity toward a studio lachey's uncircumcised penis would result in an episode where she would masturbate him. It is believed Marilyn would take part in a stag film of which Joe DiMaggio shortly after her death would attempt to purchase for $25,000. Marilyn would engage in lesbian sexual encounters including a one night stand with actress Joan Crawford. In a government memo Marilyn's name would appear reporting multiple sex parties within the New York Hotel Carlyle. Other names among this list would include Robert and John F Kennedy. The result of these affairs would lead to multiple miscarriages and dozens of abortions increasing Marilyn's insecurities. In 1950 Marilyn would receive her first serious acting job, and would begin to receive more serious roles over the next two years. Marilyn Monroe would marry Joe DiMaggio on January 14, 1954 after a two year relationship. In this same year Marilyn would fail to appear at a movie set and receive a suspension by Fox. Overseas in Korea, she would entertain 60,000 troops, star in the film The Seven Year Itch possessing the famous skirtblowing scene, and divorce DiMaggio this same year as the marriage would last a short nine months. She would marry playwright Arthur Miller on June 29, 1956 and start her own production company. Three days after her marriage she would convert to Judaism as her husband was Jewish. The two would move to England and Marilyn would not return to Hollywood until 1958. Marilyn's marriage and health would deteriorate. Her work would continue, yet she would develop a severe addiction to tranquilizers and barbiturates resulting in her forgetting lines and showing late for meetings. Despite never experiencing an orgasm, she would be the country's sexual icon. DiMaggio's sister June would once ask Marilyn if she would at least have an orgasm during sex, of which she would reply "What's that?" (Monroe, 2005).

Marilyn would begin seeing Dr. Ralph Greenson in 1960, who as a renowned psychoanalyst would treat Hollywood's elite. The focus of their therapeutic relationship would be her orgasmic difficulties.

Carley, S. G. (2013). *Serial killers, mass murders, & disorders.* Boston: SGC Production.

Months before she would die, Marilyn would tell Dr. Greenson she never cried so hard as when she would have her first orgasm. She would state to f#!% in every way possible both women and men, going down on her without receiving an orgasm. She would claim these to be wasted years (Monroe, 2005). The relationship among Greenson and Monroe would continue until her death. The atypical characteristics of their relationship would not keep Marilyn from crediting Dr. Greenson with bringing happiness to her life. Marilyn Monroe and Arthur Miller would divorce in 1961. Marilyn would begin to see Dr. Greenson daily, and even at times multiple times during the same day. Marilyn would become Dr. Greenson's only patient hiring a live-in housekeeper to stay with Marilyn, permitting Greenson to maintain an increased control of her life. Evidence of an unusual relationship would grow when Marilyn would tell Dr. Greenson, it would have been nice to be his daughter and not just his patient. She would state, "I know you cannot do so while I am your patient, but that perhaps afterward you could adopt me." She would state to have the father she was always looking for and his wife could be his mother and children her brothers and sisters (Monroe, 2005). Dr. Greenson would cater to this attachment by bringing her home for sessions.

It would be through her work with Dr. Greenson, Marilyn would first be capable of achieving orgasm. Greenson would practice many of the techniques of Sigmund Freud. The encouragement of Dr. Greenson of Marilyn would be to free associate, a popular method although unsuccessful in this case. Improvements in Marilyn's sexual difficulties would not occur until Dr. Greenson would explain to her how to achieve orgasm on her own through masturbatory techniques. Such a useful approach is atypical as a form of traditional psychotherapy (Haley & Richeport Haley, 2008). Greenson would explain after she learned to achieve orgasm herself, she could have the experience with others. This simple approach would be effective as Marilyn would claim to by now to have achieved many orgasms. Some time after Marilyn would divorce Miller in 1961, she would have this breakthrough. Greenson would fuel Marilyn's severe addiction by prescribing barbiturates and tranquilizers, yet things in Marilyn's life would appear to start to improve. Marilyn and Joe DiMaggio would start seeing a lot of each other and would remarry on August 8, 1962. Monroe would be rehired by Fox at a salary of $250,000. Marilyn's mood would fluctuate the result of her addiction, yet she was happy and by no means suicidal. Despite this three days before her marriage to Joe DiMaggio on August 5, 1962 Marilyn Monroe would be found dead in her Brentwood home.

The reported official cause of death was a suicide although Thomas Noguchi the medical examiner performing the autopsy would list the cause of death as a probable suicide. Marilyn Monroe undoubtedly died of an overdose of the barbiturate Nembutal, yet she would need to ingest 30 to 40 Nembutal pills to match the level of toxicity found in her system. Her stomach upon an autopsy would show no trace of Nembutal crystals or capsules and no needle marks of any kind ruling out intravenous use. During her autopsy the only abnormality would be bruising of her colon and large intestine. The consistency of the bruising is to a Nembutal laced enema. Self administration would be physically impossible without a loss of consciousness. Marilyn would curiously be found with a phone in her hand when she would be found. The death of Marilyn Monroe remains open to conspiracy theories.

Causes of Marilyn's Sexual Dysfunction

How could Marilyn Monroe the great American sex symbol go through the majority portion of her life without experiencing a single orgasm? Contributing to this dilemma one may point toward the repressive and strict environment Marilyn would be subject during the first seven years of her life. One may certainly assume the sexual

Carley, S. G. (2013). *Serial killers, mass murders, & disorders.*
Boston: SGC Production.

assault upon Marilyn would possess some effect, especially considering the harsh response of her foster parents. Even into early adulthood Marilyn would have very little stability in her life and would receive inadequate sex education. Another factor would be her first sexual partner and mentor being the bizarre and selfish Johnny Hyde. Further contributing to Marilyn's issue would be the sexual exploitation she would endure from studio executives in return for movie roles. Marilyn would seem to do what she had to in furthering her career and would not seem shy in doing whatever and with whomever. When a producer calls an actress to discuss a script this is not all they have in mind, Marilyn would not be the only one to sleep with a producer (Summers, 1985). This attitude of emotional detachment would not facilitate the orgasmic learning environment. Multiple casual factors are typical among cases of sexual dysfunction among both men and women. The case of Marilyn Monroe would be a minority instance in which a straightforward curative factor presents itself.

As with Marilyn Monroe the treatment for female sexual dysfunction can be simplistic and fairly straightforward. To correct the development of a distorted belief system one may make use of cognitive behavior modification. Treatment can involve counseling to facilitate sexual functioning, mild tranquilizers, and brief psychotherapy. Individuals experiencing sexual dysfunctions remain physiologically capable of sexual performance. Sexual dysfunction is the result of an inhibition of reflexive response sets the result of psychological factors (Andreassi, 2000). Psychosexual dysfunctions among a majority of individuals possesses a need to be challenged on certain problematic cognitive assumptions including, real sex only involves both of us having an orgasm, real sex cannot occur without intercourse, sex should occur with the clothes off in the dark in the bed somewhere exciting and after a show of romance. Finally sex should be routine, novel, ecstatic, special, and perfect. Treatment for sexual dysfunction often results in relapse or inhibited sexuality. When coping strategies are taught and monitored success rates improve in regard to the avoidance of relapse. Learned skills can involve undergoing booster sessions, generating a romantic mindset, reading books or pamphlets with positive information, using specific cognitive mantras, and role playing with a partner an occurrence of dysfunction.

Sexual Dysfunction

Sexual dysfunctions come in various forms as with paraphilias. Estimations are most will experience some form of sexual dysfunction during his or her life, and affecting 50% of marriages are an enduring sexual dysfunction (Masters, Johnson, Kolodny, 1991). Multiple determinants exist of individual sexual dysfunction in the form of neurophysiological, interpersonal, or psychosocial. Sexual dysfunction subdivides into four categories within the DSM-IV-TR Vaginismis or Dyspareunia, Orgasm, Arousal, and Desire. In assigning a label of psychosexual dysfunction one must be somewhat arbitrary. Erectile dysfunction by definition is a failure to capably perform intercourse 25% of the time (Masters & Johnson, 1970). A typically rare biological cause is total erectile dysfunction. More often than not the dysfunction is partial. An erection may not be persistent enough to satisfy a partner or to oneself achieve orgasm (LoPiccolo, 1993). The suggestion to impotence is a weakness to character suggesting generalized personal inadequacy. These implied traits bear no evidence of more occurrences within individuals experiencing such problems (Doctor, 1998). The traditional sex roles in society of sensitivity and warmth among females and competence for males are exactly the opposite of the suggestion of coldness among females and weakness among males.

Tim

Carley, S. G. (2013). *Serial killers, mass murders, & disorders.* Boston: SGC Production.

Tim would be silent for some time in regard to his problem yet eventually would visit his personal physician in receiving treatment for impotence. Tim would be referred to a urologist by his physician who would carefully examine Tim in ruling out various endocrinological and physical factors affecting impotence. Upon the physician's examination, he would refer him to see a clinical psychologist specializing in the treatment of sexual dysfunction. For preparation in the initiation for appropriate treatment the clinical psychologist would listen to Tim's story and his background. Tim would make a good first impression as a college educated 33 year old. Tim was both in physical good shape and a handsome man reflecting his occupation as a former professional baseball player.

Tim would relate to others with interest and warmth and was well groomed and always dresses well. Tim would leave the impression of not being interested in his work and seem as if he was not strikingly successful despite a recent promotion to bank vice-president. Despite leaving a good first impression, it would seem Tim to be an anxious individual most of the time. He would seem to need to move about during the interview and would possess trouble in articulating personal concerns. Tim would describe his father as authoritarian and perfectionistic and mother as pious and passive. Tim's upbringing may best be described as standard middle class Catholicism. Tim attends church service occasionally yet is not committed to any great depth. Tim's relationship to sports seems to be his most important focus. Tim's earliest memory would be of him at the age of three or four playing in a baseball game listening to his parents cheer as he would advance from base to base. In regard to sports, his parents were demanding, more so his father but his mother too would take some concern. These pleasant memories would be clouded by memories of his father as his Little League coach harassing him for making errors. His father was demanding on all the children but especially so with Tim. Tim's father would not show a positive response until his performance was

Carley, S. G. (2013). *Serial killers, mass murders, & disorders.*
Boston: SGC Production.

competent, which early on the instances were far and few between. Tim's father's demands would carry off of the field. Tim would view these demands as taking from the fun of growing up, but necessary to develop the skills in being a competent adult. Despite Tim's professional career being over due to injury, his parents continue to value his life in sports. Despite Tim feeling some discomfort, his parents continue to discuss the professional sporting achievements of Tim with both family and friends. Their image is as a successful athlete as they fail to see him as a developing person. The sporting needs filled by Tim would permit his parents to allow their other son Jack to pursue an interest in music.

Tim would show mixed feelings about his inability to perform as a professional athlete. Tim would slide into a base and injure his foot. When returning to early from the injury, he would alter his pitching delivery and develop a chronically sore arm. The orthopedic surgeon would inform Tim the arm would never return to its full level of function. Tim would spend a long time in the minors and would not make it to the big leagues until he was 29. Tim would be right on the edge of stardom when the injury would develop. He would develop a winning streak which was expected to continue. His team would seem to be championship caliber, and his injury would not only ruin his hopes but the hopes of the team. Sportswriters would talk about Tim's courage, stating he didn't have what it takes to stick things out after his injury.

When Tim was a junior in college he would marry his first wife moving into the role of stardom on his college baseball team. She would enjoy the degree of glamour surrounding Tim at this time as she would be a university freshman. After a short courtship the two would marry and almost immediately have a child. By then they would find they would have different parenting views and very little in common. Tim would claim there was no history of impotence in the relationship, but their sex life was sporadic at best. His wife

Carley, S. G. (2013). *Serial killers, mass murders, & disorders.*
Boston: SGC Production.

would work at a law office and have an affair with an attorney she worked with. Eventually she would leave Tim to marry the lawyer. Her new husband would obtain a prestigious job in a distant city, and she would take their child with her. Tim continues to see his 11 year old son with some degree of regularity. The distance and the early separation would prohibit the development of a strong relationship.

As of recent times Tim would date Pam who he would have a satisfying sexual relationship. Six months earlier Tim would decide not to continue his baseball career, Pam would move in with him 18 months prior. Pam never valued Tim's sporting career highly. Tim may not necessarily love Pam, but there is a sexual attraction at least during the early courtship and during the first several months of dating, the two would possess a very active sex life. Pam's initial attraction to Tim would pertain to his athletic appearance, although she was mostly unresponsive to his baseball career. The two would talk of marriage but aren't confident in making such a commitment. Tim's parents never make any mention of Pam to their friends as they are upset the two cohabitate without a marriage.

Tim believes his impotence may have started through his worries of the sportswriters' criticisms of his lack of desire to return to the game. His initial incident with impotence would occur after a heavy night of drinking after reading an article about how he cost his team a shot at the championship. Tim would also possess uncertainties pertaining to his relationship with Pam. These factors compounded would result in an apprehensive and distracted mental set. Creating even more anxiety would be Tim's awareness he did not have a full erection deflating any erection he had obtained. Pam was neither critical or supportive, perhaps she too would be drinking heavily at the time. Tim felt humiliated and his continuing problems in maintaining an erection would bring about even more anxiety. Tim did not consciously take his religious views seriously as he would

Carley, S. G. (2013). *Serial killers, mass murders, & disorders.* Boston: SGC Production.

possess prohibitions against almost all types of sexual behaviors. An older male friend would teach him to masturbate, and the first girl he dated Barbara in high school, he would often engage in petting and fondling. A good friend of Barbara, Carolyn, would be Tim's first sexual experience. It was very anxiety provoking yet enjoyable to Tim. It would occur in Carolyn's home in the living room and as they got started Carolyn's father would scare Tim by asking if anyone was down there. His erection would temporarily fade, yet they would finish as Tim's high drive level would come to the rescue.

Causes of Tim's Impotence

After Tim's physical examination the physical causes of impotence would be ruled out. After spending an evening at the university sleep lab the indications of the test were normal in terms of nocturnal penile tumescence (NPT). The duration, strength, and sufficient number of erections during sleep would suggest psychological rather than physiological factors. Typically found among men are a display of few to no NPTs in the demonstration of physically based impotence (Masters, Johnson, & Kolodny, 1991). Organic factors can play a part in the following cues suggestive of erectile dysfunction: loss of masturbatory and nocturnal erection, ability to initiate but not maintain an erection, normal libido, sequentially deteriorating erections, and gradual onset. General indicators of psychogenic erectile dysfunction include: loss of libido, normal morning and nocturnal erections, brought on by life stresses, sudden onset, and episodic. Emerging from Tim's psychological evaluation are several factors contributing to impotence. Tim would possess a strong need to control his environment like his father, and would experience a threat from uncontrollable change. Suggesting a loss of control and generating anxiety among Tim would be the conflicting feelings surrounding his attitude toward his new girlfriend, the problems stemming from his baseball career, and his divorce. The vague feelings of anxiety among Tim would be the physical focal point of his impotence. Tim would possess performance anxiety, as unable to enjoy the pleasures of the response, the individual takes on a spectator role in the sexual act. Other characteristics would predict Tim's impotence other than Tim's obsessive features. Tim's revelations of Pam is she would move more strongly in the direction of women's liberation than he would be accustomed or feel comfortable with. She would begin to discuss her need to fulfill her own needs and find herself. Pam would begin to flirt in front of Tim as he would permit himself to do to her. Even Pam would insinuate Tim to not really put a full effort into recovery from his injury. The combination of these developments would make Pam a threat to Tim's self-esteem. These developing beliefs would become strongly enforced when Tim would experience impotence with Pam. The guilt Tim would experience from his strict Catholic upbringing would be another factor. Tim would try to maintain a standard role among the church, although they would forbid his behavior as a divorcee living with another woman out of wedlock. Tim would struggle with the church's hypocrisy whose nuns would break vows of chastity to themselves leave their calling and marry. Sexual restrictive societies tend to possess a higher concordance rate of impotence. The movement toward a more liberal value system from a restrictive belief system also is likely to possess a higher rate of impotence. The common first experience factors of impotence were present within Tim of relationship problems, fatigue, and alcohol (Doctor, 1998). Despite early successful sexual experiences a significant level of anxiety would be associated.

Treatment of Impotence

Treatment of orgasmic and erectile dysfunctions possesses numerous effective psychological, physical, and chemical techniques (Meyer & Weaver, 2007). The most effective and efficient of treatments are prescription drugs to prescribe specifically for erectile dysfunction. In the great majority of cases these drugs would act as the only form of treatment. Questionably only moderately effective is the administration of the hormone testosterone. Another seldom needed method is penile artery bypass surgery. More likely to be useful are various forms of revascularization. For organically based cases and at times in severe psychogenic cases prosthetic devices can be used. One such device is inserted into the corpora cavernosa, a semi rigid rod. This device can interfere with urological diagnostic procedures and a permanent erection can be somewhat embarrassing. An alternative is to inflate the penis with a hydraulic device. Psychological sensate focusing techniques are both safe and generally effective for orgasmic and arousal disorders. To assist a client to stop spectatoring, sensate focusing techniques can be combined with sophisticated cognitive therapies (Meggers & LoPiccolo, 2002). Carrying out these procedures with a stable partner from the client's natural world are particularly effective. The first practice of sensate focusing would occur by a practicing physician, Sir John Hunter, in or around the year 1750, who would advise his clients to go home and lie in bed and fondle one another. The beginning of Tim's treatment with the psychologist would pertain to his perfectionism, clarification of his feelings of his relationship with his girlfriend, and his guilt about his sexual experiences. As Tim would become more comfortable in his relationship with Pam, he would ask her to participate in the latter stages of his treatment program. The emphasis of the therapist would be for Tim and Pam to focus on the pleasures of petting and fondling, and would be advised for a period not to proceed into the act of intercourse. When they were becoming aroused by this, the therapist would recommend the two have intercourse but not to achieve orgasm. As arousal would increase intercourse would become successful. A year after the treatment the two would marry, as other areas of the relationship would begin to improve, as the impact of their communications and meaning would be clarified.

Carley, S. G. (2013). *Serial killers, mass murders, & disorders.* Boston: SGC Production.

Tim's relationship with his parents would improve when he would get married, yet he would need to work on his dependence of his parents' approval. This would be an issue through some follow-up therapy sessions while he would retain a caring relationship for his parents, but also distance himself from the need for their approval. Tim would take up painting and enroll in refresher courses pertaining to his work. Tim's self-esteem would improve permitting the initiation of new behaviors in the creation of a positive cycle of psychopathology.

Carley, S. G. (2013). *Serial killers, mass murders, & disorders*.
Boston: SGC Production.

Virginia Woolf

Suicide

Suicide in the United States occurs at the rate of 15 per 100,000 comparing to the rate of suicide attempts which is 225 per 100,000. The rate of suicide among those possessing psychiatric disorders shows no significant difference among this statistic. The rate of suicides among psychiatric patients is at 15% comparing to the general United States statistic of 10 – 12%. So a slight increase does exist. According to Bostwick (2000) these rates may be even lower among the psychologically disabled population. Hospitalization the result of a suicide attempt or ideation, the suicide completion rate diminishes to 8.6%. Patients hospitalized for an affective disorder for specifications other than suicidal tendencies possess a lifetime suicide completion rate of only 4%. This number further diminishes to as low as 2.2% among the general inpatient-outpatient population. Those unaffected by an affective disorder among the general population possess a lifetime prevalence rate of less than .5%. The Centers for Disease Control and Prevention in 2001 would report the completion of 60% of suicides is through use of a firearm. Behind unintentional injury and homicide, suicide is the third leading cause of death among the young population ages 15 – 24. Death from suicide is a more likely occurrence than death

Carley, S. G. (2013). *Serial killers, mass murders, & disorders.* Boston: SGC Production.

by homicide at a ratio of 1.7 to 1.0. Females who are more likely to make a suicide attempt are four times less likely to die of suicide.

Severe depression does not necessarily involve suicide (Bongar, 2002). In the presence of significant depression the threat of suicide should be a concern. Throughout history the more famous suicides would include Cleopatra, Adolph Hitler, Samson, Amadeo Modigliani, Jack London, and Ernest Hemingway. The typical profile for those attempting suicide is an unmarried white female possessing no close friend to confide and experiencing an unstable childhood. Also fitting the profile is a history of stressful events both past and present. The suicide completer matches an entirely different profile. Of a 45 year or older white male unmarried or divorced, who lives alone abusing alcohol possessing a significant history of physical or emotional abuse. According to Derkheim upon consideration of mental health professionals not all suicides are pathological. Under specific requirements the Death by Dignity Act would be passed in 1996 and upheld in 2007 by the Oregon Supreme Court, permitting the use of lethal drugs to perform a physician assisted suicide. A result of the great pains of cancer, Freud would request his physician Max Schur to end his suffering on September 21, 1939. Over a 24 hour period Schur would administer the lethal dose of morphine upon the request of Freud (Larson et al., 2007). Social factors may have played a role in Freud's decision to seek the services of Max Schur.

Emphasizing the sociological factors contributing to suicide would be Emile Durkheim. Expressing feelings of alienation and a loss of cohesiveness are subgroup members. Durkheim explains the presence of different suicidal types in altruistic, egoistic, and anomic. Altruistic is a suicide for the good of the cause, egoistic is from lack of group ties, and anomic under the conditions of normlessness (Shneidman, 1985). Among suicidals are different types of suicides involving negative self, anomic, bizarre, spite, inadvertent, altruistic, and realistic. Negative self involves a sense of chronic failure or inadequacy and chronic depression leading to the suicide attempts which in time will lead to fatality. The person's inability to cope with abrupt economic or social conditions results in suicide. The classification of bizarre is the occurrence of hallucination or delusion bringing about the act of suicide. Spite is to kill oneself to inflict pain on another. Inadvertent is a gesture of suicide as an act of manipulation of another yet a misjudgment causes a fatality. Subservient behavior to a group who approve suicidal behavior defines altruistic suicides. Realistic involves the conditions of extreme pain before death precipitating the act of suicide.

The focus of any evaluation should be on the suicidal clues such a person may leave. Suicidal individuals no longer derive pleasure from pursuits and interests and possess a feeling their life is not a continuance of past to present. The suicidal display feelings of hopelessness or helplessness and are generally depressed. When mixed with depression or a crisis another risk factor for suicide can be perfectionism. As compared to depressed individuals perfectionistic suicidals are less responsive to psychotherapy or medication. The successes within treatment a perfectionist may view as failure. Remaining consistent over the years is the basic suicide profile of an older white male living in isolation experiencing depression and feelings of hopelessness. They often possess a medical illness or schizophrenia, abuse alcohol, and are experiencing a loss. Those experiencing panic attacks, borderline personality disorder, and AIDS can fit the suicide profile. Suicidal persons possess a history of suicide attempts, and self damaging acts are part of the family history. They can withdraw from family and friends abruptly. They may revise wills or give away possessions. Suicidals after a long depression can demonstrate sudden cheerfulness. Interpersonal competition may be present with a loved mate or the person may live alone. Individuals may possess a family history of addiction patterns or personal history. Avoid crises instead of facing them and possess a preoccupation with death. Suicidals may be socially isolated and may experience chronic pain. They may have a family history of parental rejection or family instability. They may have a parent or role model who attempted suicide be experiencing depression or psychosis or may possess a family history of depression or psychoses.

Major life stress is often what can trigger the suicidal event. The source of this stress can be the loss of a loved one or a debilitating illness. Suggesting high risks for suicide among high risk mental disorders is violent impulsivity. A serious suicide attempt will be successful 10 – 15% of the time. Of those within the acute suicidal zone only maybe one in 100 will kill him or herself. The probability of attempting and completing a suicide increases under certain factors such as recent and a history of panic attacks. A remission and persistence of secondary depression after a discharge from a psychiatric unit. Cessation of psychotropic medication and absence of therapeutic or friendship alliance. Alcohol and drug abuse and sleep disruption. A high need for seeking stimulation despite suicidal thoughts, cyclical moods, and a propensity toward violence. The loss of a parent or retirement and absence of a support system of family and friends. Ease of access to lethal means and fantasies of death. Viewing oneself as shameful to significant others and increases in self-hatred the result of shameful behavior. High levels of distress or depression, idea death is a means of cessation of distress, and an inability to cope with psychological suffering are all factors in increasing the potential for a suicide attempt. These factors keep in mind are not predictors and the study bases upon long term results when the need is for short term predictions on the individual level. No data can significantly determine if a person will or will not attempt a suicide.

Carley, S. G. (2013). *Serial killers, mass murders, & disorders*. Boston: SGC Production.

Society and the individual can take part in suicide prevention (Phillips, 1974). It is an important step to educate the public in regard to the myths and facts pertaining to suicide. Demonstrating a slight decrease in the suicide rate are suicide prevention telephone hotlines. Restriction on media publicity of suicides is part of suicide prevention on the societal level (Phillips et al., 1993). Initially Phillips (1974) would compile a compilation of stories pertaining to suicide of which would appear on the first page of the New York Times from the years 1946 to 1968. With the appropriate corrections for effects of trends and seasons Phillips' would next examine the suicide statistics within the United States from the years 1947 to 1967. Phillips would conclude basing upon this research suicide attempts within the U.S. would rise after stories pertaining to suicide. This would be termed the Werther effect in recognition of German author Goethe whose fictional character would trigger imitative acts of suicide with his suicide. The four most plausible explanations of the rise in suicide rate under such circumstances are the bereavement explanation, prior conditions explanation, precipitation explanation, and the coroner explanation. The basis to the bereavement explanation in the rise of suicide rates post-story is a result of grief and not imitation. In arguing against this explanation is the fact non-celebrity deaths do not possess an effect on the rate of suicide. The prior conditions explanation is this correlation among post-story suicides is the result of prior social change such as an economic depression possessing the result of increased publicized and non-publicized suicides. This still cannot explain the consistency of post-story suicides. The precipitation explanation is these suicides are inevitable and the story only hastens the decision-making process in committing the act of suicide. If this were so the peak of suicides post-story would be followed by a drop in follow-up periods, which it does not. The coroner explanation is in uncertain cases a suicide may be placed in the category of homicide, undetermined death, or accident. The numbers of deaths among these competing categories should decrease post suicide story, which again they do not.

Research similarly shows fictional suicides on television and movies can produce this same effect. The most compelling evidence is present within research pointing to a 1981 and 1982 west German television fictional broadcast of a student 19 years of age killing himself by throwing himself in front of a moving train (Phillips, Lesyna, and Paight, 1993). After each broadcast nationwide increases of suicides in this manner would increase. The increase would be more prominent within the male population. Not fitting the data are the other competing explanations. Data regarding the Werther effect would find single program associations with suicide rate would be weak yet multiprogramming would possess an effect on the suicide rate. The predisposed groups for suicides as unmarried white males of retirement age are especially prone to the Werther phenomenon.

On the individual level several precautions can be taken in the avoidance of and prevention of suicide. Make a concerted effort in guaranteeing a suicidal individual receives professional help. Encourage suicidal individuals to engage in certain behaviors such as avoidance of self-medication, confide inner feelings among someone, engage in activities in which the individual demonstrates competence, start a diary, follow a normal routine, and regular physical exercise. A suicide attempt is often a cry for help, show some personal concern toward the suicidal person. Keep methods of committing suicide away from suicidal individuals. Depressed individuals with feelings of hopelessness one should attend and take their complaints in a serious manner. Those who voice a desire to kill themselves should be attended to seriously.

Bipolar Disorder

Hippocrates during the 4th century B.C. would suspect manic and depressive symptoms to be part of a single disorder. Since the times of Hippocrates distinguishing has occurred among unipolar and bipolar disorder, a result it is believed of etiological factors (Goodwin & Jamison, 1990). The early twenties according to the DSM-IV-TR is typically the mean age for the onset of bipolar disorder. The broad range of behaviors typifying mania include speeding up of the thought process, euphoria or variable irritability, and hyperactive motor behavior. The speech among manics is often difficult to understand, rapid, and loud. During an expansive mood manics can take on multiple tasks without completing the tasks. Manics also ramble about their worth, power, and personal plans and avoid sleep. Manics are known to complain and engage in hostile tirades when their mood becomes more irritable. Reactions among psychotic manics involve explosiveness, hallucinations, bizarre and impulsive behavior, and delusions of grandeur. These reactions are very similar to schizophrenic episodes (Cullberg, 2006). The differences are manics tend to be distracted by external stimuli, which go unnoticed by others compared to schizophrenics and schizoaffectives who are more distracted by internal thoughts. Manics are also open to contact with others whereas shizophrenics and schizoaffectives during an active phase tend to avoid relationships. Suicide is frequently a complication of bipolar depression as is seen within the case of Virginia Woolf. If untreated approximately 15% will commit suicide. When compared to the general population this is 30 times the rate and among any other medical risk or psychiatric group is by far the highest rate. Of those bipolar patients as many as 82% possess suicidal ideation (Goodwin & Jamison, 1990). The disorder tends to possess a slow onset despite discrete manic episodes which can be sudden. Personal history may display the evidence of childhood and adolescent symptoms that develop into intense and debilitating symptoms as is the case of Virginia Woolf. Bipolar disorder may not always be seen

Carley, S. G. (2013). *Serial killers, mass murders, & disorders.* Boston: SGC Production.

as a negative as at times it may spur creativity as is the case with schizophrenia.

Twenty-four hundred years ago Aristotle would ask why is it those outstanding in the arts, poetry, or philosophy to be melancholic. The English poet John Dryden 300 years ago would write that which would degenerate into the phrase, "There is a thin line between genius and madness." It is not a new concept psychopathy encourages creativity. Research would support a link among creativity and bipolar disorder. As an example artists are more likely to possess the disorder than non-artists, and the rate of alcohol use is over 50% among actors and novelists compared to less than seven percent among military officers and those involving themselves in the physical sciences. Of this group 15% of the actors and poets are believed to have experienced the disorder comparing to those involved in the physical sciences at a rate of less than one percent. Artists who have had bipolar disorder consists of an impressive list led by painter Vincent Van Gogh and poet/painter Dante Gabriel Rosetti and also including the likes of composers George Friederic Handel, Hector Berlioz, Robert Schumann, writers Honore de Balzac and John Ruskin, Virginia Woolf, Ernest Hemingway, F. Scott Fitzgerald, William and Henry James, Herman Melville, and playwright Eugene O'Neill. It is poets who are most often bipolar including John Berryman, Sylvia Plath, Theodore Roethke, Anne Sexton, Robert Lowell, Hart Crane, Gerald Manley Hopkins, Poe, Tennyson, Shelley, Coleridge, and Byron, all bipolar. It may be the inner turbulence of one's psyche causing poets to be bipolars. This pattern of bipolar among poets would continue even during the 18th century as the group would experience at a minimum subclinical hypomanic states. The relationship among bipolar disorder and poetry may be the result of the sporadic effort to effectively produce poetry does not translate to other genres. The inherent imagery present within poetry may be most similar to the severe emotional disruption of primitive thought. The mania of the bipolar mood swing fuels the emotional depth to the productivity of the depressive low. The result is the afflicted artist may avoid therapy in the fear successful treatment could hinder their creativity. It may be in some cases for this to be true.

Virginia Woolf

In terms of prose writing Virginia Woolf is one of the most talented of the twentieth century. Woolf would be one of the first writers to provide a description of the relativity to the individual experience. She would write dozens of literary reviews over the next 30 years including her book The Voyage Out in 1915. Some of her 15 other books would involve classics such as The Waves, To the Lighthouse, and her most famous establishing her as a leader of the woman's rights movement A Room of One's Own. Woolf would reflect upon the extremes of her own life within this book. Her ability to express all ranges of human emotion would make her admired by all. From the time of childhood, Woolf would experience bipolar disorder, through as explained by others, as lapses from sanity. The same highs and lows associating with the disorder would contribute to her passion in novel writing, yet at the same time lead to her destruction (Bell, 1972).

The birth of Virginia Stephen Woolf would occur in Cambridge, England in 1882. Her father was a distinguished editor Sir Leslie Stephen. Woolf would have two step sisters each having a different father and different mother to Virginia. One would have the same mother as Virginia whose father was her first husband. The other the same father as Virginia, Stella Duckworth, from his first wife, who as it turns would be institutionalized for the majority of her life for mental disturbances. On the Duckworth side of her family she would also have two half-brothers. Virginia was close to her extended family and belonged to an upper middle class family stressing the importance of intellectual achievement. Virginia was exceptionally attractive. Virginia was always reading as her father would at a time choose all the books for her to read from his personal library. By the time she reached her teens, he would have to permit Virginia to read what she should choose as she had already read so much. This was a time when this would be considered a great deal of freedom for a girl. Virginia would be envious of her brother Thoby who could attend school, at Cambridge. She could not because she was female. Virginia would receive private lessons in Greek and Latin and would teach herself English literature.

Virginia would describe her mother's death when she was 13 as the greatest possible tragedy as she and her mother were very close (Lehmann, 1975). Upon the death of Virginia's mother her father would become moody, unreasonable, and demanding. The role of their mother would be taken over by her stepsister Stella Duckworth. Virginia would experience her first breakdown as she would become uncontrollably excited and her pulse would race as she would slip ever deeper into depression. Woolf would be prescribed outdoor exercise and she would continue to read often, despite her lessons stopping. Two months after the death of her mother, Stella would pass on whom Virginia deeply loved. Virginia's father instead of showing self pity would become tyrannical. Vanessa the next oldest sister would replace Stella in the mother role. Mr. Stephen's inconsideration for Vanessa left her with mixed emotions regarding her father. Virginia would experience an even more extreme breakdown upon the death of her father in 1904. She would experience moments of intense irritation accompanied by headaches escalating to a severe manic state and feelings of guilt pertaining to her father. Virginia would make a suicide attempt by jumping out of a window, the result of perhaps evil nurses as she would refuse to eat. She would experience hallucinations finding birds to be chirping in Greek and that King Edward VII was hiding among the bushes. At this time in Woolf's life no effective treatment for her disorder had been discovered. The doctors examining her would prescribe only rest.

Virginia would deficiently develop sexually as she had been sexually abused by both of her half brothers. At the age of five Gerald would examine her genitals, and when she was a teenager George would periodically fondle her in her bedroom. Virginia would fall deeply in love during her adolescence with her cousin, Madge a girl. Virginia would next fall in love with an older woman who would assist her during her breakdowns. It is not clear whether or not these women knew the extent of Virginia's affection. Virginia and her five siblings would travel to Greece after the death of both of her parents. Thoby would die from a typhoid fever attack from impure milk another painful loss for Virginia. Virginia would be left alone with her younger brother when her older sister would marry. The weekly social group her sister started, Virginia and her brother would take over. Virginia over many weeks would become more willing to express her opinions and become more outgoing. Virginia would become known for her sharp tongue.

Virginia's career would lead her to writing book reviews for well respected magazines. Many men would pursue Viriginia, yet she would marry Lytton Strachey, who upon marrying her would confess his homosexuality. A friend of Lytton, Leonard Woolf would begin to date Virginia. In August of 1912 they would marry, despite her moderate anti-Semitic views and Leonard's Jewish heritage. Leonard would truly love Virginia, yet with her sexual preference for females she did not respond sexually to Leonard. Leonard would describe Virginia as losing contact with reality demonstrating lapses in sanity. Virginia would possess the delusion her nurses were evil and would experience intense bouts of guilt, depression, and wild excitement. One such episode she would talk continually for several days without stopping until she would fall into a stupor. During her altered states Virginia would recall most of the happenings. It would seem when Virginia to be in the late stages of her novels in which her episodes would occur. Virginia would experience no serious relapses during the 1920s a result of the forced rest and quiet bestowed upon her by Leonard. Virginia would become quite famous and would be invited to give lectures at both Cambridge and the United States to receive public honors. Virginia would make a habit of turning down such invitations. Virginia would sense another attack coming in the late stages of her writing Between the Acts in 1941. She would experience very real and endless fears and tormenting voices. Virginia was convinced more than ever the suffering would continue and never stop. Upon this Virginia would write her farewell letters to both her sister and husband Leonard. She would proceed to fill her pockets with stones and drown herself in a nearby river. This is her letter to Leonard (Bell, 1972):

"Dearest,

I feel certain I am going mad again. I feel we can't go through another of those terrible times. And I shan't recover this time. I begin to hear voices, and I can't concentrate. So I am doing what seems the best thing to do. You have given me the greatest possible happiness. You have been in every way all that anyone could be. I don't think two people could have been happier till this terrible disease came. I can't fight any longer. I know that I am spoiling your life, that without me you could work. And you will I know. You see I can't even write this properly. I can't read. What I want to say is I owe all the happiness of my life to you. You have been entirely patient with me and incredibly good. I want to say that—everybody knows it. If anybody could have saved me it would have been you. Everything has gone from me but the certainty of your goodness. I can't go on spoiling your life any longer. I don't think two people could have been happier than we have been."

Carley, S. G. (2013). *Serial killers, mass murders, & disorders.* Boston: SGC Production.

Causes of Bipolar Disorder and Diagnosis

Bipolar disorder separates into different diagnostic categories: mixed, depressive, or manic basing upon the last episode. The categorization of Bipolar I Disorder also is dependent on seasonal patterns of depressive episodes, accompaniment by rapid cycling, and the long term pattern of the illness. Occurring within 10 – 20% of bipolars is rapid cycling (four occurrences or more in a 12 month span) and females are more predisposed to rapid cycling. Virginia would fit the criteria of Bipolar I Disorder at her death showing depression as her most recent episode. The requirements for this diagnosis involve the ruling out of the similar features of other disorders such as delusional disorder or schizoaffective disorder. Bipolar II disorder is distinguished from bipolar I within the DSM-IV-TR replacing manic episode requirements with a hypomanic episode. In the case of a polar shift or greater than two month intervals between episodes the disorder becomes recurrent. The propensity for psychosis is another aspect of the disorder. According to DSM requirements under the conditions of severe bipolar illness, a subject may be classified severe with mood incongruent psychotic features, severe with mood congruent features, or severe with psychotic features. The delusions and hallucinations Virginia would experience would classify her as the third type. Common over the life course of bipolar disorder is a decrease in interval duration of manic and depressive episodes. At times although rare, patients may experience strictly manic symptoms with the absence of depression. In existence is a bipolar pattern among the overwhelming majority. Elevated and expansive moods characterize manic phases. Manic episodes are defined with the DSM-IV-TR as periods of persistent and unusual irritability, expansiveness, or mood elevation lasting a duration of longer than seven days or in the case of a hospitalization any length of time. The requirement for a diagnosis is for three symptoms or four in the case mood is irritable instead of expansive: despite high potential painful consequences extreme involvement in pleasurable activities, increase in agitation or goal directed activities, racing thoughts, talkativeness, and a decreased need for sleep. In Virginia's case she would experience both irritable and expansive variations of the bipolar. She would also possess agitation, racing thoughts, distractibility, and pressured speech.

Manic or depressive episodes can last months or years, still others can last only a matter of minutes. Mixed mania may present itself in which depression and mania are experienced concurrently. Such individuals experience energy and weariness or despair and euphoria at the same time (Goodwin & Jamison, 1990). A poorer prognosis remains for rapid cycling. While experiencing mania the imagination of the bipolar patient would seem to go into overdrive placing extreme significance on the ordinary. The patient is seemingly devoid of common sense. The poor judgment of manics possesses certain consequences such as self destructive sexual relationships, drastic career changes, extravagant purchases, and imprudent marriages. Violence toward oneself and others becomes at a heightened risk (Bongar, 2002). In time mania will gravitate toward depression. The pain of the depression is as a nightmare as sadness turns to despair. The depressions of Virginia she describes as unbearable and extreme. The common feelings of this phase involve exhaustion and hopelessness. Also typical of this phase are Virginia's self deprecatory comments and low self esteem.

Family studies would indicate the genetic transmission of bipolar disorder. This is in the concordance of dizygotic and monozygotic twins and existing correlations among biological relatives and adopted persons (Nathan, 1995). Genetic loading from either or both sides of the family increases the risks of obtaining bipolar disorder. As of yet no definitive conclusions have been drawn in regard to the location of the genetic mode of transmission. One such standard treatment of the disorder is lithium because of its ability to modify mood swings violent in nature (Cullberg, 2006). The use of lithium can occur during an active episode or prophylactically. Patients already experiencing three or more episodes, lithium may provide less protection. The effects of lithium are not immediate, and according to Goodwin (1994) the assertion is the evaluation of its effectiveness could take years, concluding the benefits of lithium to be minimal. Only half of the bipolar population may be responsive to lithium therapy. Certain factors may attribute to the ineffectiveness of lithium such as the pattern of symptoms, more rapid cycles of mania to depression, comorbid psychological and physical disorders, problematic side effects, and the initial symptom being a psychotic one. The expectations of a successful lithium treatment are really quite limited. The individual taking lithium is not immune to a manic or depressive relapse. Of users of lithium the concordance rate is 70% will not experience a relapse after one year's time. This number drops proportionately at three and five years to 50% and 35% respectively.

One such side effect of lithium are tremors in conjunction with the dulling of senses, lethargy, hypothyroidism, acne, decrease in sexual interest, altered sense of taste, problems concentrating, memory impairment, weight gain, nausea, and occasional tardive dyskinesia. Increasing suicide risk is the discontinuation of lithium. These limitations can make for the necessity for other drug treatments either substituted, alternated, or combined. Helpful as an adjunct drug is duloxetine in the case physical pain is part of the depression. Relating to the sensitivity model of bipolar disorder are the explanations for those no longer finding the benefits of lithium therapy. Relating to this model are later episodes occur without an environmental stimulus, and the primary involvement of psychosocial stressors occurs during the early episodes of bipolar disorder. According to theory after numerous episodes the bipolar disorder becomes autonomous. This explanation makes the long term maintenance and early institution of lithium therapy critical.

Carley, S. G. (2013). *Serial killers, mass murders, & disorders.*
Boston: SGC Production.

Timely treatment is a must as the neurobiological claim the disorder can possess on the central nervous system can be minimized (Post, 1993). In addition the systems supporting compliance can be critical. Families should learn to recognize the early signs of episodes, in addition to educating themselves on the course of the illness, the side effects, and the medications. A requirement in most cases also involves cognitive behavior modification and supportive psychotherapy (Reinecke et al., 2008).

Virginia's marriage to Leonard was fortunate for her as until her death, he would remain dedicated to the marriage. Often the impact this illness can have on a marriage is devastating. It may only take one bad day for loyalty, affection, and trust to dissipate among the relationship. The inconsistent treatment of spouses and children can create confusion and strong emotional reactions (McCullough, 2002). The manic state of the bipolar individual can create even more problems by engaging in affairs, inappropriate sexual advances toward others, and threats of divorce. It is important to educate both society and family. The profit motive within pharmacological research may help explain the evolution of lithium as an effective treatment. The first isolation of the chemical element lithium would occur in 1817 by a young Swedish chemistry student by the name of John Arfwedson. The name would arise because John would find the element in stone. It would occur by chance during the 1940s where an Australian psychiatrist, John Cade, would discover the positive effects of lithium on mania. This would occur in a study of whether manic depressive episodes could be caused by uric acid. Human subjects would be injected with urea from guinea pigs. In adding lithium urate to the uric acid, Cade would find the urea to become less toxic. The curative properties of lithium would be indicated through further experimentation. There would be some time between the discovery of lithium and the widespread use and marketing of the product. It would be the more exotic less available compounds receiving the attention. Two plausible explanations exist, as a naturally occurring element lithium cannot be patented and concern exists over the side effects of lithium. Of more interest to drug companies is gaining control of the market and substantial profits helping to explain the research into new synthetic compounds.

Carley, S. G. (2013). *Serial killers, mass murders, & disorders*. Boston: SGC Production.

Marna (Munchausen by Proxy Syndrome)

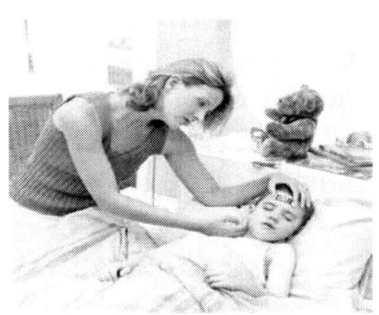

Factitious Disorder

In consideration for the diagnosis of a factitious disorder one should also consider the possibility of a malingering disorder. The labelings make reference to a client's voluntary production of symptoms to receive a labeling of physically or psychologically disturbed. It is the motivations for this presentation as the primary differences (Johnson, 2008). The motivations of the malingerer is the appearance of illness in gaining a logical goal. The possible goal being exemption from financial compensation for alleged injuries or criminal responsibility. The manifestation of the factitious disorder by psychological symptoms is the less common form. Physiological symptoms of factitious disorder are most common the pattern of which describes Munchausen's syndrome. The naming of Munchausen's syndrome is after the eighth century German equivalent to Paul Bunyan, Baron Von Munchausen (Janofsky, 1994). It is client psychology, in which the motivation to appear needful will stem, as opposed to malingering shared goals. The limitations and ranges of symptomology is a product of individual imagination, and degree of sophistication pertaining to medical information (Boyd et al., 2007). Contributing to the disorder is experience through previous hospitalizations, hospital situations, or acquisition of knowledge from family members. To elicit care from

Carley, S. G. (2013). *Serial killers, mass murders, & disorders*. Boston: SGC Production.

nurses, physicians, and psychologists persons can become reliant on their illness and ill behaviors. A commonality among factitious disorder is a lack in bonding personal relationships, providing alternative supports. Mr. McIlroy a skilled patient would receive over 200 hospital admissions in Britain subjecting himself to hundreds of painful treatments and procedures (Pallis & Bamji, 1979). The strength of compulsion of being viewed in the patient role becomes ever more obvious through the individual's willingness to submit to such rigors. Munchausen's syndrome may be rare yet continues to be a consistent disorder at the same time. The characteristics of Munchausen syndrome include physiological complaints presented by a dramatic patient. The patient exaggerates the illness exhibiting Pseudologia Fantastica. To minimize communication a patient will make use of hospital networks within different geographical locations.

Munchausen by Proxy Syndrome

A form of factitious disorder is Munchausen by Proxy Syndrome in which a caregiver induces psychological or physiological symptoms on a child followed by the continuous seeking of medical intervention. This disorder would first be described in Leeds, England, in 1977 by pediatrician Dr. Roy Meadow. This form of child abuse can often be fatal. Most often the perpetrator is the mother who will present the role of model parent only to premeditate destructive behaviors. The code for the disorder in the DSM-IV-TR is as a factitious disorder yet is referenced as a factitious disorder by proxy. The causes of the disorder are difficult to understand, but it would seem the cause to relate to the fulfillment of certain psychological needs among the caregiver. It is not uncommon for the perpetrators of Munchausen syndrome by proxy to have been one time experiencing Munchausen syndrome.

Carley, S. G. (2013). *Serial killers, mass murders, & disorders.*
Boston: SGC Production.

Marna

Marna was a former nurse and 37 year old housewife, who after her six year old daughter Prudence would be admitted to the hospital with severe vomiting, would be arrested. Upon conviction, Marna would face up to 45 years in prison for charges of fraud and aggravated child abuse. Over a 2.5 year span this particular visit to the hospital would be Prudence's 68th visit. Prudence is Marna's 4th child and until the age of four she was mostly healthy. Prudence's two older brothers would experience a similar occurrence when they were young experiencing similar symptoms. They would recover around the time Marna's third child Penny was born who would die during infancy. The diagnosis was sudden infant death syndrome. Prudence would be born one month later. During the early course of Prudence's illness several times Marna would bring her to the emergency room with reports of seizures. The physician would treat Prudence with medication increasing the dose when the seizures would seem to worsen. The medication would be discontinued when the desired effect would not occur after a few months. Marna would state her to believe Prudence to be experiencing the rare and often fatal blood infection sepsis. The hospital would notice no symptoms associating with sepsis. For three years between the ages of four to six Prudence would possess treatments for various chronic conditions including seizure disorders, immune system deficiency, and gastrointestinal problems. Prudence's trouble eating would result in the insertion of a tube into her stomach, the beginning of 27 enduring operations. These other operations would require tubes inserted into her intestines, stomach, and surgery in the area of her heart. Prudence would be part of 700 minor procedures spending a total of over 600 days in the hospital. Marna would always present herself with intense concern over her daughter's medical problem, yet verbalize confidence in the abilities of the attending staff. Marna would always show distress when leaving Prudence in the hospital explaining to the staff to take good care of her baby. Marna would

Carley, S. G. (2013). *Serial killers, mass murders, & disorders.*
Boston: SGC Production.

become attached to the charge nurse of the children's ward Lynne bringing her gifts, and explaining how they had so much in common her being a former RN. The medical bills would pile up over time adding up to over one-million dollars in payouts by Medicare. Marna would organize fundraisers and would even have a couple of professional athletes and local celebrities visit her daughter. The abnormal frequency of Prudence's symptoms would cause the medical staff of the hospital to over time become suspicious. The staff would make note of Marna closing the curtains and door prior to the worsening of Prudence's symptoms. They would note a commonality of the increase in symptoms when discharge was a day or two away. They would also learn contradictions in Marna's stories pertaining to her past. Lynne would have lunch with a nurse who used to work with Marna, where she would find out Marna was an LPN and not an RN. Lynne was told of her husband she loved very much, who was never at any of their functions. Lynne would recall never hearing any mention of Marna's husband herself.

Nursing staff would take a more extensive lab analysis of Prudence's vomit during her final admission. They would find discontinued antiseizure medications in a toxic dose. Marna would be arrested and Prudence put into foster care. The condition of Prudence would improve and she never again would deteriorate. The investigation that would follow would involve the examination of thousands of medical documents pertaining to Prudence's medical records. They would find doctor's orders in Marna's handwriting and that Marna would tamper with the speed of her IV pump. During the trial expert witnesses would testify Prudence to show no evidence of the symptoms of the illness in claim, beyond the explanation by Marna's intervention. With so many different systems it would seem unlikely for someone to suffer from problems. Marna would be sentenced to five years for Medicaid fraud and aggravated child abuse. During an appeal of the case, the case of her other daughter Penny who had died would be reopened.

Carley, S. G. (2013). *Serial killers, mass murders, & disorders.*
Boston: SGC Production.

Marna would be convicted for the first degree murder of her daughter Penny and sentenced to life in prison.

Diagnosis of Munchausen by proxy syndrome is often difficult because of both little awareness of the disorder and reluctance to diagnose such a disorder (Johnson, 2008). Facilitation of a diagnosis of MBPS can occur through a multidisciplinary team familiar with the disorder using specific guidelines (Parnell, 1997, pp. 48–50). These guidelines divide into three categories family features, mother-perpetrator features, and child-victim features. Upon suspicion of MBPS a practitioner should consider these guidelines in determining the use of appropriate intervention and to refute or confirm the diagnosis upon compiling all necessary and pertinent data. Child-victim guidelines in the identification of MBPS involve unexplained persistent and recurring illness by a consulting physician following a thorough examination. Diagnosis of a rare disorder descriptive of symptoms. Unresponsive symptoms to a common treatment regimen, and inconsistent laboratory findings with the reported history. Symptoms and physical findings at odds with the general healthy appearance of a child. A temporal relationship among the mother's presence and the symptoms of the child. An unsubstantiated pertinent medical history and complaints of lethargy, fever, vomiting, diarrhea, apnea, unconsciousness, and bleeding seizures.

Mother-perpetrator features involve while the child is in the hospital showing a reluctance to leave the child. Close personal relationships developing among the hospital staff. A desire to be employed by the medical staff or background in the medical field. In terms of child care an unusual calmness when facing problems. Unusual symptoms of medical problems similar to those of the child. Fabricating information pertinent to one's personal life. Family features guidelines involve the unexplained death or illness of a sibling of the child in care. An emotionally distant marital relationship. Family history of emotional, physical, or sexual abuse. A pattern of illnesses within the family origin.

Treatment Options

Treatment of MBPS would involve two parties one for the child victim and the other of the parent perpetrator. Upon a diagnosis of MBPS mental health professionals should work closely with the medical team in formulating treatment goals. For victims of MBPS over the age of three psychotherapy is a necessity. Depending on the age of the child when he or she is rescued from the mother (or father) the treatment options can vary (Ayoub, Deutsch, & Kinscherff, 2000). In general three and four year olds take the blame for separation from a parent. These children should have it made clear their removal from a parent is for their own safety, and they have in fact committed no wrongful or unjust act. Victims at this age are accustomed to the accompanying symptoms of their illness developing a sick child identity. The therapeutic goals are to increase individual autonomy in forming a new more healthy identity. Children over the age of seven may develop with the perpetrator an enmeshed relationship difficult to alter. The reason is the isolation of the child by the parent, limiting social interaction among other children. Engaging in normal social functions is replaced with the induction and fabrication of sickness. Upon rescue from the situation a conflict of loyalty is experienced by the child. Adolescent victims of MBPS possess little formation of identity outside the one associating with their mother. Adolescence should be a time of separation from caregivers and the development of identity. Common among cases of MBPS is a lack of autonomy and extreme dependence upon mother. When not in the presence of mother a child may even feign illness. The core belief of the dysfunctional child as helpless and irreparably impaired should be addressed through therapeutic sessions. The therapist should provide services only to the victim and not the family as the role of the therapist should be central toward the victim's improvement.

Psychotherapy toward the mother-perpetrators of MBPS tends to be ineffective (Ayoub et al., 2000). The extreme perpetrators such as Marna will continue their behavior during or after legal system and psychotherapeutic participation. The recommendation is for an absence of treatment is not in the case of an induction of illness upon a child by a mother. The child should be removed from the mother's care. Successful therapy is possible and through the meeting of certain conditions reunification may even be an option. These conditions involve the acknowledgement of the presence of MBPS. Participation in intensive individual therapy by an experienced mental health professional in treatment for MBPS. Participation in the treatment by other family members who possess an understanding of the disorder and have made repeated attempts to protect the child. Therapeutic improvement is dependent on the recognition of the creation of alternative coping methods with feelings of abandonment, recognition of inappropriate behaviors, and cessation of such behaviors. In lessening sensations of perpetrator isolation marital therapy can be useful. Should young children at home not feel threatened the initiation of family therapy may occur. The participation of a child-victim may be necessary within the presence of a therapist. Crucial for success and reunification is the treatment of a father permitting the behavior to occur and who remains in the marriage. The separation or divorce of a father before the presence or noticing of any abuse may be more willing to acknowledge the presence of child abuse. The therapeutic goal is the maintenance of support toward a child by the parents, especially so should the perpetrator continue to deny the presence or existence of any form or type of abuse. The primary concern is always the safety of the child. Termination of parental rights should always be considered should a child be at a high risk factor for injury or death.

Carley, S. G. (2013). *Serial killers, mass murders, & disorders.*
Boston: SGC Production.

The popularity of detecting deception through physiological measurements possesses of numerous approaches. At times this process can be a simple measure. The most common method of detecting deceit is the polygraph otherwise known as the lie-detecting device. The polygraph functions through measurements of physiological arousal arising from numerous emotional responses such as sexual arousal, anger, fear, and lying. The naming of the polygraph is such as it measures several functions of the body including blood pressure, heart rate, and respiration. The influence of the results obtained from the polygraph occur through a client's willingness to accept a belief, examiner skill in making the client believe deception will be noticeable, and the employment of questioning techniques. The variety of arousal sources the polygraph can detect may result in the inaccuracy of the polygraph record. The claim of professional polygraphers is the polygraph is in fact highly accurate in making sound judgments (Boyd et al., 2007).

Carley, S. G. (2013). *Serial killers, mass murders, & disorders.* Boston: SGC Production.

Jack Ruby

Childhood and Adolescence

Many still remember where they were on Friday November 22, 1963 when Jacqueline would motorcade through the streets of Dallas, Texas, with President John F Kennedy as he would be assassinated. The person responsible for this murder or at least who would be kept captive would be Lee Harvey Oswald who would consequently be imprisoned in a Dallas, Texas, jail. A short two days later on November 24 Jack Ruby would enter the basement of the jail Oswald was being imprisoned during a transfer to a new facility. Through a legion of police Ruby would somehow manage to fatally shoot Oswald. Controversy would build surrounding Ruby's motives for Kennedy's assassination through his many connections with crime. In diagnosing Ruby's mental status several approaches could occur. One such approach may be to view the early years of Jack Ruby followed by alternative theories focusing on Ruby's adult life (Summers, 1980).

Ruby would be born Jacob Rubenstein the fifth of eight children, he would be born in Chicago, Illinois, in 1911. The marriage of Ruby's parents would be an arrangement through a Polish Jewish marriage broker. His uneducated mother Fannie Rubenstein would come with a dowry. She was an incessant talker and emotionally unstable individual much like Ruby. Joseph Rubenstein Jack's father was short, stocky, and mean. Jack's father would have no trade to speak of and had the tendency to curse, drink, and abuse women. It would be a frequent occurrence where Joseph would abuse Fannie physically. The couple was originally from Poland and would move to America in 1905. Jack would grow up in a poor unhappy home and the frequent violence and fights among his parents would result in his mother filing assault and battery charges against Joseph. On a regular basis Joseph would slap his children insisting their education end after grade school. Jack's parents would separate when he was just 10 years of age. Jack along with his siblings would be placed in foster homes. Jack would occasionally stay with his mother who would abuse him physically and emotionally. Jack's mother was compulsive, lazy, and demanding throwing temper tantrums when she would not get her way. Jack's mother would announce her dislike for her children. At the age of 61 in 1937 she would be committed to a mental hospital with a diagnosis of deteriorating paranoia. The term would reference a degree of organic deterioration.

When Jack was eleven he would become noticeably defiant and depressed. Jack would be disobedient to authority and constantly skip school. Jack was described by the welfare department of possessing an adequate IQ, and that he was impulsive, would possess an inability to pay attention, and was self centered. Jacob would spend all of his time in the streets at age 16 having dropped out of school. His attempts at a job would be unsuccessful a result of tardiness and a violent disposition. Jack would make money through different means selling chocolates at strip shows, peanuts at athletic games, pushcart novelties, and race track tip sheets. Jack would also scalp tickets and run errands for Al Capone. Jack would make it a habit to work out in the gym and wearing expensive clothes would be seen by many a ladies' man. Jack's reputation was for

Carley, S. G. (2013). *Serial killers, mass murders, & disorders.* Boston: SGC Production.

committing senseless acts of violence. It was Jack's determination to prove to the world he was a man. Those expressing anti-Semitic feelings, Jack would get in fights with defending his Jewish heritage. When Jack was a teenager he would fight in a gang against those who would otherwise taunt Jews. Jack Ruby's murder of Oswald may possess different theories along with different facts relevant to the case to each theory.

Social Psychological Theory

Behavior from a social psychological view is the result of interactions among the person and environment. An explanation for Jack's tendency toward violence and crime could be the learned behavior from his parents during his childhood. It would seem Jack to learn, his parents would not love him. An individual with two conflicting beliefs according to cognitive dissonance theory experiences stress or tension, and motivation is the result of searching for the different means of removing any existing conflict. Ruby's childhood conflicts could involve "My parents love me and the feeling is mutual," and "My cruel parents do not like me." A means of resolving such conflict may be to form the conclusion "I really don't need my parents, so it really doesn't matter what I think of them, and consequently what they should think of me for that matter." Jack's resort to criminal activities may be a learning process of not caring for the values of society. When Jack was 26 years of age he would become an organizer for the scrap iron workers' union. Ruby would work alongside Jimmy Hoffa, head of the Teamsters Union and leader of the underworld. It would be Hoffa who would threaten the life of John F Kennedy. Ruby would be entrenched among some of the most notorious criminal leaders of Chicago by the age of 28.

Another theory on Ruby's tendency to commit crimes would be the diathesis stress theory claiming, individual weaknesses and

Carley, S. G. (2013). *Serial killers, mass murders, & disorders.*
Boston: SGC Production.

strengths can cause behavior as stress increases individual weaknesses can surface. In Ruby's twenties his gang would attack anti-Semites, and when in his thirties upon being called a Jew bastard, he would beat a sergeant senseless. The diathesis to Jack is being a Jew among groups of people who possess dislike for the Jewish culture. Ruby's predisposition to violence could act as another diathesis triggering stress when taunted, or exposed to hatred for being a Jew or otherwise. Of recent times the role of the media in facilitating societal violence has gained increasing awareness. Researcher Edward Donnerstein would find physical aggression rates among television programs has held a steady figure for several years at or near 60%, yet can escalate to even higher rates during prime time. The study consensus would find the attractive and good characters and child role models commit more than 40% of the violent acts. In featuring bad characters more than a third of them go unpunished, condoning their physical aggression. Children often will not make the connection when in the end the bad guy is punished. Aggressors 70% of the time will show no remorse for violent actions, and experience no penalty or criticism when the violent act should occur. Television violence, half of which is no evidence of physical injury, or suffering from a victim or negative community or family impact.

Genetic Theories, Biological Theories, and Organic Theories

The deteriorating paranoia found in Ruby's mother would give indications of inherited genetic predispositions to organic dysfunction resulting in false beliefs or delusions. Let us look at Ruby's mid-fifties, while in jail for shooting Oswald, he would be of the belief Jews may receive torture and punishment for his crime. This belief would be even more apparent after his conviction for first degree murder. As Ruby's mother got older, she too would experience an increase in delusional behavior. The organic explanation for Ruby's behavior would be used as his defense in his court trial. Ruby would profess his innocence on the grounds of temporary insanity, the result of psychomotor epilepsy. The two major subgroups of epileptic seizures include partial and focal epilepsy. Such seizures begin in a limited section of the brain, and either stay in the vicinity or spread adjacently. Such forms of epilepsy may or may not associate with loss of consciousness. Involving larger areas of the brain are generalized epileptic seizures definitively involving loss of consciousness. A complex partial seizure can be described by psychomotor epileptic seizures. Such seizures involve the experience of illusion and behavioral responses to the stimulus of an illusion. With the application of such a diagnosis to Ruby, his behavior before and during the shooting would be seen as outside normal consciousness. Ruby may have had hallucinations experiencing visions he would find real, and his shooting would be a response to these hallucinations. Ruby's lawyers would claim the shooting to place in the midst of an epileptic blackout. This diagnosis could not explain the fact the act was planned. Besides Ruby did not exhibit the physical course associating with psychomotor epilepsy. Making a persuasive argument this was Ruby's first seizure would be difficult to prove and unusual, no evidence would exist of subsequent seizures. The course of a psychomotor epileptic seizure is one in which after the initial seizure the production of future seizures would take less stimulation. No evidence would exist Ruby would be prescribed anticonvulsant drug therapy for his condition. A brain tumor at Ruby's autopsy however would support the diagnosis.

Testimony supporting psychomotor epilepsy would be making the claim of a loss of Ruby's consciousness; however, a more appropriate diagnosis would seem more along the lines of a dissociative disorder. The predominant condition of such a feature is an interruption of the integrated mechanisms of consciousness. This diagnosis too would seem difficult in proving possessing no subsequent events with similarities to the dissociative experience.

Carley, S. G. (2013). *Serial killers, mass murders, & disorders.*
Boston: SGC Production.

Using psychomotor epilepsy as the defense, it would be of no surprise Jack Ruby would be charged with first degree murder and receive a sentence of death. An alternative biological perspective on violence contends it is only the human, which will kill members of the same species without reason of survival. Contrary to this statement in Gombe National Park in Tanzania eight chimpanzees would travel to the border of their range entering the territory of a neighboring chimpanzee. They would attack and mortally wound the young male chimpanzee and return to their quarters. This would mark the first lethal raiding among chimpanzees. The significance of the event is in the deliberate killing of one's own, killing with no purpose and among a specie closely related to humans as compared to other species. Gratuitous violence would exist among other species upon further research.

Affective Disorder Theory as an Explanation for Ruby's Criminal Tendencies

It is possible Ruby would suffer from an affective disorder along the lines of cyclothemia, bipolar disorder, or atypical depression. In existence is insufficient evidence in determining Ruby's proneness to mania or uncharacteristic activity. It is known Ruby would experience depression such as when the welfare department would describe Ruby as a depressed child. Ruby would admit as a means of fighting depression to overeat (Williams et al., 2008). To gain energy Ruby would take medication to suppress his appetite. Ruby who would become obsessed with his hair loss would then stop taking the weight loss medication. Antisocial personality disorder as an example manifests itself throughout the person's life. Depression and related affective disorders risk and possess the opportunity for remission. A sort of remission would occur in 1944 when Ruby would lose his mother and join the U.S. Army Air Force. Ruby's previous behavior patterns would contradict his behavior in the Army Air Force. As an aircraft mechanic he would rarely get in fights and would even be awarded a medal of good conduct. Upon his discharge in 1946 he would be a private first class. Ruby was not seeking out the life of a criminal. Upon his return to civilian life he would struggle for eight years in his business with his brothers who would sell key chains, punch boards, and other miscellaneous items. The three would constantly fight, and for a few years after leaving the business Jack would not speak to his brothers. This may have brought about the return of Ruby's mood swings. During this time, Ruby would receive instructions from organized crime members to travel to Dallas, Texas. With depression comes psychosis and with a verdict of electrocution, Ruby would lose all hope (DeBattista, 1998). Ruby's delusions of the death of all Jews would reoccur, and the realization of never seeing his dogs again would set in. On death row Ruby would attempt suicide multiple times, one such method would be to smash his head off the concrete wall in hopes of cracking his skull. Ruby's depression was more evident than ever.

Ruby's Bout With Psychopathy

Ruby's criminal life beginning during childhood would support a diagnosis of psychopathy or antisocial personality disorder for that matter. Through connections with Cuba, Ruby would be linked to the underworld of the U.S. government. This would take place through the smuggling of guns and ammunition to Cuba's Fidel Castro. To ensure good relations, organized crime would support Castro upon the end of the revolution. This same group in time would turn on Castro as he would not endorse their activities. The wishes of the underworld for the death of John F Kennedy may not have been a coincidence. Ruby would demonstrate consistent activities characteristic of antisocial personality disorder. As an example the very name Ruby would associate with the expansion of Dallas' organized crime network. Ruby would operate bootleg whiskey and smuggle narcotics. Ruby would open nightclubs the

Carley, S. G. (2013). *Serial killers, mass murders, & disorders.* Boston: SGC Production.

underworld figures could regularly attend. Those who crossed Ruby he would beat up without punishment. In all Ruby would be arrested nine times for violent acts while operating the night club. The only punishment he would ever receive would be for a traffic violation. This would be reflective of the manipulation and the extent of his contacts with judges and law enforcement officials. The willingness to kill for money is a trait associating with antisocial personality disorder. It is believed this would be the compelling force causing Ruby to kill Oswald. Prior to Kennedy's assassination in 1963 Ruby would experience financial difficulties. Ruby would be forced to sell one of his night clubs the result of debt and unpaid taxes. Ruby would agonize over finance yet before the assassination would feel confident his financial troubles would soon end. Three days before Kennedy's assassination on November 19, 1963 Ruby would explain to a lawyer he had a connection permitting him to pay his debts. Evidence suggests after Kennedy's assassination Ruby would receive large sums of cash. Deceit is yet another characteristic of antisocial personality disorder (Boyd et al., 2007). Following the assassination Ruby would frequent public places displaying grief over President Kennedy's assassination. This a possible reflection of the dissociative process. The deceit would continue as after killing Oswald, Ruby would deny his connections to the Cuban underworld. Ruby would explain his motives to killing Oswald to alleviate the discomfort Mrs. Kennedy would endure through a painful trial with Oswald. Contradictions may exist toward the psychopathy-antisocial personality disorder theory. The most evident is the manner in which Ruby would kill Oswald. Ruby would know for sure he would be caught and punished for his crime, a psychopath would surely avoid this action. The appropriateness to these theories would not free Ruby from a first degree murder conviction for taking the life of Lee Harvey Oswald on March 14, 1964 and sentencing by penalty of death. While awaiting a new trial to overturn the death penalty conviction Ruby would die of cancer in 1967.

Carley, S. G. (2013). *Serial killers, mass murders, & disorders.* Boston: SGC Production.

Causes for Violent Behavior and Strategies of Intervention

Causes for violent behavior are numerous along with the consensus strategies for intervention. Violence would seem an inherent part to human nature. Intervention can involve psychotherapy in the attempt to modify basic personality patterns. Medication can minimize inappropriate reaction and diminish anxiety. Psychosurgery is even an option to interrupt brain functioning patterns. A second potential cause for violent behavior is as a consequence of social learning. Interventions can involve family therapy to facilitate the coping mechanism in the family setting. Group therapy can assist in the enhancement of appropriate coping mechanisms within the social setting. To better assert oneself without the use of violence one can make use of assertiveness and social skills training. Systematic desensitization can diminish inappropriate reactions. To strengthen appropriate responses removal of environmental reinforcers can occur, extinguishing violent behavior through the processes of token economy, time out, or social isolation. Another means of extinguishing violent behavior is through classical conditioning in a similar means to aversive conditioning. Parents Anonymous a form of parent effectiveness training can enhance the adequate coping skills providing for a supportive peer group. A third cause for violent behavior is as a consequence to the situational factors leading to frustration. One means of releasing such frustrations is through traditional psychotherapy and changing patterns of coping. Other means involve family therapy, group therapy, and assertiveness and social skills training. A token economy should provide for opportunities to extinguish violent behavior in concurrently reinforcing positive experiences (Carley, 2012). Parent effectiveness training is also a useful means in suppressing violent behavior. Violence as a means of communication is yet another cause for violence. Interventions involve expressive therapies offering substitute or alternative means of expressing violent feelings. Assertiveness training, systematic desensitization, and parent effectiveness training can each be effective in suppressing violent tendencies and the tendencies causing violent behavior. A final cause of violent behavior is the aggression and violence present within the protection of territory and body space. Effective means of intervention include systematic desensitization, assertiveness training, and individual psychotherapy improving one's self concept and self esteem.

It may be a formidable task to predict violent behavior before its onset. This can be one of the major tasks of the mental health professional. The lack of consistent accuracy would make for the term risk assessment. On a personal level it may be an unpleasant and anxiety provoking situation bringing psychologists ever too close to the dark side of the human condition. The California Supreme Court would increase professional difficulties with their ruling in the Tarasoff vs. Regents of the University of California case. After a ritual New Year's Eve kiss among Prosejit Poddar and the object of his affection Tatiana Tarasoff, Poddar in a therapy session would claim he felt like killing Tarasoff. As the campus police would be sent to pick Poddar up, he would convincingly pose himself no problem, and the campus police would leave. Poddar would later kill Tarasoff and her estate would sue. The California Supreme Court would find the therapist to possess the duty of warning Tarasoff of Poddar's threats, an amended duty to protect. It would be the low base rates in predictability of behavior causing the therapist to make such a decision as accurate prediction is next to impossible and overprediction common (Meyer & Weaver, 2006).

Carley, S. G. (2013). *Serial killers, mass murders, & disorders.* Boston: SGC Production.

O.J. Simpson

American Consciousness

The forefront of American consciousness would be conquered by O.J. Simpson and the grucsome details of the events leading to his late wife Nicole Brown. Even before this we all knew a little bit about O.J. who would become quite a popular actor in movies such as the Naked Gun, The Towering Inferno, Hertz-Rent-A-Car commercials, and his role as commentator on Monday Night Football. This would all come about from OJs sporting career which would start as a Heisman Trophy award winning running back while attending the University of Southern California (USC). OJ would break into the NFL with the Buffalo Bills and the 49ers becoming the first running back in NFL history to break the 2,000 yard rushing mark in a single season. In 1985 OJ would meet induction into the NFL Hall of Fame in Canton, Ohio. OJ was truly an American living icon. Some would describe him as Michael Jordan before there was a Michael Jordan. The last time OJ would move our consciousness would occur that memorable Friday night on June 17, 1994 watching OJ and his friend Al Cowlings being chased by a hoard of police cruisers in his white Ford Bronco. This chase would occur in a similar fashion as

Carley, S. G. (2013). *Serial killers, mass murders, & disorders.* Boston: SGC Production.

a funeral procession down the LA freeway. On this night OJs easy going and friendly personality would disappear from the consciousness of the public replaced with visions of a very different picture.

Childhood of OJ Simpson

The birth of OJ would occur in 1947 on July 9. Orenthal James Simpson would take his name after the obscure French actor Orenthal. OJs father would abandon his family when he was just a toddler and his childhood would be altogether unremarkable. Rumors are his dysfunctional father may have experienced with homosexuality helping to better explain OJs macho attitude. Contrary to OJs father his mother Eunice would be both supportive and strong throughout OJs life caring for him and his three siblings as an orderly in a psychiatric unit. OJ who would be diagnosed with rickets and a calcium deficiency would wear braces on his legs until the age of five. The child they used to call pencil legs would go on to become one of the greatest running backs in the history of football. His deformed extremities leaving him pigeon toed and bowlegged would create the illusion of possessing an oversized head. This fact would subjugate OJ to taunting with names such as Headquarters or Waterhead.

Carley, S. G. (2013). *Serial killers, mass murders, & disorders.* Boston: SGC Production.

Adolescence and Emerging Adulthood of OJ Simpson

OJ would become more offensive in his adolescent years becoming close to being a hardcore delinquent. OJ would join a fighting gang when he was 14 the Persian Warriors and he would bully other kids. The ladies auxiliary of the gang would sexually initiate OJ and he would be caught stealing from a liquor store. OJ would be pushed back onto the positive path as myth has it through a communication with baseball great Willie Mays. The reality of the matter is his mother would place OJ in a Catholic school with a more positive peer group allowing him to associate more with his positive identity and focusing on his emerging athletic talents. During his senior year in high school he would lead the city in scoring. Despite the flocking of recruiters OJs grades would not be adequate for a major college. For this reason OJ would enroll in the City College of San Francisco. OJ would be a football star at City College of San Francisco and with his adequate grades would accept a scholarship to USC. As an All-American football star he would accept the Heisman Trophy in 1968 as Division 1s football player of the year. While at USC OJ would become a smooth dresser and talker communicating in both an easygoing and amicable image. OJ would continue to have trouble with his grades at USC and would drop out before earning a degree. This would not keep him from going on to stardom in the NFL.

OJ the Womanizer

OJ would have a less than admirable private life having the reputation as a womanizer. OJs first wife Marguerite of eleven years claims she would be abused during the relationship of which OJ would deny (Kubany, McCaig, & Laconsay, 2004). Reports also would state OJ to possess a drug problem. A Buffalo bar owner would state OJ would often smoke cocaine during his playing days of which he would come close to getting in legal trouble. OJ would only ever admit to trying marijuana and even then claims his use to limit to a single try. OJs most publicized instance of abuse would occur in 1989 where Nicole OJs wife during his second marriage would come out of the bushes bruised in a bra stating "he is going to kill me" to responding police officers. Nicole would drop the charges and OJ would explain to the Hertz CEO the situation was not a big deal. Olsen would believe OJ as would the rest of the public.

In June of 1977 OJ would meet his second wife 18 year old Nicole Brown. This would occur when she was waitressing at the nightclub she would work. OJ and Nicole would quickly become involved despite OJ being in the tenth year of a marriage and wife Marguerite carrying their third child. Marguerite and OJ would not divorce until 1980. OJs stormy relationship with Nicole would start from the beginning as OJs controlling nature and unfaithful behaviors would create an unstable environment. In 1985 Nicole would be pregnant with their first child and a prenuptual agreement would occur between the two. Their first child would be born on October 17 of this year only nine days before the police first response to a distress call at 360 Rockingham. Nicole would be found sitting on the hood of the car of which OJ had knocked the front window out with a baseball bat. Over the next four years the distress calls would continue with up to the occurrence of 30 distress calls.

Carley, S. G. (2013). *Serial killers, mass murders, & disorders.* Boston: SGC Production.

OJ In and Out of Prisons

Public and private conflict would continue by the two catered to with the abuse of drugs and alcohol. Nicole and OJ would divorce in October of 1992 although the two would reconcile and break-up from this time to Nicole's death on June 12, 1994. It was more clear than ever to OJ there would be no chance for reconciliation among the two. Fifteen hours before the killings a model Paula Barbeiri who was dating OJ at the time left a message on his phone stating their relationship would be coming to an end. Three hours before the grizzly murders Gretchen Stockdale would state OJ said he was "finally . . . unattached with everybody." Evidence suggests OJ would murder Nicole and Ron Goldman who was returning a pair of sunglasses. Goldman a friend of Nicole was possibly her lover. OJ would plea to find the killer. Significant evidence exists to hold OJ accountable for the murders of Nicole and Ron. Since 2007 OJ continues to possess significant legal problems including charges of kidknapping, armed robbery, and assault with a deadly weapon. This would occur with the alleged involvement of OJ in a robbery of the Las Vegas hotel. Simpson is currently serving a nine to 33 year prison sentence. Simpson will not be eligible for parole until 2018 when he will be 70 years old.

OJ would not be found innocent but would be found not guilty by a unanimous majority jury (Meyer & Weaver, 2006). In a civil trial Simpson would be found legally responsible for the deaths of Nicole and Ron. Many claim race would play an issue in freeing Simpson from his murder conviction pointing to a largely black jury deciding the verdict. This is contrary to the white jury in the civil trial who would find OJ guilty. In any case the standards of proof apparently were not met for the guilty verdict in the criminal trial requiring beyond a reasonable doubt. In a civil trial a reasonable doubt will only require over 50%.

Carley, S. G. (2013). *Serial killers, mass murders, & disorders.*
Boston: SGC Production.

Abnormal Behavior

Whether or not OJ would kill Nicole his behavior could certainly be viewed as abnormal perhaps warranting a diagnosis for the DSM-IV. OJ would seem to experience along with Nicole substance codependency and abuse. Evidence supports both were experiencing depression or anxiety and OJ would experience thoughts of suicide after the incident. Other syndromes may apply outside of the DSM-IV including codependency and battered spouse syndrome. The credibility of the DSM-IV diagnosis possesses the tendency to be more credible than the syndrome (Greenberg, Shuman, & Meyer, 2004). In recent years many syndromes have been publicized including the battered spouse syndrome withstanding the test of time. The first successful employment of the battered spouse syndrome the then battered woman syndrome would occur in 1977 in the case State vs. Grieg. This case occurring in a Yellowstone County, Montana court would argue the violence a woman would receive in her relationship could create a situation in which she was unable to leave her husband. An acquittal would occur in this case and since such time the battered spouse syndrome has been used in numerous cases at times succeeding. Battered spouse syndrome (BSS) would fall along the lines of the DSM-IV diagnosis of post traumatic stress disorder (PTSD) (Melton et al., 1997). The early legal uses of PTSD and BSS to some extent would portray a severely disordered and psychotic victim the result of trauma. More recently these effects of trauma have been viewed as a normal reaction (Kubany, McCaig, & Laconsay, 2004).

Syndromes are groups of symptoms or signs of condition, disturbance, disease, or lesion in plants or animals. General definitions agree the observance of the behavioral group occurs with consistency. Syndromes are observable behavioral patterns precipitated by some event and predictable. Within any syndrome difficulties can arise in defining abnormal behaviors. First the implication is critical behavior is forced. As an example the establishment of BSS in murder or assault cases the purpose is to void the perpetrator's responsibility for any unethical behaviors. The implication is the syndrome's existence would void responsibility. Concurrently very few of the abused assault or murder their abusers. The variables among those who do and don't murder and assault their abusers are not clear. It may be the existence of the self defense claim may make the syndrome unnecessary in any case.

The validity of the estranged spouse syndrome (ESS) is ever present in the OJ Simpson case consisting of all of the essentials describing the syndrome. OJ is still in love with the spouse. Nicole disengages from OJ yet because of his feelings she continues to send mixed messages. OJs understanding of the relationship being over seems to transform. OJs sense of loss triggers severe emotions leading to feelings of jealousy and betrayal. Anger grows in OJ along with feelings of depression. The catalytic event is OJ catching Nicole with a new lover causing peaks in arousal and disruption spilling into anger and homicide. The patterns of behavior in the OJ case are consistent with the requirements for ESS. The consistency of ESS should be viewed as equal to that of BSS (Meyer & Weaver, 2007). The consistency of behavior creates a dilemma as what is being inferred is that the behavior was in some way or form compelled thus permitting a perpetrator to argue an absence of responsibility for any ensuing behaviors. In clear cases of BSS legal cases will accept compulsion basing upon consistency but this is not the case with most other syndromes. Definitive conclusions are difficult with limited scientific data permitting the dominance of political issues.

A judgment of abnormality may be no more than a sociopolitical assumption (Greenberg, Shuman, & Meyer, 2004). At other times earlier in history such abnormal behavior one may view as romantic.

Carley, S. G. (2013). *Serial killers, mass murders, & disorders.*
Boston: SGC Production.

As an example let us look at Hector Berlioz composer of Symphonie Fantastique the inspiration for which would be Irish actress Harriet Smithson. Berlioz would be engaged to marry 19 year old Camiile Marie Moke a pianist. His fiancee's mother would send Berlioz a letter stating her plans to marry another man. His memoirs would state him to be so angry he planned on killing them all. Needless to say many would see this as an example of Berlioz' romanticism and not abnormality. This would be a product of the times plus the fact Berlioz never actually committed any acts of violence toward these parties. Berlioz would eventually marry Harriet his inspiration for Symphonie Fantastique.

Guidelines for judging abnormality have evolved throughout history consisting of certain criteria. The existence of mental disorder may be indicative of recurring behaviors. One such recurring behavior is an inability to inhibit behaviors self-destructive in nature. Hallucinations others cannot see and outbursts of violence. Poor and ineffective interpersonal skills and academic and vocational failure. Depression and anxiety and inabilities to conform to behavioral codes are each criteria for judging abnormality and abnormal behavior. Of criteria deciding abnormality the most consistent are deviant behaviors not conforming to societal roles and norms, continuity or disordered behavior, and the degree to which interpersonal function becomes disordered. The continuum of behavior possesses on one side normal adjustment and on the other abnormal adjustment. Much of behavior may occur within this middle ground making it difficult in distinguishing normal from abnormal behavior. Predispositions to abnormal behavior may exist as a genetic determinant. Abnormal behavioral pattern causations tend to possess multiple sources and not a single source. Signs of abnormality do not have to be flagrant. Many times abnormality and the presence thereof can be subtle. Judgments pertaining to abnormality are affected by social value systems. In terms of interpersonal relationships a psychological handicap is more

Carley, S. G. (2013). *Serial killers, mass murders, & disorders.*
Boston: SGC Production.

detrimental than a physical handicap. An individual labeled with a psychological handicap may continue to be labeled even when the disorder is no longer present prolonging the disorder. Mental abnormality often coincides with criminal behavior.

Conclusion

One man enters making a crowd of three. One man leaves and two never take another breath. We all remember the day the cheers rang out when the OJ verdict was finally made. OJ would leave the court room on this day not necessarily an innocent man but a man found to be not guilty by a reasonable doubt. Those cheering may not have considered the families of two deceased persons who had a lot of life to live. Some did not want OJ free others did not want OJ imprisoned. Others still just wanted the law to handle the matter and put a guilty man behind bars. What if an innocent man were placed behind bars? What if OJ really didn't viciously murder two lovers in a wild jealous rage? Did you do it OJ? We may never know for sure but the memory still haunts us of dead bodies and court room acquittals. When the jury system cannot enforce justice what is to keep all of us safe from the rage, fury, anger, and jealousy of others. Should we be scared, perhaps. As the world changes with the demographics perhaps justice becomes no more than a matter of numbers. The OJ case can demonstrate this, we know this. A jury consisting of 75% African Americans would let OJ go claiming reasonable doubt was not efficient. A civil court of white folk certainly would find the evidence sufficient. Is the white jury wrong for finding OJ guilty of his crime in the civil court? Is a black jury guilty for not finding OJ guilty of his crime? Love turns to hate and jealousy to rage and the once great in the eyes of the social world has turned into a villain. To many OJs release was not going to make him an innocent man. The many who still believe OJ would take Nicole and Ron's life would find him to be no more than a guilty man walking the free road. Take a look over your shoulder

Carley, S. G. (2013). *Serial killers, mass murders, & disorders.*
Boston: SGC Production.

OJ, someone's out there that doesn't believe a word coming out of your mouth. Rumor had it family members of the victims were having thoughts of committing the ultimate act of hate themselves. Can you blame them, what if somebody killed your son or daughter? Maybe OJ is safer in prison where he will be spending a minimum of the next five years behind bars still professing his innocence whenever parole trials come around. Only now OJ claims he had nothing to do with robbing the hotel. Pattern of violence forming, I think so. Are we fooled, I think not. They say all the money in the world cannot make you a happier man. Maybe it's true, I know I would feel better if I had a handful of money. Money as they say makes the world go round but at the same time can't buy everything. It seems as if OJ still had his heart set on little Miss Nicole and although their marriage may be over he would continue to show feelings of control over her decisions. That's OJ Simpson, no one like him ever before and hopefully never again.

Carley, S. G. (2013). *Serial killers, mass murders, & disorders.*
Boston: SGC Production.

Elvis Presley and Dr. S

Prescription Drug and Polysubstance Abuse

Of substance abuse patterns among the DSM-IV-TR prescription drug abuse is not specifically discussed. The pattern of prescription drug abuse cuts across personality patterns focusing on client characteristics instead of the abused drug. Of the high level of prescription drug abuse present within society physicians and drug companies should take at least part of the blame. In existence are common signs of prescription drug abuse, such as an increase of alcohol use as a supplement to the effect of pills, and withdrawal from friends, interests, or activities. Anxiety increases especially pertaining to obtaining more pills. Contact with health care workers may increase, and resistance-avoidance may occur toward any health care professional who confronts the pattern of prescription drug abuse. Back-up plans may occur in obtaining the drugs, and quick refill efforts can occur.

Not included in the DSM-IV-TR or other versions of the DSM for that matter is the term polysubstance abuse. Included in the DSM-IV-TR is a category of Polysubstance Dependence involving the use of three or more substances in a period of six months, as no one substance is predominately used. The gateway to adolescent drug

Carley, S. G. (2013). *Serial killers, mass murders, & disorders.* Boston: SGC Production.

abuse and dependence often occurs through the polysubstance abuse of alcohol, marijuana, and nicotine. The neglect of polysubstance abuse is a belief system that all psychological and physiological disorders are curable (Garner & Garfinkel, 1997). The polysubstance abuser possesses a high need for sensation seeking or new experiences combining the expectancy of an external agent to cure all worldly problems. More attention would be given to the increase in polysubstance abuse among high school and college aged individuals after the arrest during the summer of 2007 of Al Gore's son Albert Gore, III. Al Gore is the former Senator, Vice-President, and presidential candidate.

Elvis Presley

Elvis Presley as one of the most popular entertainers of all-time may compare to other cultural icons, such as James Dean or John F. Kennedy. Known as the king of rock his music would change the music industry forever. Elvis' first recording hit was in 1951 and 21 years later at the age of 42 his untimely death would occur. In existence is speculation whether or not Elvis' death was a suicidal prescription drug overdose, yet it is no mystery Elvis would abuse prescription drugs. Elvis Presley was born in January 1935 in the town of East Tupelo, Mississippi. Elvis' only sibling was his twin brother Jesse. Elvis' father would spend three years in prison when he was at an early age causing him to grow closer to his mother (Elvis Australia, 2012). In 1949 Elvis' family would move to Memphis Tennessee where Elvis' music career would take off (Meyer, Chapman, & Weaver, 2009). Worldwide Elvis would mount 142 gold records. The Army would draft Elvis in 1958 the same year his mother would pass away. Ten years later Elvis would marry his wife Priscilla and have a child Lisa Marie. Elvis would become promiscuous sexually, promote unhealthy eating habits, sleep at odd hours, and gain increased dependence on prescription drugs. In 1973 Priscilla would divorce Elvis, as Elvis would become alienated and experience numerous physical disorders. His drug use would result in collapsing and canceled shows. After Priscilla involved herself with another man in 1973, Elvis would find himself living in complete isolation as his drug use would increase in 1976. Elvis' depression would lead to wild spending sprees as he would grow irritable and his drug abuse would continue to increase.

Two years and eight months before Elvis' untimely demise he would receive prescriptions for an unbelievable 19,000 doses of narcotics. Elvis would claim his passion for painkillers was a dental issue. David Stanley who would work close with Elvis believed the overdose to be a suicide. A doctor had found the cause of death to be cardiac arrhythmia and not a drug overdose finding heart disease to be the presiding factor. At the time of Elvis' death however there were many drugs found in his body: codeine, ACTH, valium, ethchlorvynol, demerol, amobarbital, phenobarbital, and methaqualone. For this reason the Van Nuys Bioscience Laboratory would find polypharmacy as the cause of death (Meyer, Chapman, & Weaver, 2009).

It may be Elvis may possess a predisposition toward addiction when considering the dependency of Elvis' mother on alcohol and sleeping pills permitting her to relax and sleep. As Elvis would become famous just as his mother he would begin to show signs of anxiety and depression. His father would most likely abuse alcohol and would show signs of antisocial patterns. Other factors exist contributing to Elvis's addictive behaviors such as the willingness of dentists and physicians to prescribe Elvis medication. The seclusion and alienation a result of his fame and the immense pressures of his occupation could also contribute to an addictive personality. Abusers remaining in contact with reality should be described as psychotics. Behavior deteriorates from the use of drugs over long periods. These deteriorating behaviors involve motivation, interpersonal relationships, and work and school performance. Upon the manifestation of emotion the affect is flat. Just as the alcoholic promises are often broken despite protesting the advent of change. It is not deceit keeping the addictive personality from changing as despite the intellectual commitment to change, the individual cannot generate the motivation or behavior necessary in actuating change (Boyd et al., 2007). Elvis would never promise to make a change to anyone or appear to protest in anyway the advent for change of his behaviors pertaining to drug use.

Biological, Psychological, and Social Factors of Case of Elvis

The biological factors involved in the case of Elvis involve his dependence on prescription drugs. This dependence on narcotics, which Elvis would claim was a response to dental problems, may have led to psychological and social factors contributing to his drug dependence (Kowalski & Westen, 2009). At the same time social and psychological factors would contribute to his addiction to painkillers. Not to ignore other biological factors contributing to Elvis' excessive use of prescription drugs was his medical history possessing of an excessively long colon, glaucoma, a deformed leg, and heart palpitations. Despite these biological necessities incorporating the use of prescription drugs it seems the loss of his mother may have first lead to Elvis' addiction to pain medication. To further compound social factors leading to Elvis' depression and isolation is the divorce with his wife Priscilla. As depression and isolation would set in this factor may have led Elvis further into the use of prescription drugs until dependence would set in. As one who is always performing Elvis may have taken prescription drugs to enhance his performance. These social and psychological factors compounding one another and working off one another would increase Elvis' addiction. Even Elvis' death, which would be found a biological heart problem may have been the social and psychological factors he was dealing with contributing to as speculation suggests his suicide.

Carley, S. G. (2013). *Serial killers, mass murders, & disorders.* Boston: SGC Production.

Psychotherapeutic Interventions, Biological Interventions, and Social Interventions. Different interventions can be appropriate in the case of Elvis, including psychotherapeutic interventions, biological interventions, and social interventions. The implication of psychotherapy is simply to cure problems. The rationale in selecting such an intervention is psychotherapy as a behavioral and psychological intervention can form an assessment and ensuing discussion regarding the biological and social influences on behavior. During psychotherapy these influences can meet consideration. A psychotherapist could gain insight into Elvis' past to try to distinguish if this could have a bearing on Elvis's drug addiction leading to depression and biological ailment. As it turns Elvis' father was in prison when Elvis was very young at which time Elvis would become very close with his mother. The death of Elvis' mother would play a role in his drug dependency and psychological state (Tripod, 2012).

The therapist may have tried to ease the pain of Elvis' loss in an attempt to alter any unwelcome behaviors. Within a psychotherapeutic intervention the approach to helping the patient is an individual approach (Plante, 2011). This means simply the therapist meets and attempts to cure the patient through means of psychotherapy. The participants of this form of treatment would be Elvis and his psychotherapist. Although a discussion of many individuals within the life of Elvis may occur, ultimately it is only the therapist and Elvis who would work together to right any unwelcomed behavior. In working with a psychotherapist the involvement of other trained professionals may occur in some manner. These trained professionals can include psychologists, psychiatrists, social workers, nurses, counselors, and others. The psychotherapeutic intervention setting would be a professional setting, such as the office of a service provider equipped with seating permitting a private conversation. The setting can occur outside the professional setting yet the clinician should have a compelling reason to do so (Plante, 2011).

In selecting a biological intervention in treating Elvis with substance abuse the rationale would be providing Elvis with different medications would counteract his addiction to prescription medication. In taking a biological intervention in treating Presley for substance abuse a clinician would prescribe the appropriate psychotropic medication (Corner, 2005). Perhaps with the onset of Presley's depression he may receive a prescription for an antidepressant to deal with this aspect of drug addiction (Liveleak, 2012). In treating withdrawal symptoms biological treatments to help people withdraw from substances include: detoxification, antagonist drugs, and drug maintenance therapies. A psychiatrist would play the larger role in the biological intervention of substance abuse. The psychiatrist's role would be to prescribe the medication, which would best treat Elvis for his substance abuse disorder. Other trained professionals can also take part in the treatment of Elvis for his substance abuse disorder such as psychologists, social workers, nurses, counselors, pharmacists, and others. Biological intervention settings would begin in the professional office setting in which a diagnosis would occur in which a psychiatrist may prescribe a psychotropic medication (Plante, 2011). Elvis would next possess expectations to take part in the treatment plan in a natural setting outside the care of the clinical setting.

In selection of a social intervention the aim may be to improve psychological and social functioning. In creation of the social intervention the design of a program would occur by a clinical psychologist making use most likely of the psychoeducational approach (Plante, 2011). Often the implementation of a community program can occur. The participants of the social intervention, including Presley would be first a clinical psychologist who would design and evaluate Presley's program. Other individuals with similar problems would be present within the community program along with other counselors. The social intervention would occur first within the clinical setting and move toward a sort of classroom setting with the community program (Plante, 2011).

Areas the interventions target. The intervention seems to target in the case of Elvis as a psychotherapeutic intervention, the psychological factors stemming from childhood should a psychodynamic approach occur. These psychological factors can be the result of childhood social or biological factors. In this case the social factors can involve Elvis' father spending three years in prison and bonding with his mother during this time. In adulthood Elvis' childhood would contribute to each biological, psychological, and social factors contributing to diminished well-being. Elvis would experience drug addiction causing depression and leading to the break-up with his wife and eventual as speculation would contend own suicide. Psychotherapy does not necessarily focus on childhood yet the occurrence of the passing of Elvis' mother, a social factor leading to his drug addiction, a biological factor would be a good direction in terms of "course of action" and therapeutic intervention (Kowalski & Westen, 2009). Elvis' drug addiction would in turn promote depression a psychological factor regarding Presley's well-being.

Nicotine Dependency

In Cuba in 1492 natives would dry and smoke some plant leaves observed by two members of Columbus' crew, Rodrigo de Jerez and Luis de Torres. When de Jerez would try some for himself, he would become the first confirmed European smoker. De Jerez would be imprisoned back in Spain for smoking, as the smoke coming out of his mouth would lead them to believe he was possessed by the devil. Jamestown as the first English settlement would do poor economically until the husband of Pocohontas, John Rolfe, would plant some tobacco seeds. As the plants would flourish, tobacco would become the critical cash crop. In terms of requiring health care, smokers are 50% more likely than non-smokers. The smoke the smokers disperse is also harmful, second hand smoke. The warnings from the Surgeon General's office pertaining to the risks of smoking tobacco have had little success in deterring smoking. The individuals who do quit are often susceptible to relapse. Other historical anti-smoking campaigns include China's 1683 law authorizing the beheading of those possessing tobacco, and the Turkish law where addiction to tobacco could be punishable by torture and execution. These campaigns also would be relatively ineffective.

In initiating and maintaining tobacco addiction in existence are seven major factors to consider. Physiological addiction to nicotine is the primary component. Smoking subgroups exist of moderate smokers who do not become addicted. The addiction to nicotine is the result of the intensification of the glutamate flow increasing the firing rate of neurons. Nicotine addiction occurs within the insula. This would be known, as an individual who had a stroke and damaged this brain region, would no longer possess the urge to smoke. The neural intensification acts as a reward system within the limbic system of the brain. Other factors initiating tobacco addiction involve fulfillment of personality needs, tranquilizing effect of nicotine, habit, genetic predisposition, peer pressure, and modeling (Petraitis, Flay, & Miller, 1995). Nicotine abuse and dependence is catered through a failure to discriminate use from abuse among society, tolerance for adolescent smoking, accepted patterns of daily use, and legality of substance. Nicotine Dependence is defined in the DSM-IV-TR along the criteria of other substance dependencies. Nicotine dependence will occur within 90% of those smoking regularly through the age of 20.

Carley, S. G. (2013). *Serial killers, mass murders, & disorders.* Boston: SGC Production.

Dr. S

Dr. S would experience an irregular heartbeat at the age of 38 the result of a severe flu attack. Upon meeting with his personal physician Dr. F, he would be told the cause was his habit of smoking cigars, and he would be advised to stop. Dr. S. would try to stop, but his pulse rate would worsen and he would become depressed. He would make several attempts at stopping before returning back to his 20 cigar a day habit. At the age of 67, DR. S. would develop jaw cancer and undergo 33 operations. The result of cancerous and precancerous conditions would be the removal of his entire jaw. Dr. S. would stop smoking at the age of 73, which would help relieve his chest pains from heart disease (angina pectoris). He would continue his attempts at the cessation of smoking and fail each time. After many years of suffering from heart disorder, cancer, and operations, he would die from the cancer at the age of 83.

This is not a recent case as Dr. S. would be born in Freiberg, Moravia on May 6, 1856 currently part of the Czech Republic. His father Jacob Freud was a Jewish wool merchant, and along with his wife Amalie, and son Sigmund who was four years old at the time, would move to Vienna. Sigmund would remain in Vienna until 1938 fleeing Austria to escape Nazi persecution (Larson et al., 2007). The difficulty of changing this behavior (in engaging in tobacco products) can be attributed to Dr. S., being Sigmund Freud. The modern era uses every tactic possible in the cessation of smoking tobacco yet possess little or no success. The success rate at the Mayo Clinic as an example is only 40%, and this is under an intense inpatient program combining all and any medications and techniques known to help. According to the DSM-IV-TR of the individuals who try to quit smoking each year only a small percentage of 5% will succeed. Most individuals can control their smoking during the treatment phase only to relapse. Even a single lapse of one or two cigarettes results in total relapse 50% of the time. Most prone to relapse are heavy smokers.

Different treatment techniques can be used gearing toward the cessation of smoking tobacco products. A delay strategy can be used where one can delay smoking his or her first cigarette up to the point of quitting. Alternatively a "quit day" can be set. To mute the craving for nicotine the drugs naltrexone and buproprion can be useful. Fade the addiction through "isolated nicotine" by using the nicotine patch. Psychotropic medication can assist, especially the NicVAX injection. Hypnosis and relaxation training along with counseling can increase motivation and emphasize the need to quit. Create aversion-extinction responses by smoking very quickly. Place more importance on one's diet and exercise. Find outlets which the economics to smoking do not cater toward. Treat any existing depression or anxiety and participate in support groups. Facilitate the support of others by working with them.

Success in quitting smoking tends to proceed these stages. Think about the possibilities of quitting and consider change. Form a goal and consider the financial and health costs. The quitting time is chosen and the commitment is final. The preparations are already in place, and the quitting period has begun with new behaviors replacing smoking. A healthier lifestyle begins and plans are made in the case of relapse. The continuation of success usually requires the support of those significant others taking part in the process of cessation. Friends and family who smoke may make cessation more difficult even if they should pledge their support. It would seem more important as with other commonly abused substances to focus more on prevention as opposed to finding a cure. The importance of this can be seen in the statistic 90% of 20 year old smokers become long-term smokers. The smoking rate has dropped in the United States by more than 100% from the years 1966 to 1997. So prevention would seem the key ingredient. Another factor

Carley, S. G. (2013). *Serial killers, mass murders, & disorders.* Boston: SGC Production.

contributing to tobacco use would be socioeconomic status as those of low status seem to possess a higher likelihood to abuse tobacco.

Karen Carpenter and Christina Ricci (Anorexia Nervosa)

Anorexia Nervosa

Hardly recognized not even until the late 1960s would be the presence of eating disorders. The significance of eating disorders would not be brought into popular awareness until the death of Karen Carpenter stemming from this disorder. As obesity increases to epidemic proportions so too have eating disorders become an epidemic within the United States (Burton, & Shaw, 2004). The translation of the term anorexia nervosa is "not eating because of nervous causes." The DSM-IV-TR consists of essential requirements in diagnosing anorexia nervosa. The major requirement is a refusal to maintain 85% of one's normal weight for their height and age or failure to meet the 85% minimum during growth periods. This is accompanied by the intense fear of becoming fat despite being underweight, and the denial of the seriousness to one's low body weight or distortion of body image. Anorectics do not experience a significant loss of appetite. Despite losing weight the fear of weight gain should persist among the anorectic. Amenorrhea is common among postmenarcheal females.

Carley, S. G. (2013). *Serial killers, mass murders, & disorders.* Boston: SGC Production.

According to the DSM in existence are two types of anorexia binge eating/purging type or the restricting type.

The presence of anorexia nervosa is most common among those females of the middle and upper socioeconomic status. Anorexia and bulimia of recent years is becoming increasingly more evident among older women, young adult males and adolescents, and preadolescent girls (Grilo, 2006). The occurrence of anorexia typically first occurs during puberty as the young woman becomes increasingly aware of her self-image. The mortality rates of those experiencing anorexia are between five and 15 percent. The majority of cases occur between the ages of 12 to 18, a total of 75% of all cases, and in this age range 1 in 200 to 250 females are expected to develop anorexia. This equates to a death toll of 1 in 2000 women will die from anorexia. In an act of cleansing the body of food, women will induce vomiting or make use of laxatives. Among the male population anorexia nervosa is far less common. Systematic differences exist within male anorectics comparing to female anorectics in the case it should occur. Males are less likely to die from the disorder, more likely to report enjoyable sexual experiences and to overexercise, less likely to experience premorbid large appetites, less conscientious about schooling, and less likely to make use of laxatives or diet. In general anorectics will show signs of bulimia, and compared to anorectics who do not binge-eat are more disturbed (Heffner & Eifert, 2004). Anorectic parents tend to be very controlling, but are typically caring. The anorectic in control of this behavior uses the disorder in making a statement of independence from the family. The personality characteristics associating with anorexia nervosa include persistent stubbornness and selfishness, perfectionism, introversion, and excessive sensitivity and dependency (Bruch, Cyzewski, & Suhr, 1988). Anorectics lacking bulimic characteristics are typically stubborn, confused about sexuality, perfectionistic, passively controlling, and shy. Anorexics with bulimic characteristics are controlling of peers, industrious perfectionists, and typically extroverted. Many bulimics are overweight whereas many others are normal weight comparing to anorexics who tend to be cadaverously thin. Through socialization and recognition, food is the focus of the anorexic and bulimic family. Anorectics will only eat small portions of exotic meals in which they cook for others. Bulimics tend not to cook in the fear they will eat all of the food before the guests even arrive.

Karen Carpenter

Anorexia nervosa would be brought into the public eye for the first time. It would take the death of one of America's best and most loved voices before eating disorders would be recognized and taken seriously. Karen would idolize her brother at a young age who would tease her by calling her fatso. Others too would tease Karen about her weight. At the age of 17 Karen would lose 25 pounds to weigh around 120. She would maintain this weight during her late teens and into her early twenties. Karen and her brother when she was 19 would sign a record deal with A & M records by Herb Alpert. This opportunity would push Karen into the limelight increasing her self-consciousness. Karen would always view her brother as the reason for their success. Karen's critical mother would display favoritism toward Karen's brother. The devotion of the family was to the career of her brother as little recognition would be given to Karen. Karen's brother too would find himself the main reason for their success. Karen's soaring career would be marked by critical statements about her weight by the media and brother. Karen would begin dieting at the age of 24, and would be forced into two months of bed rest at the age of 26, the result of excessive exercise and little caloric intake. As Karen's immune system would begin to fail she would start to miss shows, and in the hopes of burning more calories, she would become addicted to laxatives and overdose on thyroid pills. Karen would marry a man she knew only for a few months at the age of 30, and the marriage would fall apart within a year. Her

Carley, S. G. (2013). *Serial killers, mass murders, & disorders.* Boston: SGC Production.

husband at the time would admit to being too controlling. Karen would be treated for anorexia and without any family support to speak of would gain 25 pounds under the supervision of her therapist in New York. Karen would experience a relapse and upon her return to California she would induce vomiting with ipecac. The heart failure causing Karen's death was most likely facilitated by her use of ipecac of which she would increase her intake to a bottle a day. It would be the story of Karen Carpenter first publicizing anorexia nervosa.

Christina Ricci

Christina would break into the movie industry at the age of nine appearing in the movie Mermaids starring Cher and Winona Ryder. She would also appear in the Addams Family movies as Wednesday, and as the girlfriend to Charlize Theron in Monster. Christina would co-star alongside Johnny Depp in Sleepy Hollow. She also appeared in numerous independent films such as Prozac Nation. With Christina's gothic style and sarcastic nature she has never been prized as one of America's sweethearts as Karen would be. Instead along with Christina's nonexistent nightlife she is more a subject of confusion than fantasy or adoration.

The birth of Christina Ricci would occur on February 12, 1980 in Santa Monica, California, as the youngest of four children. Her father was a primal scream therapist and mother a perfectionist model. Starting at the age of five Christina could be seen in commercials for cereal and toys. At the age of 13 in 1993 Christina would begin to enjoy her notoriety having just finished the filming of the movie The Addams Family. Her family would be torn apart this same year by a divorce. Compounding the stress upon young Christina at her young age of 13 would be her casting into a role bringing her body image to the forefront as co-star of the film Now and Then starring Demi Moore and Rosie O'Donnell. Christina would be playing the younger version of Rosie O'Donnell as a cute, slightly chubby child. The young Melanie Griffith would be played by her friend and co-star Thora Birch. Christina's body type was being portrayed as one destined to be the overweight member of the peer group. Christina would make off the wall comments to the media about incest and how she could buy a gun now that she was 18. In October of 1997 Ricci would state her not wanting to be part of a romantic comedy as this is not a happy planet. Ricci would be a heavy smoker. During her teens Ricci would deal with the media angrily as she would appear to possess more trouble regulating herself than most teenagers. According to Ricci statements, she would feel removed from ordinary semblances of reality.

At the age of 13 Ricci would experience a lack of control in her life with the divorce of her parents and the parallel drawn between her and Rosie O'Donnell. Her neurosis would develop into anorexia during the film Now and Then. Ricci would despise her changing body and would burn herself with a cigarette lighter in a demonstration of her self-hatred. She would continue to burn herself until the age of 17. She once would show a reporter the burn marks upon rolling up her sleeve explaining she was testing her tolerance for pain. Christina's obsession to be thin would grow. In Christina's case, it would seem her anorexia to stem less from the pursuit of perfectionism and more on an addictive and neurotic personality (Forbush, Heatherton, & Keel, 2007). Christina was a Hollywood rebel, yet she would possess trouble controlling her pressures to be thin among her teenage world. At one point Christina would eat a single meal every three days in conjunction with a daily six mile jog. Christina would weigh only 61 pounds.

Ricci would begin talking about her disorder during her mid-twenties claiming the movie industry not to warn her of the dangers of anorexia but instead to become an anorectic. Ricci would claim to obtain advice from a Tracy Gold movie pertaining to anorexia.

Carley, S. G. (2013). *Serial killers, mass murders, & disorders.*
Boston: SGC Production.

Her act of burning herself and self infliction of pain would be a justification of the emotional pain she would experience. In Ricci's fight against anorexia she would show great courage, and although continuing her dark, disturbed persona, states she is happy to have that part of her life behind her. Ricci in her early thirties feels less a need to compete with Hollywood's nightlife and stays in most nights. She would become pregnant in her late twenties and is at peace with her body stating she feels someone truly loves her.

Causes of Anorexia Nervosa

The reasons for the anorexia of Christina Ricci and Karen Carpenter are different although both would experience a serious case of the disorder. Karen Carpenter would have attention brought upon her pertaining to her weight from those closest to her. This may attribute for her perfectionist persona. This compares to the self loathing Ricci who would be driven into anorexia by a tumultuous family life. Unlike Carpenter it would be Ricci's career first bringing attention to her weight. Unlike Carpenter, Ricci would be capable of overcoming the obsession of being thin associating with the disorder. It may be the greater body of knowledge of anorexia, including the story of Karen Carpenter, permitting Ricci to deal with the disorder. Just as Ricci and Carpenter anorectics tend to be female, white, young, ambitious, and talented. In terms of anorexia, Karen would be one of the older victims of the disorder, typically appearing prior to puberty at a time appearance enters the young woman's consciousness. With public exposure Karen's anxiety would increase in regard to her appearance. Karen's use of laxatives and self induced vomiting classifies the binge eating/purging type anorexia. The restrictive type of anorexia according to the DSM-IV-TR does not include the actions of bingeing and purging. Even when emaciated anorexics possess the belief they are too fat. Anorexics set a goal for an ideal weight, and upon reaching this goal a new goal is set for an even lower weight. The anorexic in the process of losing additional and continual weight continues to possess a fear of becoming fat or gaining weight (Heffner & Eifert, 2004). Upon Karen's entry to the stage with her bony structure, audiences would gasp as she would continue to lose even more weight keeping her eating behaviors a secret. Karen would constantly deny the presence of an illness and minimize any effects her illness may show. In maintenance of the disorder deception is central. The cycle of self starvation continues in theory as the person experiences lack of control, disapproval, or rejection. Attempts to be perfect increase as anger turns inward. The individual convinces him or herself if he or she improve things will get better, similar to obsessive-compulsive patterns. The individual becomes driven to extreme eating behaviors as the perfectionist lifestyle creates even more stress (Agras, 1995). Karen was told at a young age she would most likely be fat by her mother claiming obesity to be a trait of the family. She would be teased growing up for her weight and as an adult would continue to see herself as fat. This would be despite being severely underweight. This is the prevalent characteristic of anorexia nervosa, such a distorted body image. The origins of this illness according to theory focus on individual levels of self control over one's life. Anorectics turn inward exercising control over their bodies the result of a feeling of powerlessness. The anorectic continues to maintain control over this aspect of their life, the disorder. Evidence suggests a predisposition to anorexia may be prenatal exposure to female hormones.

Treatment for Anorexia Nervosa

The goal in the treatment of anorexia nervosa is weight restoration, change the relentless pursuit for thinness, and the treatment of physical complications. It may be inpatient treatment to be necessary involving forced or even intravenous feeding, in life threatening situations an anorectic may experience. Nutrition counseling can take place and a behavior modification program in the development of helpful feeding behaviors. The critical issue is building up the feeding behaviors with reinforcements (Agras, 1995). Helpful in the treatment of anorexia is megace ES (megestrol acetate). As a person moves into normal functioning a more psychodynamic approach can be useful focusing on emerging narcissism, perfectionism, and ambivalence over dependency (Bruch, Czyzewski, & Suhr, 1988). As the patterns of behavior associating with anorexia are often relating to family control dynamics, family therapy may be necessary. Within cases of both anorexia nervosa and bulimia nervosa relapse prevention can be critical. For high risk situations clients should receive exposure training and cognitive training in discriminating lapse from relapse and the elimination of negative self talk (Dattillo, Davis, & Goisman, 2008). Most anorectics do not experience the same tragic outcome of Karen Carpenter. Still many show long term problematic patterns, yet despite possessing residual symptoms of the disorder, in time will function normal.

Individuals with problems eating should require some form of counseling pertaining to control of eating behaviors and dieting facts. This includes the more common problems of persistent eating disorders, general obesity, and binge eating without purging. Counseling for eating disorders should focus on specific factors in returning an individual to normal functioning patterns. Critical in generating weight loss is a restriction of caloric intake and change in energy burning patterns and amounts of exercise. Control should be directed toward *what* foods an individual may possess a biological predisposition toward bingeing, as much as *when* and *how much* of this food an individual consumes. Keep in mind it is not difficult to lose weight, it is difficult to maintain weight loss. It is easier to lose weight during a first diet than a second diet. The breaking of diets most often occurs during the late afternoon. Keeping fluid intakes high is important for an individual trying to lose weight. When undergoing weight loss the body requires more water than any other fluid. Weight gain should occur upon cessation of smoking granted the activity level remains the same. Prior to the menstrual period in women food cravings will increase making them more vulnerable to lapses. The recommendation is for those experiencing binge eating disorder or overeating to monitor their daily eating habits. In existence are dieting tips which can assist in a day to day program. At least eight glasses of water should be drunk daily. Avoid meals less than two hours before going to bed and eat a high carbohydrate breakfast. Before a meal have a cup of soup, eat a salad, or have a low calorie beverage. For many hot tea can be effective. Savor the flavor of the meal slowing down the pace of eating including chewing slower. Try to eat in the company of others. Do not eat in the car or on the run. Don't eat while talking on the telephone, watching the television, or standing up. Develop a feasible eating routine of two to three larger meals and two smaller snacks daily at predetermined times. One does not have to be extremely hungry to engage in a meal. Do not have drinks with alcohol or sugar. Visualize yourself eating before sitting down to a meal. If you are about to binge use thought control and yell "Stop," or at least whisper it to yourself if you are in public. Other than planned foods avoid keeping food around. You'll be less likely to snack if you brush your teeth after every meal. Plan activities incompatible with eating, and identify the times when you are more prone to binge eating. Unless specifically prescribed avoid weighing yourself. Integrate an effective exercise program into your life. When possible walk don't drive. Do not leave any unresolved conflicts as this can promote thoughts of food or body image. A half hour before you go to a supermarket or a party drink lots of water and have a high fiber snack. Take some time each day to reflect on how you are doing in this area and in life in general. Affirm yourself in the areas you are doing well, and the areas you are not doing well visualize methods of improvement. Get help from family and friends or other helpful resources. Do not keep your decision to lose

Carley, S. G. (2013). *Serial killers, mass murders, & disorders.* Boston: SGC Production.

weight a secret and have others spell out how they can assist in the common goal.

Tom & Tabetha (Child Abuse)

Tom

Living in a medium sized city in Alabama is 39 year old civil engineer Tom. Most who know Tom would characterize him as a model citizen as he makes a good salary working for a large construction business. Tom belongs to a number of civic organizations and is a long time church member despite not particularly professing any strong religious beliefs. Tom would have what one may consider a normal childhood and would never seek help for any type of psychological disorder. Tom would marry at the age of 25 and at the beginning the marriage was perfect. The two would be delighted, Tom and his wife, when they would have a baby girl, Tina. Tom would be 30 at the time. Sometime shortly thereafter the marriage would start to deteriorate. Tom's wife didn't enjoy the functions of mothering although did enjoy the status of the role. To escape the demands of child care, she would hire sitters while she would return to her job as secretary. In the attempt of dissolving anxiety and guilt, she would increase her social drinking habit and would drink more often and secretively. After years of binge drinking she would develop a pattern of alcoholism. She was mostly non-functional as a wife and mother and could barely hold onto her secretary job.

Carley, S. G. (2013). *Serial killers, mass murders, & disorders.* Boston: SGC Production.

Tom would develop a close relationship with Tina and much contrary to his wife would enjoy fathering. Away from home Tom would possess few interests or friends. Tom and his wife would rarely engage in sexual encounters and at this point would mostly tolerate one another. Tom would satisfy his sexual needs through masturbation to videotapes, prostitutes, or the occasional affair. Before going to bed, Tina would become accustomed to lying down with her father for 15 minutes or so placing her head on his lap. On one occasion when Tina would be eight years of age her father would permit her to lie with him for close to an hour. The feeling of closeness would not be available to Tom elsewhere. Tom would quickly send Tina to bed when he would become aroused sexually. Several nights later while lying with Tina again Tom would become aroused. Instead of rushing Tina off to bed, he would instead lie there for a while. Tina would move around a bit causing Tom to ejaculate. Tom would be upset over the occasion yet would repeat the behavior during a few subsequent occasions.

A week would pass and the situation would escalate. As Tom's arousal would increase he would raise Tina's nightgown and proceed to rub his penis upon her buttocks until reaching orgasm. Tom would tell Tina it was OK and not to be upset, and she wasn't. This sexual act among the two would seem to break any inhibitions. Tina at times upon request would reach behind her rubbing Tom's penis. Tom would make contact with Tina's genitals and rub his penis between her legs. During a point of extreme arousal Tom would ask Tina to lick it and would ejaculate on her face. Tom would emphasize the need for her to keep their game a secret. At times Tom would make an attempt to penetrate Tina's vagina, but she would complain of discomfort and he would back off. For six months this pattern would continue and Tom's wife it is believed would at least suspect the happenings among her husband and daughter. She would do nothing except grab another bottle of booze and hide somewhere. Tina would be playing with a neighbor when the word penis would come up. She would blurt out, "Daddy let me lick his penis." Tina's friend's mother would ask what she meant by the comment and in vivid detail would describe everything. The neighbor would call her husband who was a physician and would report the incident personally.

Tom would break down and confess when confronted by the child protective services division. Tom would be convicted for his crime and the sentence would be probated on the recommendation of the social worker and psychologist. This would be under the stipulation of mandatory treatment and community service. Tom never again would sexually abuse Tina and his treatment would be a success. Within the year Tom and his wife would divorce and the amount of psychological damage Tina would incur is unclear. It is most likely substantial, and over time Tina may pay the highest price of all.

Tabetha

In the mountains of West Virginia Tabetha would be born to a poor family. She would move to Akron, Ohio, at the age of four with her family where her father would be trying to get a job with her uncle at a tire factory. This was a time jobs would be scarce and after years of struggling on welfare the family would move to Tennessee to attempt to obtain employment at a new General Motors plant. Her father would spend his time at home when he was around by drinking, eating, sleeping, or beating his wife or kids. During Tabetha's childhood were no dramatic incidents. Little value seemed to be placed toward education in her home, and her father who was rarely home she would seldom interact with. Tabetha's mother loved her five children yet could only provide basic needs for them. Tabetha would complete high school with poor grades, and would have an abortion during her junior year, her parents would never find this out. A month after graduating she would again become pregnant and the father would marry her. They would move

Carley, S. G. (2013). *Serial killers, mass murders, & disorders*.
Boston: SGC Production.

in together and upon giving birth to a baby girl, Tabetha would become pregnant again, almost immediately. The labor this time would be difficult and the baby boy may have sustained neurological damage.

Tabetha's husband would leave town and rarely be heard from thereafter. Tabetha did not possess many marketable skills, and was neither bright nor especially attractive. She would not attract the most eligible men with no money and two children. Her live-in boyfriends along the way would often beat her children especially her son. The tasks of childcare would overwhelm Tabetha. Her daughter was mostly docile yet her mobile son would be seemingly uncontrollable. With few skills or resources she would turn to physical beatings as the means of discipline. Another boyfriend would abruptly leave her, and her son would break the vase her grandmother would give her. Tabetha was furious and dragged him to the kitchen by the arm to initiate a brutal beating leaving her young son bloody, bruised, and battered. When her son could not move his arm the next day, she would be forced to take him to the emergency room where they would recognize the signs of probable child abuse. Tabetha would deny before admitting to the abuse and forced to take therapy to alter her behaviors. Repeat incidents would occur and Tabetha would leave town with her new boyfriend. It is most likely the abuse to continue creating a legacy her children may carry into their role as parents.

Carley, S. G. (2013). *Serial killers, mass murders, & disorders.*
Boston: SGC Production.

Daniel Paul Schreber (Paranoid Schizophrenia)

Daniel Paul Schreber

A severe and interesting disorder common to each of us is paranoid schizophrenia. Certain symptoms must exist in the application of a diagnosis of paranoid schizophrenia of which the individual must meet the overall criteria of the disorder. When the symptoms involve the domination of a preoccupation with persecutory or grandiose delusions, audial hallucinations, or delusions of jealousy the schizophrenia is said to be paranoid. On virtue of the attention given to him by Freud, Daniel Paul Schreber would become a famous psychiatric patient. In analysis of Schreber, Freud would make use of Schreber's book describing himself, his thoughts, and his beliefs. Prior to Freud's discovery of Schreber's book, he would treat and keep a woman in psychoanalysis to learn more about her paranoia despite feelings this treatment would not be helpful. Upon discovery of Schreber's book, Freud's consummation would be the writing of the case history of Schreber marking a classic case of paranoia. Captivating Freud would be the eloquent style in which Schreber would speak of his condition. To the delightment of Freud would be the phrase Schreber would use to describe his condition using terms such as nerve contacts and soul

Carley, S. G. (2013). *Serial killers, mass murders, & disorders.* Boston: SGC Production.

murder. The grandiose descriptions Schreber would make use page after page of his universe and affairs would provide Freud the opportunity to amplify aspects sexual in nature pertaining to the psychoanalytic theory. It would be the paranoia of Schreber according to Freud causing Schreber to explain the universe as a survival mechanism.

The birth of Daniel Paul Schreber would occur on July 25, 1842, as he would be the second son and third of five children born to a family of generations of professionals. Little evidence exists of the childhood of Schreber. Schreber was a good student and father a well known physician. His father Dr. Schreber would write a book on raising children from infancy to adolescence. Dr. Schreber's advice he would use on his children is to place as much pressure on children during the earliest years, in avoidance of later troubles. Dr. Schreber would believe to toughen an infant, he or she should be bathed in cold bath water, and the use of negative reinforcement may be necessary to keep a child from crying. Children should learn to restrain their emotion and undergo intense physical training. A favorite subject of Dr. Schreber would be children at all times should maintain perfect posture. In creation of a straight posture, Dr. Schreber would recommend children between the ages of two to eight to wear an orthopedic device designed for this purpose. He would emphasize the maintenance of this device during sleeping, creating a device with iron rings and a chain ensuring posture during sleep. Dr. Schreber would also recommend a caregiver to control every waking moment of the child's day. Children should be well groomed and organized, making use of negative reinforcement should children not adhere to these activities. Dr. Schreber would recommend a list detailing weekly disobedient acts to be punished accordingly at the week's end. Part of this ritual of punishment is to better ensure children do not masturbate during the later years.

Carley, S. G. (2013). *Serial killers, mass murders, & disorders.* Boston: SGC Production.

Schreber was described as a nervous child, he and his siblings would grow up in complete passivity, a result of their father's upbringing. At the age of 16 in 1858, Dr. Schreber would have an accident as a ladder would fall on his head resulting in headaches, delusions, and homicidal ideations. Dr. Schreber would experience a nervous breakdown and when Schreber was 19 his father would die. Schreber would grow to become a successful lawyer and later a judge. At the age of 35 Schreber's brother Gustav would commit suicide. Schreber would run for political office at the age of 42 and would be defeated. Schreber's first mental breakdown would occur after this defeat. Schreber would begin to experience delusions hypochondriacal in nature, with beliefs he would die of heart attack, and the belief he was emaciated. Schreber's initial hospital stay would last six months experiencing high emotionality, hypersensitivity to noise, two suicide attempts, and a speech impediment. Upon the discharge of Schreber who would gain two pounds during his commitment, he would be of the belief he had gained 30 pounds. The next eight years Schreber would spend happily with his wife. Schreber's disappointment would be the two would bear no children. Schreber would be appointed among the country's highest court as a presiding judge. Schreber would have a dream of the return of his mental illness, and upon the worsening of Schreber's anxiety and insomnia, he would contact his former psychiatrist Dr. Paul Emil Flechsig. Upon the worsening of Schreber's condition, he would receive yet another hospitalization for a lengthy eight year duration. Schreber would be 51 years of age, the same age when the ladder would fall upon his father's head.

During Schreber's second hospitalization he would write Memoirs of my Nervous Illness recording his hallucinations, delusions, and thoughts. He would claim to write the book to his wife so she could understand his religious ideas and personal experiences to better understand the oddities which his behavior had become. This book would provide information of Schreber's psychological condition.

Carley, S. G. (2013). *Serial killers, mass murders, & disorders*.
Boston: SGC Production.

Upon Schreber's second hospitalization his medical records would reflect him to experience delusions of persecution, and the belief he was going to die. Schreber would believe his penis was twisted off with a nerve probe and that he was a woman. He would consistently experience audial and visual hallucinations. Schreber would claim God to speak to him and that he was going to die. At times Schreber would scream out of the window "God is a whore." His thoughts would change from feelings he was going to die, to thoughts of flowering into a female as he would bare his naked chest to his doctor. Sexual thoughts would preoccupy Schreber. Schreber in letters to his wife and family, with amazing insight, would speak of his illness, at a time Schreber would spend much of his time naked in front of a mirror, ribbons covering his body. At the age of 53, Schreber would appeal his permanent commitment arguing his nervous illness to be a result of true objective problems. The court would find Schreber to be capable of caring for himself, despite believing him to possess a mental disturbance. Schreber's intent to publish his Memoirs the court would view as evidence of his poor decision making and judgment. Despite this, they would find Schreber's writing as possibly financially rewarding, and despite the lack of reality present within the writings, the book would reflect genuity of interest in pursuit for the truth.

Schreber's memoirs would consist of three levels of content his analysis of the cosmos, his personal experiences, and his history of illness and his appeals to his involuntary commitment. The information Schreber would receive of the cosmos would arrive from the souls which would speak to him, who would do so in fragmented sentences. Schreber would experience compulsive thoughts. Schreber's preoccupation of being transformed into a woman would continue. Schreber viewing Flechsig as a soul murderer, would claim this process to be a product of his work. Schreber claimed Flechsig would want him to become a prostitute. Schreber through a series of miracles to ensure his survival would agree to become a woman. His description of this transformation would occur through multiple attacks on his body. These attacks would involve bodily saturation with female nerves, little men in his feet pumping his spinal cord from his body, and the destruction and replacement of his internal organs. Upon surrendering to this force Schreber references himself as a joint of pork claiming his goal of becoming pregnant by God. Upon winning his appeal of the permanent commitment, Schreber's second stay in the hospital would come to an end. This would occur at the age of sixty after an eight year commitment. Schreber would go home where he would live for the next five years. He would live with his mother who would die, and his wife shortly thereafter would suffer a stroke and die. When Schreber's wife would die, at the age of 65 Schreber would return to the hospital until his death at the age of 69. Schreber would spend 12 of the final 17 years of his life committed to the mental institution. The same year of Schreber's death, Freud would publish his essay on paranoia basing upon the Memoirs of Schreber. The final position of Schreber would be as panel president in the Dresden Superior Country Court of judges. Throughout Schreber's life, he would protest publicly the devices his father would use on him.

In interpreting Schreber's delusions, Freud would find this manifestation of paranoia the cause of homosexuality of which Schreber would reject. Freud's theory of paranoia would be fueled by Schreber's writing. The repression of Schreber's homosexuality and foundation for his paranoia would mask themselves in Schreber's inability to recognize his own desires. According to Freud, Schreber would transfer his love of his father and brother onto Flechsig and God. The development of Freud's psychoanalytic theory of paranoia would be a construction from the Schreber Memoirs. Freud's interpretation of Schreber's womanly desires would justify his loss of masculinity, explaining the father-complex, viewing Schreber's homosexual fixations as unresolved Oedipus

Carley, S. G. (2013). *Serial killers, mass murders, & disorders.* Boston: SGC Production.

conflicts. Schreber would experience the threat of castration from his father, resulting in the abandonment of his mother's love, yet to identify with her concurrently.

Causes of Schreber's Schizophrenia

Consistent with the symptoms of paranoid schizophrenia the onset in Schreber's case would take place later in his life. The reason for Schreber's condition is most likely the controlling and extreme steps taken by his father in controlling his children through inhibition of expressing feelings and normal functioning. Schreber's family history does not display a history of the disorder, placing him into a smaller percentage who acquire the disorder later during the course of his or her life. During Schreber's episodes of schizophrenia, his hallucinations were constant and delusions bizarre and grandiose. Schreber would display the classic symptom picture of paranoid schizophrenia with his preoccupation of turning to a woman, his compulsive thinking through messages from souls, and involvement with God and nerves. Schreber would maintain sufficience in meeting his needs despite experiencing extreme episodes. During the course of experiencing delusions and hallucinations, he would write a meaningful and logical letter to his wife. Schreber would also remarkably make a successful appeal of his permanent commitment. This is not uncommon among paranoid schizophrenics, who often present themselves of a normal disposition. It is also not unnormal for paranoid schizophrenics to be of high intelligence as Schreber could be described.

The use of harsh and shaming techniques by his parents in disciplining him may be a contributing factor to his paranoia. Very early on paranoid individuals use symbol processing procedures in handling humiliating experiences, in blaming others in the event of wrongdoing other than oneself (Colby, 1977). Shaming techniques can predispose the individual to anticipate shameful experiences, and to engage in various mechanisms in protection of the ego from such an experience. In terms of processing information, paranoids would differ from those deemed normal through the use of projection. Freudian theorists would initially hypothesize projection, referencing the inner conflict over homosexual impulses. More recently formulations do not require homosexual conflict. Contradicting Freudian theory is the overt homosexuality among paranoids. Holding up well through the years would be Freud's hypothetical projection of the role of the unconscious (Weston, 1998). Much of the projections of paranoid delusionals are internal concerns and ruminations.

Treatment Options

Treatment for paranoid disorders often involves some form of coercion through spousal pressures, hospitalization, or imprisonment. The inherent nature of the paranoid unsurprisingly is to be suspicious of many and to trust very few. Therapeutic intervention pertaining to interpersonal problems requires a willingness to admit vulnerability and a degree of self disclosure. The willingness to admit vulnerability are the antithetic qualities making a person paranoid. A fear among paranoids is to permit others to see their vulnerabilities, making them more open to attack in a delusional state. Gaining client trust is critical (Cullberg, 2006). Severely disturbed paranoids are disorganized or dangerous and likely to be hospitalized. In hopes the paranoid will forget the content of their delusions, clinicians have administered electroconvulsive therapy (ECT). The effect of the ECT diminishes self control and increases vulnerability of the client, which unsurprisingly results in little success for this form of treatment. There is little evidence the ECT has any therapeutic value except perhaps in cases of severe depression. Psychosurgery for paranoid disorders similarly shows few if any therapeutic benefits. Chemotherapy on the other hand has been shown an effective strategy in the reduction of the bizarre components of persecutory delusions more so than with erotomanic and somatic delusions (Buckley & Meltzer, 1995). The paranoid fearing most treatment approaches can make long term psychotherapy difficult. It may be the therapist's ability to generate trust, which can lead to a significant cure.

Therapeutic intervention for paranoia rarely occurs without some form of coercion. Gaining a client's trust through empathy is part of the treatment of paranoia. The gaining of trust is not necessary in participating in patterns of the disorder. It is important to articulate to the paranoid, the consequences associating with behavior such as feelings of being misunderstood or isolated, or the apparent unfairness of interpersonal rejection. Frequently paranoids are correct in assuming people are against them, these groups often consisting of the sensory impaired, the elderly, or immigrants.

Carley, S. G. (2013). *Serial killers, mass murders, & disorders*. Boston: SGC Production.

References

ABC News, (2011). Woman wrestled fresh ammo clip from Tucson shooter as he tried to reload. *ABCNews.com.*

Agras, W. S. (1995). Treatment of eating disorders. In A. Schatzberg & C. Nemeroff (Eds.), *Textbook of Pyschopharmacology.* Washington, DC: American Psychiatric Press.

Andreassi, J. (2000) *Psychophysiology.* Mahwah, NJ: Lawrence Erlbaum.

Atkinson, L., & Goldberg, S. (2004). *Attachment issues in psychopathology and intervention.* Mahwah, NJ: Lawrence Erlbaum.

Ayoub, C. C., Deutsch, R. M., & Kinscherff, R. (2000). Psychosocial management issues in Munchausen by Proxy. In R. M. Reece (Ed.), *Treatment of Child Abuse: Common Ground for Mental Health, Medical, and Legal Practitioners,* (pp. 226–235). Baltimore: Johns Hopkins University Press.

Bartol, C., & Bartol, A. (2008). *Criminal Behavior.* Belmont, CA: Wadsworth.

Beck, A. (1976). *Cognitive therapy and the emotional disorders.* New York: International Universities Press.

Bell, Q. (1972). *Virginia Woolf: A biography.* New York: Harcourt Brace Jovanovich.

Bongar, B. (2002). *The suicidal patient*. Washington, DC: American Psychological Association.

Bostwick, J. M. (2000). Affect disorders and suicide. *American Journal of Psychiatry, 157*, 1925–1932.

Boyd, A., McLearen, A., Meyer, R., & Denney, J. (2007). *The assessment of deception*. Sarasota, FL: Professional Resource Press.

Bruch, H., Czyzewski, D., & Suhr, M. (1988). *Conversations with anorexics*. New York: Basic Books.

Buckley, P., & Meltzer, H. (1995). Treament of schizophrenia. In A. Schatzberg & C. Nemeroff (Eds.), *Textbook of Psychiatry*. Washington, DC: American Psychiatric Press.

Burney, I. A. (1999). A poison of no substance: The trials of medico-legal proof in mid-Victorian England. *Journal of British Studies, 38*(1), 59-92.

Burnside, S., & Cairns, A. (1995). *Deadly innocence: The true story of Paul Bernardo, Karen Homolka and the schoolgirl murders*. New York: Time Warner.

Caplan, L. (1984). *The insanity defense*. Boston: Godine.

Carley, S.G. (2012). *Foundation of psychology as a scientific discipline* (4th Ed.). SGC Production. Boston, MA.

Castillo, S. (1999). Stones in the quarry: George Cable's strange true stories of Louisiana. *Southern Literary Journal, 31*(2), 19-34.

Chambless, D., Sanderson, W., Shoham, V., & Johnson, S. (1996). An update on empirically validated therapies. *The Clinical Psychologist, 49(2)*, 5–18.

Clausen, C. (2007). The Rorschach murders. *Queen's Quarterly, 114*(2), 268-277.

Colby, K. (1977). Appraisal of four psychological theories of paranoid phenomena. *Journal of Abnormal Psychology, 86*, 54–59.

Coughlin, C. (2002). *Saddam: King of terror.* New York: HarperCollins.

Corner, R. J. (2005). *Fundamentals of abnormal psychology* (4th ed.). New York: Worth.

Coward, D. (1992). The Marquis de Sade. *The misfortunes of virtue* (Trans., with an introduction). New York: Oxford University Press.

Cullberg, J. (2006). *Psychoses.* New York: Routledge.

Datillo, F., Davis, E., & Goisman, R. (2008). Crisis intervention with medical patients. In F. Dattillo & A. Freeman (Eds), *Cognitive-behavior Strategies in Crisis Intervention.* New York: Guilford.

de Sade, D.A.F. Marquis. (1995). Les infortunes de la vertu; Justine, ou les Malheurs de la vertu; *La nouvelle Justine (Vol. 2 of Oeuvres).* Paris: Bibliothèques de la Pléiade.

DeBattista, C. (1998). Mood disorders. In H. Friedman (Ed.), *Encyclopedia of mental health.* San Diego: Academic Press.

DePaulo, L. (2005). The strange, still mysterious death of Marilyn Monroe. *Playboy, 52*(12), 76, 78, 82, 195–195.

DiLalla, L. (2004). *Behavior genetics principles*. Washington, DC: American Psychological Association.

Doctor, R. (1998). Sexual disorders. In H. Friedman (Ed.). *Encyclopedia of mental health*. San Diego: Academic Press.

Dunea, G. (1994). Lethal injection. *British Medical Journal, International Edition, 308*(6943), 1575.

Elder, R. K. (2010). *Last words of the executed*. Chicago: University of Chicago Press.

Esmail, A. (2005). Physician as serial killer- The Shipman case. *The New England Journal of Medicine, 352*(18), 1843-4.

Federal Bureau of Investigation. (n.d.) Multi-disciplinary perspectives for investigators. *FBI.gov*. Retrieved from http://www.fbi. gov/about-us/cjis/ucr/ucr

Flannery, D. J., Modzeleski W., & Kretschmar, J. M. (2013). Violence and school shootings. *Curr Psychiatry Rep, 15*, 331.

Forbush, K., Heatherton, T., & Keel, P. (2007). Relationships between perfectionism and specific disordered eating behaviors. *International Journal of Eating Behaviors, 40*(1), 37–41.

Game, J. H. H, & Odell, R. (1989). *The new murderers' who's who*. London.

Garner, D., & Garfinkel, P. (Eds.). (1997). *Handbook of treatment for eating disorders*. New York: Guilford Press.

Gee, J. (2000). Police probe 40 deaths at private clinic. *Daily Express*, 23.

Goodwin, F. K., & Jamison, K. R. (1990). *Manic-depressive illness*. New York: Oxford University Press.

Goodwin, G. M. (1994). Recurrence of mania after lithium withdrawal. *British Journal of Psychiatry, 164*, 149–152.

Goulde, L. L. (1997). A sniper in the tower: The Charles Whitman murders. *The Journal of American History, 84*(3), 1150.

Grilo, C. (2006). *Eating disorders*. New York: Routledge.

Greenberg, H. R. (2004). Monster/Aileen: Life and death of a serial killer/Aileen Wuornos: The selling of a serial killer. *Psychiatric Times, 21*(6), 16-17.

Greenberg, S., Shuman, D., & Meyer, R. (2004). Unmasking forensic diagnosis. *International Journal of Law and Psychiatry, 27*(1), 1–15.

Hafner, Heinz, Mauer, K., Loftier, W., & Riecher-Rossler, A. (1993). The influence of age and sex on the onset and early course of schizophrenia. *British Journal of Psychiatry, 162*. doi: 10.1192/bjp.l62.1.80.

Haley, J., & Richenport-Haley, M. (2008). *Medically unexplained illness*. Washington, DC: American Psychological Association.

Hare, R., Hart, S., & Harpur, T. (1991). Psychopathy and the *DSM-IV* criteria for antisocial personality disorder. *Journal of Abnormal Psychology, 100*, 391–398.

Harris, J. M. & Harris, R. B. (2012). Rampage violence requires a new type of research. *American Journal of Public Health, 102*(6), 1054-1057.

Hazelwood, R.R., Dietz, P.E., & Warren, J.I. (1992). *FBI Law Enforcement Bulletin, 7*, 1-8.

Hazelwood, R.R., & Michaud, S.G. (2001). *Dark dreams: Sexual violence, homicide, and the criminal mind.* New York: St. Martin's Press.

Heffner, M., & Eifert, G. (2004). *The anorexia workbook.* Oakland, CA: New Harbinger.

Hickey, E. W. (1997). *Serial murderers and their victims.* Washington DC: Wadsworth.

Hiifner, Heinz, Wolfram, Heiden, Behrens, S., & Qattaz, W. F. (1998). Causes and consequences of the gender difference in age at onset of schizophrenia. *Oxford Journals, Schizophrenia Bulletin, 24*(1).

Hilshafer, D. (2013). The mass murder problem. *Skeptic, 18*(1), 24-32, 64.

Hoekstra, M., Cheng, & Cheng. (2012). Does strengthening self-defense law deter crime or escalate violence? Evidence of castle doctrine. *TAMU.edu.* Retrieved from http://econweb.tamu.edu/mhoekstra/castle_doctrine.pdf.

Holmes, S. T., & Holmes, R. M. (2002). *Profiling violent crimes* (3rd edition). Thousand Oaks: Sage Publications.

Jackson v. *Indiana.* (1972). 406 U.S. 715.

Janofsky, J. (1994). "The Munchausen syndrome in civil forensic psychiatry." *Bulletin of the American Academy of Psychiatry and the Law, 22,* 488–489.

Johnson, S. (2008). *Medically unexplained illness.* Washington, DC: American Psychological Association.

Karloff, K. E. (2002). Jack the Ripper and the London Press. *Journalism and Mass Communication Quarterly, 79*(3), 776-777.

Kernberg, O. (1984). *Severe personality disorders.* New Haven, CT: Yale University Press.

Kinnell, H. G. (2000). Serial homicide by doctors: Shipman in perspective. *British Medical Journal, International edition, 321(7276),* 1594-7.

Kocsis, R. N., Irwin, H. J., & Hayes, A. F. (1998). Organised and disorganised criminal behaviour syndromes in arsonists. *Psychiatry, Psychology & Law, 5,* 117-131.

Kowalski, R., & Westen, D. (2009). *Psychology* (5th ed.). Hoboken, NJ: Wiley.

Kroll, J. (1993). *PTSD/borderline in therapy.* New York: Norton.

Kubany, E., McCaig, M., & Laconsay, J. (2004). *Healing the trauma of domestic violence.* Oakland, CA: New Harbinger.

Larson, R., Graham, E., & Baker, K. (2007). *A history of psychology.* Upper Saddle River, NJ: Prentice-Hall.

Lasch, C. (1978). *The culture of narcissism.* New York: Norton.

Laws, D. R., & O'Donohue, W. (2008). *Sexual deviance* (2nd ed.) New York: Guilford.

Lehmann, J. (1975). *Virginia Woolf and her world*. New York: Harcourt Brace Jovanovich.

LoPiccolo, J. (1993). "Paraphilias." In D. Dunner (Ed.), *Current psychiatric therapy*. Philadelphia: Saunders.

Marvasti, J. (2004). *Psychiatric treatment for sexual offenders*. Springfield, IL: Charles Thomas.

Masters, W., & Johnson, V. (1970). *Human sexual inadequacy*. Boston: Little, Brown.

Masters, W., Johnson, V., & Kolodny, R. (1991). *Human sexuality* (4th ed.). Glenview, IL: Scott, Foresman.

McCooey, D. (2012). Poetry, terrorism, and the uncanny: Timothy McVeigh's Invictus. *Criticism, 54*(4), 485-505.

McCullough, J. (2002). *Skills training manual for diagnosing and treating chronic depression*. New York: Guilford.

Medvedev, R., & Medvedev, Z. (2003). *The unknown Stalin*. Woodstock, NY: Overlook.

Meggers, H., & LoPiccolo, J. (2002). Sex therapy. In M. Hersen & W. Sledge (Eds.). *Encyclopedia of psychotherapy*. San Diego: Academic Press.

Melton, G., Petrila, J., Poythress, N., & Slobogin, C. (1997). *Psychological evaluation for courts* (2nd ed.). New York: Guilford Press.

Meyer, R., & Weaver, C. M. (2007). *The clinician's handbook: Integrated diagnostics, assessment, and intervention in adult and adolescent psychopathology* (5th ed.). Long Grove, IL: Waveland Press.

Meyer, R. G., & Weaver, C.M. (2006). *Law and mental health: A case-based approach.* New York: Guilford Press.

Meyer, R. G., Chapman, K. L., &. Weaver, C. M. (2009). *Case studies in abnormal behavior*, (Eighth Edition). Allyn & Bacon. Pearson Education, Inc.

Money, J. (1990). Forensic sexology, paraphilic rape (biastophilia) and lust murder (erotophonophilia). *American Journal of Psychotherapy, 44*, 26-36.

Montefiore, S. S. (2004). *Stalin: The court of the Red Tsar*. New York: Weidenfeld and Nicholson.

Moolenaar, R. L. (2011). Mental illness surveillance among adults in the United States. Centers for Disease Control and Prevention (CDC). *Atlanta, GA: Office of Surveillance, Epidemiology, and Laboratory Services, Morbidity and Mortality Weekly Report, 60.*

Mosier, J. (2004). *The Blitzkrieg myth.* New York: HarperCollins.

Murder detectives. (2000). *Channel 5.*

Nathan, K., Musselman, D., Schatzberg, A., & Nemeroff, C. (1995). Biology of mood disorders. In A. Schatzberg & C.

Nemeroff (Eds.), *Textbook of Psychiatry*. Washington, DC: American Psychiatric Press.

Novak, G., & Pelaez, M. (2004). *Child and adolescent development*. Thousand Oaks, CA: Sage.

Pallis, C., & Bamji, A. (1979). McIlroy was here, or was he? *British Medical Journal, 1*, 973–975.

Parnell, T. F. (1997). Guidelines for identifying cases. In T. E. Parnell & D. O. Day (Eds.), *Munchausen By Proxy Syndrome: Misunderstood Child Abuse,* (pp. 47–67). Thousand Oaks, CA: Sage.

Penrose, V. (1996). *The bloody countess: The atrocities of Countess Erszebet Bathory*. London: Creation Books.

Pctraitis, J., Flay, B., & Miller, T. (1995). Reviewing theories of adolescent substance abuse. *Psychological Bulletin, 117,* 67–86.

Phelps, L., Brown, R., & Power, T. (2002). *Pediatric psychopharmacology*. Washington, DC: American Psychological Association.

Phillips, D. (1974). The influence of suggestion of suicide. *American Sociological Review, 39*, 340–354.

Phillips, D., Lesyna, K., & Paight, D. (1993). Suicide and the media. In R. Maris, A. Berman, & J. Maltsberger (Eds.), *Assessment and Prediction of Suicide*. New York: Guilford Press.

Plante, T. G. (2011). *Contemporary clinical psychology* (3rd ed.). Hoboken, NJ: John Wiley & Sons.

Post, R. M. (1993). Issues in the long-term management of bipolar affective illness. *Psychiatric Annals, 23*, 86–93.

Ramsland, K. (2005). *The human predator*. New York: Berkley Books.

Ramsland, K. (2009). The measure of a man: Cesare Lombroso and the criminal type. *Forensic Examiner, 18*(4), 70-72.

Reinecke. M., Washburn, R., & Becker-Weidman R. (2008). Depression and suicide. In F. Dattillo, & A. Freeman (Eds.), *Cognitive-behavioral Strategies in Crisis Intervention*. New York: Guilford.

Roesch, R. (1979). Determining competency to stand trial: An examination of evaluation procedures in an institutional setting. *Journal of Consulting and Clinical Psychology, 47*(3), 542–550.

Russell, S. (2002). *Lethal intent: The shocking true story of one of America's most notorious serial killers*. New York: Pinnacle Books.

Schechter, H. (2003). *Fatal: The poisonous life of a female serial killer*. New York: Pocket Star Books.

Schechter, H. (2003). *The serial killer files*. New York: Ballantine.

Shneidman, E. (1985). *Definition of suicide*. New York: Wiley.

Simola, S. (2003). Ethics of justice and care in corporate crisis management. *Journal of Business Ethics, 46*(4), 351-361.

Smyth, E. (1992). Sam Sheppard crimes of passion. *Crimes and Victims*. Leicester: Bookmart.

Stone, M. H. (2009). *The anatomy of evil.* Amherst, NY: Prometheus Books.

Stone, M. H. (2010). Sexual sadism: A portrait of evil. *Journal of the American Academy of Psychoanalysis and Dynamic Psychiatry, 38*(1), 133-57.

Strupp, H., Lambert, M., & Horowitz, L. (Eds.). (1997). *Measuring patient changes in mood, anxiety and personality disorders.* Washington, DC: American Psychological Association.

Summers, A. (1980). *Conspiracy.* New York: McGraw-Hill.

Summers, A. (1985). *Goddess: The secret lives of Marilyn Monroe.* New York: Scribner.

Walk-up, J. T. & Rubin, D. H. (2013). Social withdrawal and violence -- Newtown, Connecticut. *The New England Journal of Medicine, 368*(5), 399-401.

Warren, J. I., & Hazelwood, R.R. (2002). Relational patterns associated with sexual sadism: A study of 20 wives and girlfriends. *Journal of Family Violence, 17,* 75-89.

Warren, J., Reboussin, R., Hazelwood, R. R., Cummings, A., Gibbs, N., & Trumbetta, S, (1998). Crime scene and distance correlates of serial rape. *Journal of Quantitative Criminology, 14,* 35-59.

Weston, D. (1998). The scientific legacy of Sigmund Freud: Toward a psychodynamically informed psychological science. *Psychological Bulletin, 124,* 333–371.

White, J. H., Lester, D., Gentile, M., & Rosenbleeth, J. (2011). The utilization of forensic science and criminal profiling for capturing serial killers. *Forensic Science International, 209*(1), 160-165.

Williams, M., Teasdale, J., Segal, Z., & Kabat-Zin, J. (2008). *The mindful way through depression.* New York: Guilford.

Wilson, C. & Seaman, D. (1992). *The serial killers.* London: Virgin.

Zugibe, F. & Carroll, D. L. (2005). *Dissecting death.* New York: Broadway Books.

9 781492 734192